Social Care and Social Exclusion

Social Care and Social Exclusion

A Comparative Study of Older People's Care in Europe

Edited by

Tim Blackman

Sally Brodhurst

and

Janet Convery

palgrave

First published 2001 by
PALGRAVE
Houndmills, Basingstoke, Hampshire RG21 6XS and
175 Fifth Avenue, New York, N.Y. 10010
Companies and representatives throughout the world

PALGRAVE is the new global academic imprint of
St. Martin's Press LLC Scholarly and Reference Division and
Palgrave Publishers Ltd (formerly Macmillan Press Ltd).

ISBN 0–333–91964–5

This book is printed on paper suitable for recycling and
made from fully managed and sustained forest sources.

A catalogue record for this book is available
from the British Library.

Library of Congress Cataloging-in-Publication Data
Social care and social exclusion : a comparative study of older people's care
in Europe / edited by Tim Blackman, Sally Brodhurst, and Janet Convery.
    p. cm.
Conference papers.
Includes bibliographical references and index.
ISBN 0–333–91964–5
    1. Aged—Care—Europe—Congresses. 2. Social isolation—Europe–
–Congresses. I. Blackman, Tim. II. Brodhurst, Sally. III. Convery, Janet.
HV1480 .S63 2000
362.6'094—dc21
                                                        00–048336

10   9   8   7   6   5   4   3   2   1
10   09 08 07 06 05 04 03 02 01

Printed and bound in Great Britain by
Antony Rowe Ltd, Chippenham, Wiltshire

Contents

List of Tables

Acknowledgements

Many people have contributed to this book and to the international seminar series from which it originates. The seminars were funded by the UK Economic and Social Research Council (Ref. R45126456496). We are grateful to the ESRC and for the generous hospitality and support that we also received from the School of Social Sciences and Law at Oxford Brookes University, Ruskin College Oxford, the Social Studies Department of Trinity College Dublin, University College Dublin, the Irish Association of Older People, IMPACT, Dun Laoghaire Corporation, the Norwegian Social Research Institute (NOVA), Bærum Kommune and the First KAPI of the Municipality of Keratsini in Greece. Thanks are due to the following for assisting with organization of the meetings: Roberta Woods (Oxford); Evangelos Paroussis, Anna Amera, Dora Baka, Evangelia Hatzi and the employees and members of the First KAPI of Keratsini and the Municipal Board of Keratsini (Athens); Mia Vabø and Gunvor Erdal (Oslo); and Sheila Simmons and Janet Convery (Dublin).

Seminar participants from the United Kingdom were Helen Bartlett, Tim Blackman, Sally Brodhurst, Caroline Glendinning, Chris Gostick, Evangelos Paroussis, Maria Parsons and Bridget Robb. Participants from Denmark were David Bunnage and Merete Platz; from Norway, Gunvor Erdal and Mia Vabø; from Greece, Anna Amera; from Italy, Elisabetta Cioni; and from Ireland, Janet Convery and Sheila Simmons.

Tim Blackman
Sally Brodhurst
Janet Convery
February 2000

Notes on Contributors

Anna Amera is a Professor at the Department of Social Work, TEI of Athens.

Tim Blackman is Director of the School of Social Sciences and Professor of Sociology and Social Policy at the University of Teesside, Middlesbrough.

Helen Bartlett is Director of the Oxford Centre for Health Care Research and Development, and Deputy Head and Professor in the School of Health Care at Oxford Brookes University.

Sally Brodhurst is Joint Commissioning Manager for Older People, Oxfordshire Health Authority and Oxfordshire County Council.

Elisabetta Cioni is Professor of Sociology of the Family, University of Florence, and during 1997–98 was Chief Coordinator of the Social Policies Department of the Municipality of Pistoia, Italy.

Janet Convery is a former social worker and is currently Lecturer in Social Work at Trinity College Dublin and a member of the National Council on Ageing and Older People.

Gunvor Erdal is a team leader with Bærum Kommune home care services.

Caroline Glendinning is Reader in Social Policy at the National Centre for Primary Care Research and Development, University of Manchester.

Evangelos Paroussis is Senior Lecturer in Social Work at Oxford Brookes University.

Merete Platz is a Senior Researcher at the Danish National Institute of Social Research, Copenhagen.

Bridget Robb is Principal Lecturer in Social Work at Oxford Brookes University.

Mia Vabø is a Researcher at the Norwegian Institute of Social Research (NOVA) in Oslo.

Introduction

Tim Blackman, Sally Brodhurst and Janet Convery

Origins

This book originates from a series of international seminars examining the provision of social care for older people in six European countries: Denmark, Greece, Ireland, Italy, Norway and the United Kingdom. A group of academics and practitioners participated in four two- to three-day meetings over 18 months during 1997–99. A considerable amount of additional research and writing also took place outside these meetings, producing briefing papers and preparing comments on draft chapters. We hope that the end product is a book, created jointly by academics and practitioners who have engaged in an international project of mutual learning and debate, which can enlighten and benefit others as much as the experience has enlightened and benefited us. In particular, the book should interest anyone who wants to inform their work in this field – whether in policy, practice, teaching, learning or research – with a cross-national perspective on Europe's diverse laboratory of approaches to the social care of older people. The contributors include sociologists, gerontologists, social policy academics, social workers, health care professionals, planners and volunteers, spanning a wide range of ages, social backgrounds and nationalities. We hope that our readership will be as diverse.

The first meeting was held at Ruskin College, Oxford, from 12 to 14 September 1997. Prior to the meeting, participants prepared and circulated papers describing the policy and practice background for their countries. These were discussed at the meeting, along with four case studies of older people which were used to elaborate the level and type of care services each older person would be likely to receive in each country. A matrix was also constructed summarizing the key features of each country's care system. Following this meeting, the work of the group was concerned with producing papers on access to, and eligibility for, social care services; the role of family care; the roles of publicly and privately funded services; and the extent of user charges for services.

The second meeting was held in Athens at the Hotel Poseidon from 26 to 29 March 1998 (amid storms and an electricity blackout!). An extended overview paper based on the Oxford proceedings and other material was circulated in advance. Further work was undertaken to clarify descriptions of the care system of each country, including types and levels of care; social, cultural, political and ideological contexts of care provision; and examples of special features. The case studies were also elaborated further, using these 'micro' pictures of individual cases based on four hypothetical older people, ranging from low to high levels of need, as typical examples of how needs are addressed in each system. The meeting discussed criteria for state intervention in the care of older people; the role of the family and a 'duty to care'; public spending and charging; and the role of pressure groups. Finally, the group considered how the concept of social exclusion could be applied to social care, including aspects such as professional gatekeeping of resources and the use of discretion; 'client–patron' features of policy and practice; gaps in care provision; resource issues; discrimination; and choice and powerlessness. The group received tremendous hospitality from local people and professionals in Athens, including a memorable visit to the First KAPI of the Municipality of Keratsini.

The third meeting was held in Oslo from 10 to 13 September 1998, hosted by NOVA, the Norwegian Institute of Social Research. This meeting was concerned with reviewing the group's work to date, defining social exclusion (exclusion from rights, integration into social life and preventing dependency), and discussing the concept of 'inclusive services'. Bærum Kommune very generously organized visits to sheltered housing, a nursing home, a day centre and a senior centre.

The structure of the book was worked out during one of the sessions in Oslo, and first drafts of chapters were prepared for the final meeting in Dublin. This was held at the offices of the Irish Association of Older People in University College Dublin from 11 to 14 March 1999, hosted by University College Dublin and the Irish Association of Older People. The group also visited two housing schemes for older people. The drafts were discussed and further writing was planned, which took place between April 1999 and February 2000.

Issues

At the heart of this book is the issue of how the values and structures of Europe's diverse welfare regimes predispose these societies towards particular configurations of social care for older people. Three important questions follow from this. To what extent can these configurations, or 'systems of care', be regarded as successful in tackling social exclusion among older people? What can the concept of social exclusion reveal about the situation of older people and the strengths and weaknesses of social care? Do welfare regimes, and the systems of care that exist within them, determine particular patterns of responsibility, provision, access and entitlement?

The book begins in Chapter 1 by defining social care and explaining the rationale for selecting the six countries as illustrating the range of approaches to the social care of older people in Europe. The chapter considers the wide variation in expectations of informal family care across the six countries and the contrasting types of formal care provided. The concept of dependency is explored in relation to differences in the type of care older people receive. The chapter concludes by introducing the concept of social exclusion, to which we return in the final chapter after exploring in detail the care systems of each country.

Chapter 2 considers issues involved in the comparative study of older people's care. Does the balance between State, family and market involvement in the care of older people enable general models to be identified? To what extent can we talk of a 'mixed economy' of care in Europe generally? The chapter examines the extent to which economic, political and cultural factors create unique systems in each country, and discusses the extent of similarities and common pressures and trends.

The following six chapters describe in detail the social care systems of each country, including wider contextual descriptions of health care and pension provision. Each chapter is organized under the following topics: state, family and individual responsibilities; structure, funding and organization of services; coverage and variations in provision; charges and older people's incomes; access and entitlement; and issues of choice and information availability. Chapters 3, 4 and 5 consider the three countries where local authorities have a formal comprehensive duty to assess need and provide care management: Denmark, Norway and the United Kingdom. Chapters 6, 7 and 8 consider the three countries where there are no such comprehensive duties and a greater emphasis on family responsibility: Ireland, Italy and Greece. Each chapter ends with a short bibliography of sources.

While Chapters 3 to 8 describe the social care each of the six countries provides for older people at the 'system' level of family, public, voluntary and private institutions, Chapter 9 turns to what this means for individual older people who need assistance with activities of daily living because of ill-health or disability. Four contrasting cases of older people needing help with their care are considered country by country. Similarities and differences are discussed, and the situation of each case is used to illustrate key features of care in the six countries.

Chapter 10 takes this analysis a step further by using the concept of social exclusion as a means of evaluating the adequacy of care, especially the quality of care in different care settings. The idea of 'welfare culture' is introduced to take account of national differences in the role of the family. The chapter considers whether social exclusion can be used as an evaluative concept across different welfare cultures, focusing on issues of access and entitlement, including variations in the provision of services, the extent of assessment and discretion, and the balance between informal family care and formal, organized services. The chapter concludes by reviewing the strengths and weaknesses of social care in each country, and the developments which appear to hold most promise in tackling social exclusion among older people through improved services.

Chapter 11 concludes the book. It reviews a number of issues that arise from the material presented and discussed in previous chapters, returning to the questions posed at the start of this section of the Introduction. It points to some possible solutions to the problems encountered with the social care of older people, identifying the various strengths that exist in both policy and practice, especially where these help to prevent the types of exclusion discussed in Chapter 10. The chapter begins by returning to Chapter 2's discussion of the extent to which it is possible to generalize about welfare regimes and care systems, and considers whether such generalization helps to understand why countries have different approaches to the social care of older people. This is followed by a short discussion of Denmark as a possible exemplar of social care provision, and a wider discussion about cross-national policy transfer. Issues and solutions are then considered, drawing upon the experiences of all six countries explored in the book and, where appropriate, other research evidence. The decentralization and integration of social and health care services are discussed, together with the assessment of need, supporting informal care, the relevance of a social model, and the empowerment of older people. A final section draws together the main themes and conclusions of the book.

Terminology

Terminology is always a problem for comparative studies. This section seeks to clarify a number of terms, although discussion of 'social care' and 'social exclusion' is left to the main chapters of the book.

In general terms, 'older people' is used to describe people who have retired from full-time paid employment and are eligible on grounds of age alone for some type of pension. In Norway and Denmark this includes people aged 67 or older; in the other four countries it includes people aged 65 or older (ignoring gender differences in statutory retirement ages, which are being phased out where they exist in the European Union). The book's focus on social care means that the main concern is with people experiencing age-associated disease or disability that results in their needing assistance with their activities of daily living. These needs are particularly concentrated among people in their 80s and older. However, it is recognized that there is no necessary relationship between ageing and needs for social care, and that most older people are active and independent. Despite this, the prevalence of these needs increases significantly with age, and ageing raises particular issues for the provision of social care, as discussed in subsequent chapters.

We use the term 'local authority' to describe the local tier of administration responsible for organizing social care services. In Denmark and Norway this term is used to describe the municipalities, which are the lower tier of local government responsible for, among other things, community health care and social care services. The upper tier of local government in these two countries consists of county councils which are responsible for the hospitals. Where reference is made to these local authorities, they are described specifically as county councils. In England, social services authorities are responsible for social care and can be county councils (upper tier) or unitary councils, metropolitan authorities or London boroughs (single-tier local government). In Greece, prefectures are the local level of organization of the Department of Health and Social Welfare and employ social workers, while municipalities also employ some social workers and nurses, and organize some care services. In Ireland the relevant organization is the area health board which employs community nurses and social workers. In Italy, the equivalent of the English local authorities is the commune, which has responsibility for social care provision, but health and some social services are run by separate local health units (AUSLs). We describe all of these as 'local authorities' unless there is a need to clarify the particular unit of administration. We use the term 'central government' to describe national government or what in Norway and Denmark is termed 'the State', and 'regional government' to describe provinces. Other sub-national units of administration are described as they would be in the appropriate country, although translated into English.

In Norway, Denmark and Italy 'home care services' include both home helps and home nursing. Home helps assist with practical domestic tasks such as cleaning and shopping. In the UK, 'home care' (or domiciliary services) refers to personal care such as washing, dressing, toileting and feeding *and* domestic help such as cleaning, shopping and preparing meals, although cleaning is now often not included, a trend also evident in Norway and Denmark. It does not include nursing care. In Ireland, 'care attendants' provide personal care. We use the term 'home care' in the UK sense to include both personal care and domestic care, although when necessary the more specific terms of 'home help', 'personal care' and 'nursing care' are used.

'Institutional care' is used in the book to describe care in residential or nursing homes – that is, outside the hospital but not in 'ordinary' or 'supported' housing – although there are no residential homes in Denmark and a declining number in Norway. In both these countries the main distinction is between institutions (mainly nursing homes) and supported housing (often converted residential homes). We use the term 'supported housing' to include what in the UK is still more commonly called 'sheltered housing'.

Another source of confusion is residential care. In the UK there is a clear distinction between residential homes and nursing homes, although an increasing number are 'dual registered'. In Ireland there is no such distinction made and the predominant residential care model is the nursing home model. In Norway, this distinction has been blurred by the upgrading of residential homes to nursing homes, and in Denmark there are no residential homes – in both countries the distinction between 'institutional care' and 'community care' is also breaking down to some extent. Short-term 'institutional' care is accessed by community users, and care staff may be integrated in teams that provide services to residents both in the community and in institutions. The generic term 'institutional care' includes residential and nursing homes, as well as the increasingly less common provision of long-term care in hospitals. A similar generic term is 'supported housing' which consists of grouped independent residential units, suitably adapted and with facilities and a warden, commonly called 'sheltered housing' in the UK and Ireland, and 'service housing' in Norway. Denmark in particular has reduced its number of nursing home beds in favour of expanding independent adapted dwellings, although they are not all staffed at the level of nursing homes.

'Informal care' and 'family care' are used interchangeably to describe support with personal care and help with domestic tasks received from family members or, much more rarely, neighbours and friends. As discussed in Chapter 1, however, the meaning of 'care' in this context varies greatly across the six countries. 'Formal care' is used to describe any organized care provided by the public sector, voluntary organizations or private-sector providers. In the UK it is very common for local authorities to pay in full or part for services provided by the private sector to people who are assessed as needing services and unable to pay in full themselves.

'GPs' (general practitioners) and 'family doctors' are also used interchangeably in the book to describe medical doctors providing primary care.

Another term which is ambiguous in the international context is 'means testing'. In the UK this term is used to describe the financial assessment of a person's income, savings and assets, together with those of anyone else living in their immediate household, to determine what they should contribute to the cost of services. Many older people experience this assessment as intrusive and humiliating. There is a standard national means test for residential and nursing home charges, but great variation between local authorities in charges for domiciliary services. Liability can range from zero to the full cost of providing the service. Unlike Italy, Ireland and Greece, where certain social care services are exclusively for 'deserving' poor or low-income older people, publicly funded social care services in the UK are in principle available to all. However, in practice they are concentrated among those with low incomes because others do not apply due to charges, either going without or using (sometimes cheaper) private services.

Means testing also exists in Ireland, Italy and Greece, but is more informal than the UK's formal assessment process, with the exception of Ireland's formal means test for a grant towards the cost of private nursing home care. This is largely because so many voluntary organizations are involved in providing social care and determine eligibility themselves (although guidelines are used by Italian local authorities). Special mention should be made of Ireland's medical card system, whereby 75 per cent of older people are eligible on financial grounds for the card, which gives them access to free health care and, where they exist, free or very low-cost domiciliary social care services. This entitlement extends to long-stay beds in health board hospitals, although patients must relinquish most of their pensions to the hospital while resident.

In Norway and Denmark means testing could also be said to exist but is termed 'co-payment' for those services that are not free and involve income-graded payments. Co-payment can be distinguished from means testing by the relatively small charge that is levied, its minor role compared with means testing in generating income for the local authority, and its main purpose of discouraging unnecessary use of services. It should also be viewed in the context of Norway and Denmark's good pension provision, and the public availability of tax records which obviates the need to ask older people themselves potentially stigmatizing questions about their income and savings. Charges are much higher for institutional care, but are a fixed percentage of the user's basic pension and any supplementary income, and exclude savings or property. 'Normal' provision such as meals requires payment.

Means testing for social care and disability benefits is absent in Greece. Disability benefits are provided by social insurance organizations and depend on the level of disability rather than income, and services such as those provided by community day centres (KAPIs) are made available on the basis of a very small annual fee and small charges equivalent to a bus fare. It is also of note that these centres, which provide an increasingly important part of Greece's services for older people, are open access and avoid the stigma of either means testing or charity. For example, only 'normal' light meals are provided; more substantial provision is considered to be a duty of the Church and only given to elderly people who are struggling to meet subsistence needs.

While in general we discuss England, Wales, Scotland and Northern Ireland as the 'United Kingdom' or UK, it is important to note that Scotland and Northern Ireland have separate legal systems and that Scotland, Wales and Northern Ireland have their own regional parliaments. This means that important differences in the structure, funding and delivery of services can exist and are likely to become more prominent in future. While it is possible to generalize in many respects, when we discuss detail this is in relation to the situation in England. A similar issue arises with the Italian regional system. Thus, while in general we seek to recognize regional differences, especially between the less developed south and the northern and central regions of Italy, more specific examples, such as the case studies in Chapter 9, are more typical of the northern and central regions where services are more developed. Local variations in services exist in all countries and are discussed in the relevant chapters.

Throughout the text amounts of money are given in euro to facilitate comparison of expenditure between countries. At the time of writing €1 was equivalent to £0.62 and $0.90.

1
Social Care in Europe

Tim Blackman

This chapter considers the range of responses to needs for 'social care' in Europe's ageing societies, including the responsibilities of family members and the coverage and intensity of formal, organized social care services. Social care encompasses personal care such as washing and dressing, practical assistance with the preparation of meals and house cleaning, and opportunities for socializing and leisure activity. The extent to which any person needs help with these activities of daily living depends on their level of disability or mental health problems, and the environment in which they live. The term 'social care' is used to distinguish this type of assistance from medical or nursing care, although the distinction is not always helpful when considering the total care needs of an older person, nor necessarily evident in the care systems of some countries. It has also shifted over time: in the UK, for example, the growing extent of charges for social care since the early 1980s has been used to reduce pressure on free health services by redefining tasks such as bathing and even 'general nursing' as social care (Twigg, 1997; Loux, Kerrison and Pollock, 2000; see also Chapter 5).

The importance of distinguishing social aspects of care lies in their relevance to the quality of life of older people, beyond the narrower treatment and rehabilitation aims of medical services. These social aspects can either be reflected in the separate provision of 'social' services or in the integrated provision of medical, nursing and social care which, ideally, work together to maximize the health and well-being of older people. As is discussed in Chapter 10, meeting needs for social care is essential if older people are to avoid being excluded from the individual autonomy and social participation enjoyed by people without these needs.

Helping with an older person's personal care or with domestic tasks can be demanding work. Throughout Europe, within the family this work is undertaken predominantly by female spouses and daughters (Walker and Maltby, 1997). Care work normally has substantial emotional and social significance for both care giver and care receiver. In some European countries this significance means that care work comprises part of the values and practices that construct the private sphere of 'the family'. In other countries paid care – also almost entirely provided by women – has replaced much of the unpaid care work of family members. With the care work done by someone outside the family, there are greater opportunities within the family for more independent and personal relationships, and these different scenarios create quite different meanings of the term 'social care'. For a Greek daughter, social care can mean being the sole provider of substantial personal and domestic help for a very dependent parent towards whom she feels a duty to care, reinforced by social norms and an absence of alternatives. In Denmark, by comparison, the daughter of a frail parent is likely to be caring in a quite different way: visiting, chatting and occasionally shopping. Her parent's needs for personal and domestic help are expected to be met by the State.

This book focuses on six countries: Denmark, Norway, the UK, Ireland, Italy and Greece. These countries have been selected because they span the range of social care provision in Europe: from low to high levels of informal family care work, from high to low levels of organized care provided by publicly funded care workers, and from low to high levels of private expenditure on care services. These differences are discussed in detail in this and subsequent chapters. This chapter considers the wide variation in expectations of family care across the six countries and the contrasting types of formal care provided. The concept of dependency is also explored in relation to differences in the type of care received by older people. The chapter concludes by introducing the concept of social exclusion, to which we return in Chapter 10.

Ageing and social care

Ageing is a well-established demographic feature of all European countries as fertility has declined and life expectancy improved. Most countries have seen the proportion of their population aged 65 and over increase from around 10 per cent in 1960 to around 15 per cent in the late 1990s (OECD, 1999). Ireland and Greece are the main exceptions, for different reasons. Between 1960 and 1997 the size of Ireland's 65-plus age group increased only slightly as a proportion of the total population from 10.9 to 11.4 per cent. While Ireland's population ageing is set to continue, it will do so slowly and alongside growth in the number of adults in economically active age groups. In contrast, Greece is experiencing comparatively rapid ageing and saw a doubling in its 65-plus age group's share of the total population, from 8.1 per cent in 1960 to 15.8 per cent in 1997.

In northern Europe, the main issue for welfare systems which already depend on comparatively high amounts of tax revenue is the projected sharp growth in people aged 80 and over, who are particularly high consumers of health and social care services (Royal Commission on Long Term Care, 1999a). By the mid 1990s, people aged 80 years or older accounted for approximately one-quarter of the total population aged 65 years or older in Denmark, Norway and the UK, compared with just over one-fifth in Italy, Ireland and Greece (OECD, 1999). Southern European countries have younger age structures and are experiencing significant growth in their populations aged over 60, with a more delayed growth in their 'old old'.

Northern European countries depend on large numbers of female employees to undertake care work, and employers are under increasing pressure to offer higher pay and professional status to attract sufficient recruits to the care workforce. There is also concern about the future availability of care within the family, especially in the UK, although the likely future extent of this problem is unclear (Royal Commission on Long Term Care, 1999a). This problem is much more acute in southern Europe, however, where a key issue is whether the current dependence on the informal care of older people within the family, predominantly by female kin, will be sustainable in the absence of any significant paid workforce of carers. There are growing numbers of older people and lower numbers of family carers due to women's rising labour force participation and, in the longer term, declining fertility (Drew, 1998). New education and employment opportunities have opened up for women, who have traditionally undertaken the care of older people, and younger women are increasingly less willing to undertake unpaid care work.

Ageing has brought with it an increasing prevalence of age-related morbidity and disability, and much of the post-war expansion of Europe's health care systems has been in response to these trends. Today, all countries in Europe face economic and political obstacles to finding the tax revenues necessary to support significant growth in publicly funded services and benefits for older people. The impact of ageing on health and social care expenditure arises because older people tend to need care more frequently as they develop chronic, principally cardiovascular and respiratory, diseases. A number of European countries, including Belgium, France, The Netherlands and the United Kingdom, have found that spending on health care multiplies between 65 and 75 years compared with the younger and middle-age groups, but that among the 80-plus age group increased demand and costs fall more on social care services (Jakubowski and Busse, 1998).

All European countries have established universal or nearly universal coverage of their populations by organized medical services which are provided free or at subsidized cost through health insurance or coverage by public services, although in Ireland free primary health care is confined to people on low incomes, including three-quarters of people aged 65 years or older. This degree of state regulation of health care reflects a dependency on professional expertize that has seen medicine encroach extensively on the private sphere of individual and family life. The situation is very different with regard to social care. At its most comprehensive in countries such as Norway and Denmark, social care includes help with ability to move about indoors and outdoors, shopping, cleaning, cooking, eating, dressing and undressing, going to the toilet, washing and general hygiene, and self-medication, as well as psychological and social factors such as sense of locality, sense of sight and hearing, vivacity, self-awareness, emotional security, and ability to make contact with and communicate with other people. The coverage of this type of care varies greatly from country to country, and also varies significantly within countries because of discretion at local level about what is provided. In almost all European countries social care is a family responsibility shouldered predominantly by female kin, complemented to different degrees by public, voluntary and private services.

Ageing brings an increasing risk of enduring difficulties such as physical disability, depression or dementia, and of stressful life events such as loss of affective relationships. These changes affect individuals at different rates and with different patterns, and individual older people respond to them in different ways: they have different degrees of vulnerability and different coping styles (Titterton, 1992). There are also great differences in the coping resources available to older people, such as their family, income and wealth, and the public services available where they live. These differences determine whether the loss of adaptability that can occur with ageing also means for the older person a loss of autonomy, independence and quality of life.

Ageing is a public policy issue in all European countries but there are different perspectives on what the role of the state should be in responding to this challenge. Some European countries have highly developed welfare systems, exemplified by the Scandinavian welfare states. These provide a high level of benefits and services for older people and have generally reduced levels of social polarization, exclusion and segregation in these societies (Musterd and Ostendorf, 1998). Other welfare states are less developed, notably in southern Europe where there is a polarization between relatively well protected core sectors of the labour force and the weaker social protection experienced by peripheral groups (Ferrera, 1996). As discussed in Chapter 2, general models of welfare states are useful as descriptive and theoretical tools, but are limited in helping to understand the particular situation of older people within these different welfare regimes. In particular, by emphasizing particular concepts – such as Esping-Andersen's (1990) early concern with the extent to which welfare provision displaces market forces with different, needs-based, allocative principles – other factors are neglected. Such factors can be the key to understanding why particular types of provision vary so greatly across Europe, and social care is a prime example.

This difference in the meaning of social care is also reflected in arrangements for paying family carers from public funds. These arrangements differ between the six countries, largely because there are quite different attitudes about whether family care is equivalent to waged work. In Italy small and essentially tokenistic payments are sometimes made by the local authority, and in Greece modest payments to a family carer may be available through a contributory social insurance scheme. The United Kingdom and Ireland have national systems to provide financial support to family carers, but payments are strictly rationed, conditional and modest in amount. However, in Denmark and Norway a family carer can opt to be employed by the local authority as a waged home carer for a close relative, although in Denmark this arrangement is limited to practical help. It excludes personal care, a policy which reflects Denmark's clear policy of professionalizing this type of assistance.

Coverage of social care services

The six countries discussed in this book span the range of social care provision in Europe. Using the main components of formal social care provision – long-term care in nursing and residential homes and home care – Table 1.1 shows the position of each country in terms of the estimated coverage of these services by publicly funded provision.

Table 1.1 Receipt of publicly funded long-term care, female employment and GDP

Country	Older people resident in long-term care institutions[a] (%)	Older people receiving home care (%)	Female participation rate[b] 1997 (1987)	Gross domestic product per capita $US 1998 ($US[c] using purchasing power parities)
Norway	7	15	75.8 (72.3)	32 853 (27 497)
Denmark	4	20	75.1 (76.8)	32 934 (26 280)
UK	4	8	66.8 (62.4)	23 006 (21 170)
Ireland	5	3	50.4 (38.5)	22 287 (22 509)
Italy	2	1	44.1 (43.4)	20 323 (21 739)
Greece	1	<1	47.5 (41.7)	11 366 (14 463)

[a] Older people are defined as aged 65 or older in the UK, Ireland, Italy and Greece, and 67 or older in Norway and Denmark
[b] Female labour force of all ages as a proportion of female population aged 15–64
[c] Purchasing power parities eliminate differences in price levels between countries

Sources: OECD (1996), (1999); Eurostat (1998); Nordic Council of Ministers/Nordic Statistical Secretariat (1998).

In the two Scandinavian countries, between one-fifth and one-quarter of older people are receiving formally organized social care services funded almost wholly by taxation and allocated according to need. There is a somewhat greater bias towards care in nursing and residential homes in Norway compared with Denmark's more deinstitutionalized system, although Norway is moving further towards the Danish model. At the other end of the range, Greece and the south of Italy have extremely low levels of publicly funded institutional and domiciliary care. Family members are normally expected to meet the personal care and domestic needs of older relatives. If this is not possible, the lack of publicly funded services means that private services must be purchased out of disability pensions or insurance benefits – an expensive and often unaffordable option. Local authority and, in particular, church and voluntary organizations exist as sources of help for older people who are poor and without family support, but provision varies greatly from area to area.

Coverage is a little higher in Ireland but long-term care in institutions includes long-stay hospitals as well as nursing homes and residential units. The UK occupies a middle-ranking position, although the extent to which care provision is deinstitutionalized is comparable to Denmark.

As discussed in Chapter 2, cross-national statistical comparisons are fraught with difficulty because of lack of data and different definitions.

Table 1.1 gives an indication of where each of the six countries stands in relation to the coverage of publicly-funded social care, but this picture is to some extent misleading. While the local state is almost a monopoly provider of formally organized social care in Denmark and Norway, in the UK many older people pay privately for this type of assistance. Compared with these Scandinavian countries, the UK is a relatively low-tax country. Tax receipts represent 52 per cent of GDP in Denmark and 41 per cent in Norway, but the equivalent figure is 36 per cent of a smaller GDP per head in the UK – less than Italy's 43 per cent and Greece's 41 per cent, and closer to Ireland's 34 per cent (OECD, 1998a). Both the UK's and Ireland's state-funded social care provision is means tested and targeted on low-income older people; including private home help raises coverage in both countries to about 12 per cent, and a high proportion of older people also pay privately for nursing or residential home care (OECD, 1996). Similarly, although the coverage of formally organized home help services in Greece is extremely low, Stathopoulos and Amera (1992) estimate that social care provision reaches some 10 per cent of older people, largely through the voluntary activities of KAPI centres (see Chapter 8). By the end of the year 2000, 30 to 40 per cent of Greek municipalities will have home help and/or home nursing services connected with the KAPIs and local health services. And while, overall, Italy broadly fits the general pattern of southern European countries, with per capita welfare expenditure about half of other EU states, Italy's 'core' developed regions are more similar to northern Europe than its relatively underdeveloped south, which has strong similarities to Greece, Portugal and Spain (Pratschke, 1999). Nevertheless, Table 1.1 is a reasonable indication of the extent to which formally organized social care services are available to older people in the six countries, planned and funded by the State, although not necessarily directly provided by the public sector. In countries with lower coverage, more older people are dependent on either their families or their ability to pay, or receive no help with their care needs.

Table 1.1 reveals a close association between the coverage of publicly funded social care services and the level of women's participation in the labour market. The State's responsibility for providing care services for both older people and children is greatest in the Scandinavian countries, where political action has established these services as part of women's right to paid work. Indeed, Anttonen and Sipilä (1996) report a strong statistical relationship across 14 European countries between the level of women's employment and the provision of both publicly funded children's day care and home care for older people.

The relationship was stronger for older people's services than for child care, although the level of child care provision was strongly related to the level of participation of mothers of small children in the labour market. The explanation for this relationship lies both in the opportunity to take up paid work which the existence of care services creates, and in the employment opportunities for women which the care services themselves generate.

Given the wide scale of social care provision for older people in Denmark and Norway, population ageing is creating major pressures on public expenditure. But opposition to rationalizing provision is strong because the services are universal and a wide range of older voters and their families have a stake in them, and continue to press for improvements. The fact that these services employ large numbers of women and facilitate others in going out to work also generates political support for the high spending that sustains them. Although changes are being made, with greater targeting of services and the development of support for family carers, Norway and Denmark are essentially locked into a model of high social spending in which care work is largely a state responsibility (Kvist, 1999). Large majorities in these countries consider that meeting the future growth in older people's needs for care should be a public responsibility (Bay, 1998).

The United Kingdom presents a more complex picture. As considered in Chapter 5, its means tested system of social care for older people has been reduced in coverage in recent years. But the comprehensive duty placed upon local authorities to assess all people who appear to be in need of social care services, regardless of income, makes the system similar in many respects to those of Norway and Denmark. There is, however, less funding for care services and means tested charging for any social care services assessed as needed; research by Davis, Ellis and Rummery (1997) suggests that budgetary pressures lead to many older people being denied their right to a full assessment. Nevertheless, the formality of referral and assessment processes in the UK, Norway and Denmark creates a single access point where decisions are made about an older person's eligibility for publicly funded services. Care management is also part of this process, with one professional taking responsibility for organizing services for an individual older person.

The picture is radically different in the southern European countries and Ireland, where the role of the State is minimal and discretionary in a much less regulated way than in the UK, Norway or Denmark. The expectation has been that virtually all social care will be provided within the family. This model is under pressure from women's increasing educational achievement and rising economic activity rate, together with legislation that has promoted gender equality. As noted earlier, younger women, with higher levels of education, have become more involved in paid work than in the past, with less time to care for elderly relatives. This trend is also associated with the rapid decline in the fertility rate of southern European countries, which is likely to create a future shortage of family carers (Drew, 1998).

Ageing and dependency

Gibson (1998) argues that while dependency is often an unavoidable consequence of ageing, there are different types of dependency, with positive dependency supporting the individual's autonomy, or capacity to make decisions, and negative dependency failing to do so. This is sometimes seen as a feature of the care setting. In hospital, for example, negative dependency is often unavoidable. Platz (1998) comments, 'as a hospital patient, one is socially excluded and subject to others' authority. Possibilities for self-determination and integration are much better outside hospital, and can in themselves contribute to further recovery'. Residential and nursing homes are sometimes criticized for creating negative dependency in a similar way, but there is far less reason for this than in hospital (Jack, 1998). Older people's well-being is dependent on good social interaction and 'person-centred' care, with opportunities to make choices. In general, Hansen and Platz (1997) found no difference between nursing homes and supported housing for several measures of older people's self-reported well-being after controlling for their level of incapacity, and conclude that good care may be present or absent in any care setting. However, they did find that older people in both settings were less likely to report positive evaluations of their well-being than older people living in ordinary housing. These results are partly echoed in Slagsvold's (1999) study in Norway which compared the well-being of older people with a high level of dependency living in different residential settings. There were few differences between people living in nursing homes and in sheltered housing, but people living in ordinary housing reported a lower level of well-being. This suggests that in Norway there may be a shortfall in domiciliary provision for some users who are left with unmet needs for security, assistance and company.

While in Denmark, Norway and, to a lesser extent, the UK, many older people use publicly funded social care services, this is far less the case in Ireland, Italy or Greece. Instead, older people are often dependent on their families, sometimes voluntary services and, for those able to pay, hired private care. Family care is no guarantee against care being provided in a way that creates a 'dependent' personality. It can in fact be experienced as a type of closed institutional care and, as Giarchi (1996, p. 372) found in the city of La Spezia, it can create a gendered dependency for the cared-for person as well as the carer:

> There were moments in the interviews which picked up the sense of imprisonment of grandmothers peering through half-opened shutters at the world outside, where their husbands, male relatives and friends were enjoying the *passegiata* (promenade), or were drinking and playing cards in the *trattorie* or enjoying a game of *boccia* (a popular game of bowls). Women went out occasionally to the garden of remembrance, to Sunday Mass (here the men stayed at home), to do the shopping with their daughters, or take the grandchildren for early morning or evening walks.

Giarchi's (1996, p. 374) work in Italy draws attention to the enclosed nature of family life for some older Italians, whom he portrays as 'captive within households', with their disengagement from social life actively fostered, especially in the south. In Italy, Greece and Ireland the most vulnerable are those older people who have no family and live alone or with a family member who is also old or mentally ill. Ireland has a uniquely large group of people aged 75 or older who never married and lack family support. Giarchi (1996), however, suggests that contact with neighbours is a notable feature in Ireland where this friendliness provides some security for older people, an assessment echoed by O'Shea and Larragy (1995). Given that majorities of older people in all six countries live separately from their children, the extent of family care in Ireland, Italy and Greece relies on close residential proximity and on the willingness of one or more family member to care. In Italy, a number of studies have noted the close proximity of family members living in separate private apartments, and many older people still live with their families (Giarchi, 1996). Even in Denmark there is provision for older people to choose to move closer to a family member, taking their services with them, despite the fact that there is no expectation that families will themselves provide care. There remains, however, a growing problem in Greece, Italy and Ireland with how to care for older people with significant personal care needs that cannot be adequately met within families. In Greece, the recent initiative to expand home help services is a response to this issue.

Without state support, families have to find ways of coping. In Italy one of the stimuli for early retirement has been children retiring early to look after older parents, especially for more severe needs such as dementia (Cioni, 1998). Berry-Lound and Marsh (1996) report that in Italy an average of 10.7 working days were lost over a six-month period for each employee combining paid work with caring for an older person, compared with 3.8 days in the UK and 3.3 days in Denmark. In Greece, the lack of nursing home provision and of community nurses has led to families hiring foreign immigrants as live-in carers for frail relatives whom they cannot look after themselves. This is quite a common solution to caring for many older people; if he or she is 67 per cent or more disabled it has been possible for an illegal immigrant to acquire a legal right to work in Greece through this route. For those who do enter a nursing home the cost of nursing care means that family members will often nurse their relatives themselves. Hiring a nurse is very expensive, and private nurses are often foreign and untrained.

In Norway, where the family is under less pressure than in Italy or Greece because of the extent of publicly funded care services, family members can still feel that an older relative is dependent on them. Home care services are relatively thinly spread because provision is based on the principle of helping as many people as possible. Although, as in the UK, provision has become more concentrated on older people with a higher level of dependency, the spread of existing services means that family care is not redundant because formal services cannot entirely substitute for it. What is occurring, however, is a trend towards more people providing smaller amounts of informal care as the number of older people living alone continues to increase. But growth in the number of informal carers, rather than in the amount of help each carer provides, has meant that there is a relatively modest impact on carers' employment opportunities and incomes, and there is not the marked relationship between informal care and physical and emotional strain which has been found in the UK (Lingsom, 1997). Indeed – and this is probably even more true of Denmark – the fact that much of the care work is done by public services means that there is more opportunity for family relationships to be based on forms of positive dependency in which interactions are intimate and mutually rewarding.

Although the primacy of the family has inhibited the development of social care services organized by the state in Greece, Ireland and Italy, this has not been the case with regard to Church and voluntary sector services. In Greece, the Eastern Orthodox Church runs residential homes and community services, and involves large numbers of volunteers in caring for older people. While an important part of welfare provision in Greece, these services are variable in both coverage and quality, and in rural areas are much less developed (Stathopoulos and Amera, 1992). Other non-governmental organizations are also significant, such as the Red Cross, which runs a large home help programme in Athens.

Italy's voluntary organizations run major programmes for older people, focusing on generic rather than specialist care and usually organized in partnership with the local authorities; the main organizations are social co-operatives, Caritas, the St Vincent de Paul Society, parish groups and the Italian Red Cross. Similarly, Ireland has a large number of local and national organizations based on volunteering and running care services for older people, often organized through the parish. One estimate is that one-quarter of older people in Ireland are users of voluntary organization services, although the range and intensity of these services varies greatly (Mulvihill, 1993).

While there may be issues about the quality of care in all care settings, the association of any care setting with dependency is symbolic as well as real. 'Admission' to care in many countries symbolizes that the older person has lost their struggle to remain independent and is now to be isolated from the mainstream of society. But residential care can equally enable an older person to remain independent of a need to 'burden' their family. In Denmark, 'normal' independent living in nursing homes has been promoted by measures such as residents not paying for services in their nursing home as a total package deducted from their pensions. Instead, they receive their pensions and 'pay as they go' for services, in the same way as someone living independently in the community would pay for what they need (other than the care services themselves, which are free).

Choice depends on the availability of alternative sources of provision, and the reduction in nursing homes in Denmark has caused some opposition for this reason (Leeson, 1997). There are concerns that very dependent older people who now receive services in the community are being denied the quality of care, security and opportunities for social interaction that good nursing home care should be able to provide with its one-to-one resident–staff ratios. This 'care gap' in the community has also caused some concern in Norway (where compared with Denmark the level of provision in the community is lower although increasing) because of the contrast with high-quality care in institutions. The situation can be contrasted with the UK, where social care services are deinstitutionalized to the same degree as Denmark, and where there continues to be a strong consensus that nursing or residential home care is a last resort. This type of care, however, is often used because it is less expensive than intensive packages of care at home. While this is also a factor in Denmark and Norway, it is not the case to the same extent because the lower cost of institutional care in the UK reflects lower-quality standards than in Scandinavia. Residential and nursing home care is rarely a positive choice in the UK, partly for symbolic reasons but also because of this quality issue – which is only now starting to be addressed with national quality and training standards (Department of Health, 1998a).

Although the apparently progressive philosophy of ageing at home, with care staff working with an older person's accustomed way of life and encouraging them to do things for themselves, has come to be widely accepted across Europe, it is not unchallenged. Home care services in Norway, Denmark and the UK emphasize avoiding negative dependency by supporting the abilities of older people to help and decide themselves. Important principles are that assistance should not be offered for tasks that an older person can manage on their own, and that older people should have opportunities to participate in decisions about their care. As an ideological principle applicable to all older people this may have unintended consequences. Vabø (1998) found that very frail older people can feel worried about taking decisions, confused when faced with choices, and find too much self-help tiring and stressful. Her examples include, 'one woman who did not get help to dress in the morning because she was supposed to keep on going. The "dressing exercise" tired her so much she had to go to bed after breakfast ... Another woman felt that she had lost the ability to decide what was best for herself and just wanted a home helper who could help make the best choices' (Vabø, 2000).

The idea that the State should provide comprehensive services would be alien to most Greek citizens, where it is not the State but the family which takes responsibility for older people. Thirty per cent of older people live with their adult children. The family is the primary unit which 'a Greek trusts and respects, feels responsible for, and is dependent upon' (Stathopoulos and Amera, 1992, p. 180). The role of the family is reproduced through strong bonds of reciprocal care and responsibility. Grandparents are usually extensively involved in the everyday care of grandchildren, participate in family socializing and may help out their children financially. The increased participation of women in the labour market has served to bolster grandparents' role in child care, as well as strengthening family finances. Such practices are born of necessity in a country with a relatively low level of economic development, but they are also culturally reproduced. Attitudes to family care and the role of the State in both Italy and Ireland are much closer to Greece than to Denmark, despite considerably higher GDPs.

Ferrera (1996) and Katrougalos (1996) trace the smaller role of the State in Italy, Greece and other south European countries to their weak or divided socialist movements and to the absence of a post-war class compromise based on social democracy. The role of the Roman Catholic Church in the histories and cultures of Italy and Ireland is also significant. Although the extent of this influence on social policy is disputed (see Katrougalos, 1996), it is nevertheless the case that Roman Catholic teaching affirms the primacy of the family as a social unit, equating responsibility for the care of older parents with that for children. Catholic social teaching emphasizes subsidiarity in the sense that

> obligations should in the first place be exercised at the closest possible level to the person, with higher social bodies like the state intervening only when more proximate social networks at lower levels are unable to meet the requirements … Ordinarily, people who are within these networks will be able to support and to be supported by the others around them – in most cases the family, the workplace, and sometimes the community. (Spicker, 1997, p. 135)

Dependency for older people who need help with personal care and domestic tasks is inescapable. What is at issue is whether the dependency is negatively reinforced or whether the help provided promotes remaining areas of independence, especially the care recipient having reasonable control over what is provided and by whom, and being informed of the options available to them. Given the powerful voice of many older people within their families in Greece, Italy and Ireland, this control may exist there to a greater extent than for older people in Denmark or Norway, who are more dependent upon what the State provides. But by creating universal access to social care services, Denmark and Norway have established extensive stakeholding in these services which creates a powerful force for their continuing improvement. In other words, the quality of care is not a private issue but a public concern. An important feature of Norway and Denmark's social care services is that they are used across the social class spectrum and redistribute across the life cycle rather than from rich to poor. High taxation thus benefits a wide section of the older population. This not only generates quantitative pressure on services but also qualitative pressure. Many users are middle income and are more likely to complain about poor services than low income users, and this is reflected in survey data about complaints. Leeson (1997) reports that up to 57 per cent of Danish home care users expressed dissatisfaction with either the quantity or quality of care, a much higher proportion than has been reported in UK surveys (ECCEP team, 1998). In countries where publicly funded services are less adequate, such as Greece, there is less stakeholding in public services, especially among the middle classes, because more people look to private services for better quality and coverage if they can afford to do so, while a 'poverty of expectation' may depress demands from low-income users of public services for a better quality of service.

Bartlett and Blackman make a distinction in Chapter 2 between the more family-oriented systems of care in Ireland, Italy and Greece, and the more individual-oriented systems of Denmark, Norway and – in less universalist form – the UK. Their discussion of care systems enables some important generalizations to be made, most significantly the extent to which these systems are defined both by different levels of economic development and, on a separate dimension, distinctive welfare cultures. Despite various tensions, the systems prevalent in each country are unlikely to change significantly in the foreseeable future because of the extent to which they are determined by these deep-seated economic and cultural factors. Chapters 3 to 8 describe the systems in much more detail, illustrating how general models do not capture the complexity of each country's arrangements. However, an important overall theme that emerges from these descriptions is the different extents to which the civil societies of the six countries are penetrated by a welfare state.

A high degree of penetration by the welfare state is often regarded in the social policy literature as a precondition for social inclusion, based on common citizenship underpinned by access to employment, income redistribution and universal welfare services (Oppenheim, 1998). Some countries, notably the UK, have retreated from this position towards a more selective approach, justified by an argument that the old welfare policies created too much dependency on the welfare state, creating work disincentives and stifling entrepreneurialism (Blackman and Palmer, 1999). This argument has appeared in the developed care systems of northern Europe as the issue of 'overcare' (Gibson, 1998). This term has been used to describe the 'learned helplessness' acquired, in particular, in institutional care where the medical model casts residents in a disempowered and passive sick role (Seligman, 1975). In those countries with relatively well-funded social care systems these criticisms had a major influence during the 1980s, especially in Denmark where since 1988 no new nursing homes for older people have been built, and many nursing homes have been closed. New building has consisted of independent living accommodation, often with the same level of care services as the nursing homes they replaced. Community services have received substantial investment with the aim of enabling older people to choose to remain living in their existing home.

Conclusion

There is a growing emphasis in aged care policy across Europe on maintaining 'normal' lifestyles, not just in the person's own home but also in residential and nursing homes. This includes attention to maintaining independence for as long as possible – the ability of an individual to cope without the help of others – and maintaining the person's autonomy whatever the care setting – the ability of an individual to do what he or she desires. Active social involvement is also an important aim. None of these aims requires a particular care setting to be achievable. Domiciliary care may not achieve the high standards that are available in residential homes, and may make older people dependent on family care against their wishes. Residential and nursing homes may be used not as a positive choice but because supporting a very dependent older person in their own home is too expensive. Extensive family care does not necessarily equate with good outcomes.

Hansen and Platz (1997) identify several factors that are important to the well-being of older people independent of the particular type of care setting: mainly the physical suitability of the living environment and good opportunities for mixing with other older people. They also point out the importance of carers having a positive attitude. 'The elderly person must feel in the centre as a person and not as a case to get over with. Perhaps this demands more time for staff, but first of all it is a question of attitudes' (Hansen and Platz, 1997, p. 16).

Social exclusion is an issue of societal attitudes and practices. Exclusion is actively produced through the norms and values that govern both civil society and public services – by denying rights to certain groups, by making unfair or inconsistent judgements, by allocating resources indiscriminately or on the basis of patronage or corruption, and by stigmatizing sections of society perceived to be less productive or deviant in their behaviour and beliefs. We return in Chapter 10 to the concept of social exclusion, its relevance to the social care of older people, and how the concept might be applied to a cross-national analysis of access, entitlement and quality of care. First, however, we consider the models of care discernible in our six countries, and then describe in more detail older people's care in each country individually.

2
Models of Care

Helen Bartlett and Tim Blackman

Introduction

The purpose of this chapter is to provide contextual information about the six countries and their models of care for older people. The six countries comprise two examples of the Scandinavian welfare model with high state spending on care services, Denmark and Norway; two representatives of a liberal welfare model with medium provision and extensive means testing, the UK and Ireland; and two representatives of the south European model with very limited state-funded social care services (Castles, 1995; Daly, 1996; Ferarra, 1996; Katrougalos, 1996; Leibfried, 1993; Rhodes, 1997).

These general models, however, do not capture important features of each country's system of social care for older people. For example, the family has a central role in the social care systems of Italy, Ireland, Greece and, to a lesser extent, the UK, compared to Norway and especially Denmark. The UK has a developed system of publicly funded social care services compared to Ireland, Italy and Greece, but charges can be high as a result of means testing, in contrast to Norway and Denmark's free or low-cost services. Pension provision for many older people in Italy is good compared with the UK, enabling older people to hire care services until these become prohibitively expensive due to higher levels of need. All countries have a strong policy emphasis on care in the community and avoiding institutionalization, but Italy, Greece and Ireland continue to have an underprovision of publicly funded places compared with the level of need, and nursing home care is a luxury often only available to affluent older people. Some types of provision also show patterns that do not fit general models: community-based day centres with open access and voluntary help, for example, are an important feature of the care systems of Greece, Norway, Denmark and, to a lesser extent, Ireland. They are less common in Italy and rare in the UK. Community nursing services are universal and free in Norway, Denmark, the UK and Ireland, but there is a great shortage of these services in Italy and, especially, Greece: in these two countries, people often have to hire private nurses, who may be unqualified.

In common with many previous comparative studies, the difficulties of cross-national comparisons have to be acknowledged. The countries included in this analysis have very divergent systems with different political and social structures, a complexity of provision and multiplicity of providers. The task of comparative analysis is particularly difficult because of the lack of nationally comparable data. Some of these challenges are highlighted by Walker and Maltby (1997) in relation to the work of the European Observatory on Ageing and Older People. The Observatory was created in 1991 as part of a wider programme of actions on older people and was designed to monitor the impact of social and economic policies on older people across the member states. Key methodological problems encountered were the incomparability of national datasets, absence of up-to-date figures, lack of independent evidence, and lack of differentiation in the reporting of age ranges. While the Observatory has produced considerable national and comparative analysis on the care of older people, more remains to be done if the situations of all countries are to be reflected accurately in any comparative analysis.

Overview of welfare models in Europe

In the absence of reliable data about health and social services generally, and care of older people specifically, a comparison of the six countries can be assisted by reference to existing models and conceptual frameworks that place countries within a social, political and economic context. Various categorizations and typologies of welfare models and welfare delivery have been developed over the years. Titmuss's (1963) work is an early example. He identified three models of welfare: 'residual', with welfare needs met primarily through the family or the market and with means testing for public services which are used as a last resort; 'achievement-reward', based on earnings-related contributory principles; and 'institutional-redistributive', based on universalism and rights to state-funded services. However, Titmuss saw these models as ways of describing where the emphasis lies in any given policy area rather than as types of welfare state.

Most widely used to describe and compare European welfare states or regimes has been Esping-Anderson's (1990) classification of social democratic, conservative/corporatist and liberal welfare regimes. The social democratic welfare model, associated with the Scandinavian countries, emphasizes universal services with the statutory sector as the primary, and often monopoly, provider. Indeed, a separate Scandinavian model later emerged to reflect the similarities within the Scandinavian countries (Daatland, 1992). The provision of care by a large workforce of paid carers is financed mainly by general taxation. Neither the family nor the independent (voluntary and private) sector plays a significant role and commercial care has been virtually non-existent, the main exception being the recent spread of a purchaser–provider split in recent years and some limited growth in both non-profit and for-profit providers – mainly in Sweden. Indeed, there are differences between the Scandinavian countries, as illustrated by Sweden's greater embrace of commercialization which still tends to be opposed on ideological grounds elsewhere in Scandinavia. Other differences include Denmark's relatively greater emphasis on services compared with cash benefits for the care of children and older people (Rostgaard and Fridberg, 1998). A consequence of this is that family care plays a more minor role as a source of help in its care system compared with Norway and Sweden.

The conservative or corporatist model is associated with central European countries, none of which were examined in this analysis, although it has been argued that Greece is a less developed version of this model (Katrougalos, 1996). Labour market solutions are central, with negotiated agreements between employers and employees covering social protection measures. Those outside the labour market have to rely on charitable provision. Katrougalos (1996) argues that Greece is close to this model but is less developed because of financial constraints. Although family care is extensive in Greece, there is no deliberate policy stance to avoid interfering in private family lives, which tends to be the case in Ireland and, to a lesser degree, the UK (Hantrais, 1999). Indeed, Greece is making a significant effort to improve the coverage of home help and home nursing services (see Chapter 8).

The residual or liberal welfare state is associated with the UK, especially under the period of Conservative government from 1979 to 1997. This is based on the role of the State as a primary provider that engages directly in health and welfare activity through agencies such as the National Health Service (NHS) and local government. The State provides a basic level of welfare, from a combination of general taxation and contributory payments from those in employment, with additional services bought from the private sector by those able to afford to do so. There has been a trend for the State to withdraw from some areas, leaving the commercial, charitable and family sectors to provide. In the case of health care, there has been a substitution of means tested social care services for some provision that was previously free under the NHS (notably, long-term institutional care, although free nursing care in nursing homes is to be introduced from October 2001, with social care elements remaining means-tested). Ireland shares some of the characteristics of this model with the UK, but a tradition of subsidiarity means that the State has never developed a major role as a provider of social care, and religious and voluntary organizations figure prominently alongside family care (Munday and Ely, 1996).

More recently, evidence for a 'southern model' of welfare has been provided by Ferrera (1996), characterized by a combination of occupationalism in income maintenance and universalism as related to health care. Italy and Greece, along with Spain and Portugal, are represented here. Their modes of care for older people are difficult to classify and to fit into the categories derived for the more northern European States (Giarchi, 1996). With the introduction of the Italian National Health Service in 1978, Italy conformed to a universalist health care model which in recent years has included improved access to social care services. The family, however, still provides the focus of a collective responsibility for social care, either provided directly or hired. In the care of older people, Greece also fits the southern model but, as noted above, this may be a feature of economic underdevelopment rather than policy. Public services are currently very limited and secondary to non-statutory informal care provided by the Church, family and established charities. The main exceptions are perhaps the Greek day centres (KAPIs) and associated home help services, although these still make extensive use of volunteers.

Esping-Anderson's early classification was subsequently strongly criticized for concentrating on the income security of regular wage earners and failing to address social policy benefits and services that are important to women (Lewis, 1992). It has been argued that too much attention is given in his classification to the relationship between the State and the labour market, ignoring the relationship between the State and the family (O'Connor, 1993). A broader perspective is advocated by O'Connor and used with interesting results by Anttonen and Sipilä (1996) in their analysis of the application of welfare models to social services (specifically services for older people and children). They conclude that certain patterns exist across Europe, justifying reference to a number of models. First, they too distinguish the operation of a Scandinavian model. The model is characterized by the high labour force participation of women outside the home, universal services, citizens' rights to certain municipal services, the involvement of local government in funding and planning social services, and the limited presence of commercial services. Second, they refer to a family care model, distinctive of Italy and Greece. Here, the labour force participation of women is low, public social services are few and most services are informal. A third model proposed is a British means tested model in which the provision of social care services is the responsibility of the State, but where access is controlled and services are tightly rationed. It is noted that Ireland has many similar features to the British model, but can also be likened to the southern European family care model. Finally, in the case of the welfare of older people, a central European subsidiarity model is distinguished, applying largely to The Netherlands and Germany. In this model it is principally the family that takes primary responsibility for the social care of older people, and public services are provided mainly through religious and political organizations with public funding.

It is clear from this discussion that general models of welfare have their limitations in helping us to understand the situation of particular population groups and the characteristics of particular services. Models have tended to be based on comparing aggregate social spending between countries (Alber, 1995). This has led to a neglect of important differences, such as the coverage and level of provision of particular services; the extent to which services are organizationally and professionally integrated or fragmented; accessibility, choice and suitability for individual older people; and the role of services in supporting independence as opposed to creating dependency. The care of older people is a complex policy area, making cross-national comparisons very difficult. Policy and practice have strong local dimensions with substantial variability within countries; differing values and assumptions lie behind the roles of the family, the State, the market and the voluntary sector; and the meaning of 'social care' itself is far from unproblematic (Tester, 1999). Nevertheless, it is possible to identify broad patterns and trends, and to identify features of the wider context in which individual countries' care systems are developing.

Factors influencing models of care

Many demographic, economic and ideological pressures are common to all European nations and act to shape the way in which services develop. First, the formulation of care models is strongly determined by population ageing. The changing demographic profile across Europe is well documented (Walker and Maltby, 1997). In 1993, people aged 60 and over represented one-fifth of the total population, but this is set to rise to more than one-quarter by the year 2020. The pace of ageing varies significantly between member states as fertility and mortality rates differ between countries. Of the six countries included in this book, Ireland has the lowest proportion of people aged 60 and over and Italy the highest: 15.5 per cent and 21.3 per cent respectively. However, as noted in Chapter 1, it is the northern European countries where there is particular pressure on public spending due to an increasing number of older people aged 80 years and older. This has been a fairly long-term trend: in Denmark, the proportion of the population in this age group increased from 1.6 per cent in 1960 to 2.8 per cent in 1996, and is projected to increase to 3.5 per cent in 2020 (Rostgaard and Fridberg, 1998). As yet, however, there is no retreat from the universal model despite growing costs, although Danish provision, as in other counties with less extensive coverage, has focused more on personal care for very frail older people. Among the reasons why Denmark has been able to sustain this level of provision is its avoidance of a universal earnings-related state pension scheme and cost containment in health and especially acute care (OECD, 1996).

Second, policies for older people may result more from economic influences than from health and welfare interests. It could be argued that the different models and systems across the six countries reflect their different stages of economic development. For example, the situation in Greece could reflect the fact that Greece is 40–50 years behind other countries in its economic development. Munday and Ely's (1996) analysis supports the view that countries with higher gross domestic product such as Denmark have more highly developed social care services than poorer countries such as Greece. However, this does not hold universally: the UK, Ireland and Italy all have a similar gross domestic product but very different social care systems. In Ireland, Italy and Greece the experience of older people needing help with their care varies greatly depending on income and geographical location. For instance, despite the adequacy of pensions for many older people with good employment records, the poverty level of many other older people is high. In addition, a large proportion of older people live in the rural areas. In some cases, such as isolated areas of Greece, this can mean very few services and possibly premature death, while in Ireland older people may actually benefit positively from the community networks of rural areas which help to coordinate a variety of voluntary services.

As economic difficulties confronted European countries in the 1980s, many governments sought ways of providing care less expensively. In Greece, the expansion of community day centres (KAPIs) which combine a small group of professional staff with volunteers has been seen as a way of providing cost-effective care for a growing older population (see Chapter 8). In the more developed care systems of northern Europe, there has been a shift – to different degrees – in the 'welfare mix' to reduce costs and keep taxation at a politically acceptable level. Johnson (1999) summarizes these changes as including reductions in services and tightened eligibility criteria; increases in charges and co-payments; and increased use of private-sector providers with competition through 'contracting out'.

The UK led the way with these type of reforms in the 1980s and 1990s, especially with the 1993 reforms which introduced 'cash limited' budgets for social care and a requirement that a minimum proportion of these budgets must be spent on services from the private or voluntary sectors. Public funds are very important in the UK where a sufficient pension and insurance base has not developed as an alternative for people who need care, and family care is less available than in, for example, Ireland or Italy. However, the extent of means testing, which leaves many older people with large bills to meet, has been severely criticized, not least by the Royal Commssion on Long Term Care (1999a). The Government has responded with a package of measures that include abolishing the means testing of nursing care in all nursing homes from October 2001 (Secretary of State for Health, 2000). Although all nursing care will be free, personal social care, accommodation and meals will still involve an older person undergoing a means test to determine what they should pay towards these services.

A third factor influencing models of care for older people is cultural: ideology, social attitudes and expectations. A preference for ensuring that older people can live in their own homes for as long as possible is widespread in Europe. Walker and Maltby (1997) report Eurobarometer data showing that 80 per cent of the general public in the 12 countries surveyed expressed a preference for older people to remain at home rather than be cared for in institutions. Nevertheless, it would be wrong to assume that older Europeans are uniform in their aspirations or life experiences. The Eurobarometer survey found considerable disparity in life satisfaction: 68 per cent of older people in Denmark stated that they were very satisfied with the lives they led, compared with just

6 per cent in Greece. Only 3 per cent of older people in Denmark said they were not satisfied with their lives, compared with 59 per cent in Greece. Despite the family orientation of Greek society, in which older people traditionally have a central position, the Eurobarometer survey found that 36 per cent of older people in Greece often felt lonely, compared with less than 5 per cent in Denmark, where the great majority of older people live independently and have less contact with relatives. Cultural expectations and attitudes may therefore exercise a powerful influence on the quality of life of older people, rather than this simply reflecting the level of either family or formal care. The social and cultural values of Greek elders would be unlikely to chime well with the way older people in Denmark live, just as there is no prospect of older people's children in Denmark being prepared to be as involved with their older parents' care as occurs in Greece. Generational changes are also relevant to this discussion: despite the pressure on universal services in Norway and Denmark, future generations brought up with this level of provision are unlikely to be willing to devote more time to caring for frail older relatives when they see this as a responsibility of the State. In Ireland, Italy and Greece, attitudes among younger generations are changing as the education and employment aspirations of women increase, and there is less willingness to devote large amounts of time to unpaid social care, especially without support or opportunities for respite.

The trend towards welfare pluralism

The arguments around the development of more pluralist mixed economies of welfare generally are well known and concern the more explicit integration of state provision with private and informal sources (Johnson, 1999). There has always been a mixed economy of care: even in countries with well-developed care systems self-care and family care are significant, and help is hired privately, especially for domestic tasks such as cleaning. However, in some countries – notably the UK – a mixed economy of formal care has been developed as an explicit policy priority associated with creating 'quasi-markets' in which competition keeps down costs and creates choice, with the State in a regulatory role (May and Brunsdon, 1999). In Europe there has been a general acceptance for some time of a trend towards a 'welfare mix' of agencies providing care revolving around the State, market, voluntary sector and informal care (Abrahamson, 1992; Anderson, 1993; Baldock and Evers, 1992; Hugman, 1994). While the role of central and local Government has not necessarily been reduced, there is generally an increased emphasis on the contribution of families, volunteers and independent organizations. In addition, the gradual emergence of for-profit enterprises in social care is observed, along with the introduction of charges to help address governments' financial problems. The trend for local government to adopt a purchaser and contractor role seems likely to spread to most EU countries in the near future. Baldock and Evers (1992, p. 291) claim that 'there has been a fundamental and logically necessary re-negotiation and reorganization of the relationship between formal, public care services and the informal, mainly family, sources of care for the dependent'. This, they argue, has come about as a result of a more flexible use of resources and ideological pressures that have facilitated individualized and home-based forms of care.

Cost considerations have dominated these developments, but they also reflect a growing recognition of the 'co-production' of welfare in which public services work in partnership with the abilities and capacities of older people, as well as the range of resources that may be available within their social network and from non-statutory providers. The involvement of the non-statutory sector in social care is now extensive in many European countries, which are seeking to institutionalize its role along with family care through contracts, partnerships and payments for family carers. More covertly, however, there is a trend towards formal care services being restricted to older people without a strong family network, and for more older people to seek private services as the costs, bureaucracy and possibly stigma of accessing rationed public services increase.

A shift away from state-dominated welfare arrangements to a more diffuse and pluralist form of social care can be observed to varying degrees in our six countries. Economic criteria are key factors involved in the shift, but there is also a quality agenda. There are arguments that private providers can provide cheaper and equally good or even better services, and in Sweden competition has been used to involve local people in choosing their service provider (Rostgaard and Fridberg, 1998). In Denmark, the voluntary sector is expanding to fill gaps in formal care provision, especially psychological and emotional care (Leeson, 1997). In Greece, the expansion of care for older people beyond medical care is utilizing volunteers.

Over the last two decades policies in the UK have pursued the promotion of informal and voluntary alternatives to social care services and market values have become increasingly evident. The NHS and Community Care Act 1990 set out policies to shift the balance of care away from public provision towards private sector provision and informal care. A commitment to enabling older people to remain as long as possible in their own homes was made, reinforcing the Government's support for community care. The 1993 community care reforms that followed the 1990 Act strengthened this mixed economy model of care, reversing the post-war development of comprehensive, state-funded universal services. The largest provider of long-stay care in the UK is now the independent (private and voluntary) nursing home and residential care home sector. NHS long-stay beds have been reduced significantly in number following changes in the organization and delivery of health services and the introduction of an internal market operated by independent hospital trusts. Whereas NHS care was universally available in the past, many older people are now referred to nursing or residential homes where charges are made for social care and, until their abolition in October 2001, for nursing care as well. Only 5 per cent of the total public, private and voluntary long-stay beds in the UK are now provided in the NHS (Laing and Buisson, 1997). In long-term care, the role of large for-profit providers is now firmly established in much of Europe, although questions still remain about their suitability to participate in the 'welfare mix' of countries with large-scale direct provision by the State.

There is some diversity of opinion in the case of Denmark. Despite debate about the advantages of a plural welfare system, there is still strong political and public support for the welfare state model. However, there is an increasing emphasis on user participation, experimental service projects and cost-effectiveness (OECD, 1996). In Norway, recent policy rhetoric encourages family care, voluntarism and welfare pluralism. Daatland (1992) comments that less State ambition is observed and that these changes seem to indicate a move away from the traditional model, but to date there is little sign of it being abandoned. Indeed, Norway plans a major expansion of formal care services for older people, including a commitment to improving standards and reducing variations in provision across the country (Ministry of Health and Social Affairs, 1999).

Ireland has a policy commitment to pursuing the concept of community care, including maintaining older people in their own homes, restoring older people to independence at home, and encouraging and supporting informal care (Department of Health, 1988). However, as described in Chapter 6, there is still very limited formal support in the community, and residential and nursing homes are growing in the private sector. In fact, Ireland suffers from an under-provision of both community and institutional (non-hospital) provision (Giarchi, 1996).

In Greece there has been a move towards developing a more formalized set of services for older people. Legislation passed in 1992 underlined the Government's commitment to building a system of state-supported home care services. A National Organization for Social Care, paralleling the National Health Service, was established in 1998 and home help services provided through local authorities are now expanding rapidly. There is a policy to promote volunteering to support these initiatives. But residential care provision remains in very short supply, and costly. In Italy the principles of welfare pluralism are also evident: for-profit agencies are important in the residential home sector, particularly in the affluent north, and places in these homes may be purchased by public agencies when alternative provision does not exist (Giarchi, 1996). As with Greece, the number of residential places is very limited. Community services vary from locality to locality, and the main issue is the need to expand formal services rather than develop informal care beyond its current – and possibly unsustainable – level.

Implications for delivery and quality of care

Whatever the 'welfare mix' in our six countries, the trend towards government withdrawal from provider roles raises questions about the quality and quantity of health and social care services and concerns about possible deterioration. While comparative studies of this nature are few, some positive findings have been reported from a four-country study of European models of long-term care (Coleman, 1995). The trends in the countries studied (including the UK and Denmark) were to emphasize informal care, decentralize finances and service delivery, expand provider systems to include private and voluntary sectors, and to introduce needs assessment. Despite concerns about rising costs, a range of promising patterns were observed: the delivery of more appropriate services to each person; discouragement of institutionalization; flexible programmes of assistance around the clock; tailor-made user services; and improved communication and co-ordination among professionals. The main issue is the withdrawal of some 'low-level' services from many older people, and the possible loss of their preventative value.

The development of a mixed economy in welfare services is also not necessarily relieving the problem of fragmentation and lack of co-ordination commonly reported between health and social care in Europe. Indeed, it is the monopoly public services model of Denmark and Norway, with integration of health and social care, and increasingly between community and nursing home care as well, that appears to be most successful in achieving co-ordination. The philosophy of care, however, is crucial and this is not just an organizational matter. The social model of care is a strong influence in Scandinavia, but in Ireland, where the influence of a medical model is much stronger, there is fragmentation between services and a serious underprovision of social care, despite personal social services, community work and other welfare services being located together within a single health system. A key factor believed to hinder the development of a co-ordinated model of aged care in Ireland is the centralized administration, which has only recently begun to be addressed with some decentralization to area boards.

By contrast, in the UK public services for older people have been distributed among different authorities and subject to different rules of allocation. For example, retirement pensions and long-stay NHS care have been universally available, whereas supplementary benefit (later income support) is subject to a means test, along with publicly funded social care in institutions or the community. Boundary problems between health and social care services continued despite the division of responsibilities which was institutionalized with the creation of new social services departments under local government in the early 1970s. Such complexity in aged care continued into the 1980s, hindering the development of a co-ordinated policy. Service provision has become diverse and fragmented, and the role of local authority social services departments has shifted to that of funding and managing rather than service provision. Fragmented structures have sometimes produced contradictory practices. In the mid 1980s this divided funding responsibility for care led the Government to inadvertently fund a massive increase in numbers of nursing homes, despite a policy of deinstitutionalization and an ideological climate that favoured private enterprise (Bartlett, 1986). Lack of effective collaboration between state and non-state provision has also contributed to the creation of inequity and inefficiency. In recent years, case managers have been introduced because of the increasing levels of co-ordination required (Challis and Davies, 1986).

The implications of a 'welfare mix' in the care of older people is that the State continues to be a major stakeholder in the work of health and welfare professionals and quality standards have to be formulated and implemented (Hugman, 1994). All six countries are tackling this question to varying degrees in relation to the independent nursing and residential home sector. For residential and nursing homes, standards are set at either a national or local level and may be mandatory or discretionary. This determines the consistency or otherwise of standards across the country and the quality of care provided. The effective enforcement of standards remains a problem in some countries like the UK where qualified and unqualified staff are difficult to recruit and retain, and where there are insufficient alternatives to residential care should closure of a home be necessary (Bartlett and Burnip, 1998). Difficulties of this nature raise questions about the appropriateness of for-profit providers' participation in the care of older people and whether the 'welfare mix', supported by public funds, should only extend to the not-for-profit sector.

The idea of partnership with older people and consumer participation is emphasised in recent UK policy, particularly in relation to enhancing the quality of care for older people (Bennington *et al.*, 1998). In practice, however, much still remains to be achieved. Where older people are highly dependent, mechanisms to involve them in service planning and evaluation are rarely found. In countries like the UK, Norway and Denmark, the reality is that residents of nursing homes are now sicker, older and more dependent than they have been in previous years. User participation is therefore a particular challenge (Munday and Ely, 1996).

There is growing attention to the relationship between models of care and the quality of life of older people. While the limitations of residential options are increasingly recognized, it cannot be assumed that, in countries where the family or informal support is the mainstay of home care, the quality of care or life for the individual is higher. Equally, it is not necessarily the case that the provision of formal social care services is undertaken in ways that equate with quality of life criteria older people themselves would use, especially if they have little control over what is provided and by whom.

Conclusion

Despite the different ways in which welfare provision can be viewed across the six countries, there appears to be a shift in ideology towards an appreciation of the need for change and innovation in the way existing care services operate. Earlier macro-level analysis of certain social services dimensions concluded that there were more basic convergences between countries than differences (Kahn and Kamerman, 1976). The notion of convergence has been supported subsequently by

Abrahamson (1992), but as later chapters illustrate, the underlying systems of social protection, financing and organizing service provision are too divergent for a common model of service provision to emerge. Furthermore, ideological preferences are likely to act against convergence. For example, one country's ideological preference for market solutions may be unattractive to countries with more corporatist or consensual traditions of policy-making and long-term relationships of commitments between partners. There is a trend, nevertheless, towards 'ageing in place', but even then shortages of institutional care are evident in Greece, Italy and Ireland. Achieving 'ageing in place' is, however, generally viewed as a societal responsibility and not solely the domain of government. Families remain very involved either providing care or mediating between older relatives and formal care services.

The chapter has highlighted the limitations of using models of welfare when applied to the care of older people. The picture is complex, and models often seem far removed from the experiences of older people themselves. Indeed, relatively little is known about the preferences of older people when it comes to health and community care, or the potential of health promotion or social involvement to improve older people's health (Anderson, 1992). Despite many shared goals in the care of older people, questions remain about how quality, choice, co-ordination and the costs of care will be determined. A new system of long-term care is urgently required in many countries, especially those which have been dependent on families in the past. Variations are evident in how countries are addressing these issues and this means differing outcomes.

In order to explore this in detail, subsequent chapters will examine the organization and delivery of services for older people, and Chapter 9 will compare the care of individual older people living in similar circumstances in each of the six countries. Chapters 3 to 5 describe the social care systems of Denmark, Norway and the UK, countries which have comprehensive assessment and care management systems for the social care of older people. Norway and Denmark differ from the UK in terms of their more highly funded and integrated health and social care services. As already noted, means testing is extensive in the UK and social care services are currently administered separately from health services, although they are increasingly planned jointly, and integration is likely in the future.

Chapters 6 to 8 describe the social care systems of the three countries which rely extensively on family members to undertake care work: Ireland, Italy and Greece. All these countries have formal social care services, but they are very limited in coverage and availability, with sig-nificant provision by voluntary organizations.

In all six chapters, health care is considered alongside social care given the extent of relationships between the two. Incomes are also considered to give an overall picture of the resources that older people have available to them.

3
Denmark

Merete Platz and Sally Brodhurst

State, family and individual responsibilities

In Denmark, health and social care are available on a universal basis, dependent on need and not age or ability to pay. If an older person is in need of care, it is accepted and underwritten by legislation that the State takes responsibility for his or her care. Families have no legal duty to care and assistance given by family members or relatives is considered as an additional input to that provided by the State, not a substitution. Although there continues to be a culture of additional support provided by family members, especially children of older people, family care seldom substitutes for state care, but it may do. There is a stable pattern in Denmark of formal or state care and informal or family care supplementing each other rather than one substituting for the other. Despite changes in public policy, this principle has remained unchanged. However, while care work is generally undertaken by formal care services for older people who need assistance, especially personal care, children's support is likely to be confined to practical tasks such as minor repair work or laundry. Spouses also often help with domestic tasks but less often with personal care.

There is a cash allowance for caring in the home, available to family members or close friends who take leave from work to care for a terminally ill person, but this is rarely taken up. In 1997, it was paid for 1500 terminally ill people of whom only about 500 were aged 67 years or over (67 was the official retirement age in Denmark for both sexes until July 1999, when it changed to 65) (Danmarks Statistik, 1999). The care allowance is only paid on loss of earnings, and therefore pensioners receive no financial remuneration for caring for an ill or disabled partner. Since 1998, a family member can work officially as a home help employed by the local authority. Respite or short-break care and temporary home help is available to provide relief for an informal carer (often the partner). Respite for the carer may be provided through arrangements for the older person to attend a day care facility, often attached to a nursing home, or to spend one or two weeks at a nursing home. Cash assistance is only given to cover extra costs for caring, for example transport and nursing aids. Extra financial assistance can be given to enable an older person to remain at home rather than move into a nursing home or remain in a local hospital, and assistance is also available to adapt the home and to provide intensive care around the clock.

Denmark was one of the first countries to adopt a community care policy. Widespread deinstitutionalization has taken place, with priority given to the provision of domiciliary care. The policy of enabling older people to remain in their own homes (with support to help their independence) has been followed up by an extensive building programme of sheltered housing and adapted housing for older people, while outdated nursing homes have been closed.

Although older people in Denmark enjoy a comparatively generous provision of domiciliary care, it is increasingly being targeted at those who have the highest social and health care needs. Between 1987 and 1996 the proportion of older people aged 67 years plus receiving home help increased from 18 per cent to 24 per cent, but among the 80-plus age group this increase was from 36 to 49 per cent (Rostgaard and Fridberg, 1998). This is associated with a shift in the type of help provided: there is concern that, because the service is focusing more on personal care, it is undervaluing the importance to older people's sense of well-being of practical help which enables them to keep a clean and tidy house.

Structure, funding and organization of services

The funding for and provision of health and social care is based in Denmark on a structure of counties and municipalities. There are 16 counties, over half of which have a population of between 200000 and 300000 people, while two have populations of less than 100000 and in two the population is over 600000. There are 275 municipalities, half of which have a population of under 10000, while only four have a population of over 100000. There is a basic distinction between care services (social, residential and health care) and treatment by a doctor (surgery, medical care), both services being financed by income taxes.

Treatment or medical care provided by GPs and care in hospitals are funded through county taxes, and social and general health care, predominantly provided to people in their own community, are funded through municipality taxes. Block grants from central government are given to compensate (to a certain degree) for variations in demography and income differences between the local authorities.

Central government (Folketinget) legislation provides the legal framework for the services in the municipalities, which may develop local policies to accommodate local conditions, within the terms of this framework. The 1998 Social Services Act provides the basic guidance, but it is left to each municipality to decide on the coverage and intensity of home help, the range of home help services and entitlement criteria. The municipality can also decide whether to have home helpers or home nurses or both on duty during the night. One of these options must be provided but, at the time of writing, one municipality has decided to have neither available overnight – and is therefore technically breaking the law. Local discretion is allowed in the allocation of funds to particular services but central government gives guidelines for local budgets, including upper limits for local taxation.

County services

The counties are responsible for hospital care, including geriatric rehabilitation services; primary health care (except home nursing); and health promotion initiatives. Long-term care is not in general a county health authority responsibility, but older people with mental illnesses, such as dementia, may be referred for care at specialized hospitals. Counties therefore are responsible for the running of hospitals, and also for the coverage of GP services. GPs are not employed directly by the county, but obtain a licence to practise, of which there are a limited number for each county. GPs receive a set payment for each registered patient plus an agreed fee for each of the services delivered. The set payment and the fees are negotiated between the GPs' organization and the Association of County Councils, and GPs receive their payment from the public health insurance system. GPs have a crucial role in 'gatekeeping' access to specialist medical and hospital care.

Hospital and GP care are free to the recipient, while nursing home rent is charged at different levels depending on the person's income. As a minimum, residents pay 10 per cent of the estimated running costs and also 10 per cent of their personal income for their rent. Meals are charged for at a standard, not income-graded, rate. The charges for medicines are subsidized to a high degree, and charges are waived for people on low incomes.

Municipality services

Municipalities are responsible for community nursing, social care and long-term care. All municipalities have a statutory duty to offer home help for both domestic and personal care, home nursing and, since 1976, to provide housing for disabled people, which includes adapted dwellings, nursing homes and attached day care facilities. Care is free of charge to the recipient wherever it is delivered in the community. Other social welfare services provided are transport for people requiring treatment (free of charge); day centres, which may offer recreational activities as well as rehabilitation (free of charge following an assessment); loan of equipment and aids; and meals on wheels (for which there is a charge).

Most of the welfare services are provided by the municipalities, but some of the nursing homes and attached day care facilities are run by voluntary or not-for-profit organizations. These organizations have contractual agreements with the municipality, which remains responsible for standards in the home, admission criteria, setting rents and services charges. In all practical ways, there is no distinction between the homes run by the municipality and those run by voluntary organizations. There are no private for-profit nursing homes. For home help and care at home, commercial providers have started to be used in some municipalities in recent years. As with the not-for-profit organizations, they hold contractual agreements with the municipality for all aspects of the care delivered. Not-for-profit organizations, such as the Red Cross and Dan Age, provide volunteers to visit older people on the basis of agreements with the municipalities' home help organizations that voluntary visitors do not take over the tasks of home helpers. However, voluntary visitors sometimes undertake additional tasks, such as feeding or accompanying to the bathroom, at the request of the older person or the municipality.

Community health and social care are integrated within municipalities. Each municipality has a statutory duty to offer home help to anyone unable to perform regular activities of daily living. These include practical and domestic activities and personal care. Municipalities also have a statutory duty to provide home nursing, adapted housing, nursing homes, around-the-clock care for people in private homes and preventive home visits, and they have a responsibility to offer older people the option of taking part in activities and receiving services which have a preventive, rehabilitative purpose and promote independence. Private organizations may take on some of these enabling functions, for which they will receive financial support. Integration between home help and home nursing means that in practice the two professions, social and health, are formally working together in integrated teams. There are integrated staff units in 86 per cent of the 275 municipalities, while in the remaining municipalities staff may work in integrated teams but formally still belong to their individual professional group. The integrated teams consist of eight to ten people who are responsible for the care of older people in a local area and together the two sets of professionals provide home care. The most recent developmental trend is the introduction of 'integrated schemes' covering both staff in institutions and home help staff working in the community.

As regards the discharge of older people from hospital, there are no regulations or standards to ensure co-ordination, although in some counties the hospitals and the municipality have reached their own agreements on co-ordination. Hospitals in Denmark, in common with hospitals in other countries, are seeking to maintain a flow through their system and therefore have an interest in discharging people as quickly as possible. This can mean that older people are discharged into the community before there has been time for the municipality to make appropriate arrangements. Hospitals are unwilling to pay for extra days in hospital and, if the prolonged stay is because community arrangements are not in place, some hospitals will charge the municipality for the cost of those extra days.

Coverage and variations in provision

As a consequence of the decentralization of responsibilities to the municipalities, there are variations in the availability of services for older people, whether social welfare, home nursing, housing services or the availability of nursing home services. Thus, older people living in similar circumstances may have their needs addressed in different ways, depending on the municipality in which they live. In 1997, home help was received on average by 13.8 per cent of households with at least one person aged between 67 and 79, and 49 per cent of households with at least one person aged 80 and over, but these percentages varied by as much as 40 per cent up or down between the different municipalities (Ministry of Social Affairs, 1998). In the municipality of Copenhagen only 6 per cent of people aged 67 and over received visits from a home nurse, compared with 13 per cent on average for the whole country. There is also variation in the number of people aged 70 and over who receive help from either a home helper or a nurse in the evening and/or during the night on a regular basis. In the municipality of Copenhagen, 3.5 per cent of the population aged over 70 received evening care and 0.5 per cent received night time care, while the national average equivalent figures are 7.3 per cent and 3.3 per cent respectively (Hansen and Platz, 1995a).

The number of nursing home places available in a municipality affects the amount of home nursing available. In the 25 per cent of municipalities with the lowest number of nursing home places, 9 per cent of the older population in the community received help in the evenings and 4.7 per cent during the night. These figures contrast with the picture in the 25 per cent of municipalities which have the highest availability of nursing home places, where 5.7 per cent of the older population received evening care and 2.1 per cent received care at night. More densely populated areas tend to have a lower provision of care for older people, but neither the geographical area of the country nor the size of the population in the municipality influence availability directly of themselves. There do not appear to be easily identifiable geographical or demographic factors that explain the variation (Hansen and Platz, 1995a).

During the last 20 years the availability of nursing home places has been reduced from approximately 40 places to approximately 20 places per 100 persons aged 80 or more. In their place independent adapted dwellings have been built, but they are not all staffed and are therefore not all as fully supportive care settings as were the nursing homes. In assessment of need for admission to a nursing home, the supply of available places is a parallel consideration, and in the late 1990s it is only the most dependent people, often with dementia, who are admitted to a nursing home.

As well as variation in levels of availability, there may be variation in types of service available: for example, a few municipalities have closed down all their nursing homes and only provide services to people in independent dwellings in the community. Other municipalities have made a decision not to offer home help for purely domestic tasks, although this means that technically they are breaking the law.

Increasingly the delivery of home help services is being delegated by the municipalities to private firms, both for profit and not for profit. In some municipalities older people requiring home help for domestic tasks are given the option of receiving cash payments from the municipality with which to purchase their own care services, but this does not extend to personal care or nursing care. Both these practices are likely to continue and become more widespread in the future, but it is unlikely that the pattern of services will change. The larger municipalities are divided into districts, which results in further variation in provision within one municipality.

Charges

Hospital care is covered by public health insurance (tax financed) and is provided free of charge to the recipient and, if people are insured in 'group 1', then GP services are also free, while ordinary dental care and pharmacy/drugs carry a highly subsidized charge. Pensioners are entitled to a medicine card, subject to a means test. Home help and home nursing are free of charge, and the charging system for people in nursing homes is similar to that for people living independently: practical and personal care, nursing care and rehabilitation are all free of charge. Other services are subject to a charge, for example linen, chiropody, meals, hairdressing and leisure activities. Residents pay rent and levels of payment are subject to means testing. Nursing home residents now continue to receive their full pension and pay for the extra services they wish to have. Debate continues about whether older people should pay for home help for domestic tasks such as cleaning, with an argument put forward that these are a personal and not a public responsibility. The National Association of Local Authorities is encouraging continued debate on this issue with a view to curbing local statutory expenditure.

Older people's incomes

It is a logical step to move from charges to look at what sort of income older people in Denmark can expect. The official retirement age for both sexes is now 65, and there is one comprehensive state pension available to everyone – the old age pension. Entitlement to the full pension is based on 40 years of residence in Denmark from the age of 15 and, with fewer years of residence, the pension reduces proportionately. The old age pension, which is financed by national taxes to which all taxpayers contribute, consists of a basic sum and a supplement. The basic sum is approximately €6400 per annum, the supplement for couples is approximately €2900, and for people living alone approximately €6300 per annum (figures for January 1999). In addition, pensioners living in difficult circumstances can receive a means tested personal allowance, and about half receive a means tested housing benefit. The basic sum is reduced if earned income exceeds approximately €27 400 for a single person or €18 500 if married (this affects very few people). The pension supplement is reduced if the total income from other pensions, work or savings exceeds approximately €5900 for single people or €12 120 for couples.

In 1997, 99 per cent of all people aged 67 and over received an old age pension and approximately half of these lived alone and were therefore entitled to the single person pension supplement. Two-thirds of the old age pensioners were granted the full pension supplement and 25 per cent received a reduced amount, leaving approximately 10 per cent who only received the basic pension because of having a high income (Ministry of Economic Affairs, 1999). Old age pension, including the pension supplement, accounts for nearly 70 per cent of the total personal income of people aged 67 and over and on average the old age pension equals 80 per cent of the average wage. Older single women, a group at risk of poverty in many other European countries, are not at such risk in Denmark. During the past ten to fifteen years an enhanced equality in the disposable income of old age pensioners has taken place. This is demonstrated by the decline in the Gini coefficient from 20.7 in 1983 to 17.6 in 1995 (Ministry of Finance, 1999). This coefficient indicates the part of the total mass of income which would have to be redistributed in order to achieve absolute equality. In 1996, old age pensioners' incomes after tax were one-third higher in the upper quartile than in the lower quartile, while the average income after tax of pensioners in general was 20 per cent lower than that of people in the workforce. In the current workforce of people aged 52 and over (the pensioners of the future), 75 per cent have labour market pensions, private pensions, capital pensions or other savings relating to retirement: this is many more than among current pensioners. Therefore, in the future fewer people will be entitled to the pension allowance and it is expected that the number who have to rely on the old age pension as their only or primary source of income will decline.

Financial support between generations does occur, though not on a large scale. It is not particularly prevalent for older parents to receive financial support from their children; it has always been more common for the older generation to offer rather than receive help. In 1997, 3 per cent of people aged 52 to 57, with parents alive, offered financial help to them. This compared with 17 per cent of parents aged between

72 and 77 who offered their children financial help and 11 per cent who offered help to their grandchildren (Platz, 1999).

Access and entitlement

Every citizen in Denmark has the right to be listed with a GP and in theory has a choice of which GP within the municipality to register with. GPs refer people to specialist services, arrange for hospital admissions and work with varying degrees of closeness with local municipality services and so may, for example, refer patients to home nurses or community social services.

An applicant for home help is entitled to an individual assessment of his or her need for care and practical assistance. A nurse, a home helper or the home help manager normally visits the applicant in his or her home to assess the need for care. Provision of care is based on the household situation and an evaluation of the capacity and needs of the individual and his or her partner, but does not take account of help that could be provided by adult children or other family members living outside the household. The range of services available to meet need, the entitlement or eligibility criteria applied, and the number and type of hours of help allocated are all dictated by the local municipality's budget and political preferences. Until 1998, the majority of municipalities tended to be generous when assessing for home help, and approximately 60 per cent of all people aged 80 and over received the service. Nearly all received help with domestic tasks and for more than one-third this was the only help they received. Since 1998 municipalities have become more restrictive in allocating home help for domestic tasks. Instead, home help is more likely to be targeted on the most dependent people who need personal care. Some municipalities may be flouting the law by withholding home help for domestic care; central government does not intervene in local decisions but the Ministry of Social Affairs can bring a case before the municipal supervisory authority and an older person can complain to the local appeal board. Since 1996, contracts between the user and home help service have been obligatory, allowing the recipient to know what services he or she can expect and how many hours of care have been allocated. While the assessor also decides whether to request visits from the home nurse, there is no contract for home nursing services.

The municipality has a responsibility for assessing people's needs for adapted or specialized housing. The number of people living in independent adapted housing, for example sheltered housing or other supported dwellings for older people, is approximately 15 per cent of the total population aged 80 and over, and the number continues to rise (Jura Information, 1996).

The municipality is obliged to ensure that those who cannot remain at home, even if they receive domiciliary and personal care, can be admitted to a nursing home or another care facility such as different forms of adapted dwellings, staffed around the clock. The municipality in most cases establishes an admission board which decides whether an older person should be admitted to a nursing home or should be offered other services which should make it possible to stay at home, with decisions being made in conjunction with the GP, home nurse, home help or other relevant people. There are no national regulations regarding admission criteria and decisions are taken on the basis of evaluation of individual needs, but the admission board takes into consideration other types of care facility which could be offered as alternatives to a nursing home. Older people can apply for admission to a nursing home or alternative care in another municipality under certain conditions, for example if they have close relatives in that municipality.

Standards and quality

In Denmark there are no minimum service standard guarantees, either for availability of services or quality of care, although some political parties have raised the question of whether there should be minimum standards for home help. Central government has requested counties to reduce waiting times for hospital treatment and requested municipalities not to reduce care services for older people, but these requests have no statutory or legal status. Local municipalities are responsible for the registration and inspection of nursing homes, but this is mainly confined to the physical environment and staffing levels, and does not encompass quality issues in the delivery of care. Municipalities are likewise responsible for the quality of home care.

There is a senior citizens council in each municipality, as required by law since 1997. Their function is mostly advisory, but they have to be consulted on all municipality matters which concern older people. They can influence policy and increase the involvement of older people in exercising choice about their care. Each municipality has a local appeal board, to whom individual users or their relatives may appeal if they wish to make a complaint about services. The appeal board consists of two members from the municipality council and someone appointed by members of the senior citizens council.

Choice

The majority of people can choose the GP they wish to register with from GPs in the local area, on the strength of belonging to Group 1 under insurance arrangements. This choice can only be exercised once a year. The GP will refer Group 1 patients to specialist medical services when required and here the patient has no choice. For people in Group 2, choice of GP and specialists is open, but they are liable to pay a proportion of the fees incurred. When referred for care in a hospital, people have the right, since 1993, to choose to go to a hospital in another county, but the majority of people prefer to attend their local public hospital. Apart from some highly specialized hospitals, there are very few private hospitals in Denmark and patients using them pay the full cost themselves or have taken out private health insurance. For social care, choice depends to a large degree on what services are available locally and on the interpretation of individual needs by the assessor. Older people have the right to have an advocate or relative with them when their care needs are assessed. The local senior citizens council may give advice and a volunteer may act as advocate for an older person. With the growth in alternative provider organizations, including municipalities beginning to contract out, the older person may be able to make a choice over which organization provides his or her care at home but is dependent on the assessing professional for advice about the different providers of care. The 1998 Social Services Act allows older people to choose to pay a relative to undertake domestic tasks. By September 1998, 86 of the 275 municipalities had introduced the option of choice of provider of care and nearly 10 per cent of older people had taken this up. In those municipalities where a market economy is being fostered, 30 to 50 per cent of older people have opted to receive their care from a private provider. This choice is offered only for the practical home care services and not personal care which, with only very few exceptions, is provided by the municipality.

Older people can choose to remain at home with enhanced services rather than go into a nursing home, although in such cases domiciliary care may prove to be more expensive to provide than institutional care (Hansen, Jordal-Jørgensen and Koch, 1991). The care manager may then encourage or persuade the older person to move into a nursing home, but this cannot be enforced. Care in nursing homes, which are state funded, is fairly standard, but the older person may exercise some choice as to which one they wish to reside in. Equally, an older person who is entitled to a place in a nursing home or a special dwelling in his or her 'own' municipality may choose to live in one in another municipality, usually for family reasons. The 'old' municipality is responsible for meeting the costs and pays these to the 'new' municipality, provided that the new municipality agrees that there is an entitlement to nursing home care and has appropriate accommodation. In 1994, 1981 older people applied for a transfer of this nature and only 95 were refused.

Choice is probably less available for very vulnerable and dependent older people with no immediate family or personal resources, who may find it difficult, or be unable, to express their views and who have no one to represent these for them.

Information about services

Some municipalities provide general information about aims, regulations and practice, but lack of targeting of this information means its effectiveness is doubtful. In 1994, 10 per cent of older people's relatives felt they had received adequate information about services (Hansen and Platz, 1995b). Since 1998, municipalities have been required to publish quality standards for the home help offered. A written statement has to be provided by the home help assessor, setting out the help to be provided and the date when care needs will be reviewed. The home helper is required to sign after each visit to show that she or he has provided the care stipulated in the agreed care plan. One disadvantage of this arrangement is that it does not allow for flexibility to suit the older person's changing needs from day to day.

Since 1996, municipalities have been obliged to offer preventive visits to older people in their homes. The visits, made by a nurse or social worker, are now offered to all people aged 75 and over at least twice a year. During the visit the older person's general lifestyle and situation are discussed, including functional abilities, social network, housing, general health and finances. The aim is to enable the older person to continue living as independently as possible by maintaining their functional ability, their social network and offering any assistance at an early stage. Visits may also be made to people in nursing homes and to older people who have been recently bereaved or discharged from hospital. An important aspect of the visit is the opportunity it provides to give information about a range of possibilities to enhance the social and health well-being of an older person.

Discharge from hospital can be a difficult time for an older person and, with increasingly short admissions, plans may not be finalized for the care an older person needs following their hospital stay. Sometimes a stay in a nursing home takes place as an interim measure while ongoing plans are made, or an older person may return home before being admitted to a nursing home. There is a danger that the older person may be denied a free choice of the care he or she would like because of two systems not being fully co-ordinated – the hospital and the community. The problem is compounded by hospital services being administered by a different organization from community services.

Reassessment or review of older people's needs is guaranteed at the time of the original assessment. For personal care this should happen every six months, while for practical care it is more likely to be every 12 months although, if needs change between review dates, the home helper, older person or relatives can request reassessment. As budgets have become more constrained, some municipalities are raising their criteria for offering assistance and, if older people can manage shopping and cleaning, they will not be offered practical help. Some municipalities have decided to take this approach and have done so without reassessing needs, although a review should theoretically take place before any changes to the care package are made. Lack of flexibility, increasing efficiency and concern over best value for money may pose a threat to maintaining older people's independence and autonomy. Now that care may be given to a tight time-scale, without any allowance for time for a chat or walk in the sun to the shops, older people may begin to feel that they are no longer individual people, but 'cases'.

The quantity and quality of care for older people receives wide publicity and is well debated in Denmark. Examples of individual cases demonstrate that standards are not always as high as the public would like them to be. However, compared with older people in many other countries, Danish senior citizens are fortunate in the care they receive and the choices they have, with most receiving enough help to maintain a fairly normal lifestyle. The greatest strength of the Danish care system is that services are universally available, and people with the same needs living in the same local area, regardless of whether they are rich or poor, are entitled to the same services and same service standards. The rich pay more for some services, especially rented accommodation, but receiving help is an equal right and there is no stigma attached to receiving state care.

4
Norway

Mia Vabø and Sally Brodhurst

State, family and individual responsibilities

Like Denmark, Norway has a long tradition of state responsibility for the welfare of older people, reflected in the high subsidy level for public services and the universal availability of health and social care according to need and not age or ability to pay. Only 5 per cent of the cost of home care services is covered by fees charged to users and only 10 to 15 per cent of the real costs of a bed in an institution is raised from fees (Daatland, 1997a).

Since 1964, families have not been expected to take any financial responsibility for the care of elderly parents. If older people have financial problems, they can claim state allowances, such as housing allowance, assistance allowance or social assistance. Family members, apart from partners, do not in general feel an obligation to provide economic support; on the contrary, surveys indicate that older people often support their children financially (Gulbrandsen and Langsether, 1999). However, over the last few years state authorities have increasingly emphasized that all members of society have a responsibility for each other and that families should mobilize their own care resources for elderly parents before applying for state help. The care system is increasingly being described as a partnership between public and family care (Daatland, 1997a).

Thus, in practical terms, family care is an essential supplement to public services, and Lingsom's (1997) research invalidates the common assumption that informal care is declining as a consequence of state provision. What has changed is the division of responsibilities: the tasks required are shared out among more people, partly as a consequence of increased sex equality. Typical family contributions towards the care of their older relations are laundry, shopping or a lift in the car, but these are being joined by new tasks, such as discovering what services are available, mediating with service providers and supporting formal provision. The younger generation is more aware of how bureaucracies work and what should be available than their parents' generation, and Lingsom (1997) suggests that this may lead to demands for the provision of more state care. Even though families are in general willing to support elderly parents, most consider that the main responsibility for care lies with the State. A recent nationwide survey indicated that more than 80 per cent of the population considered that care of older people should be a public responsibility (Bay, 1998). However, several qualitative studies indicate that people who provide their parents with assistance feel obliged to do so because state assistance is insufficient (Vabø, 1998).

Structure, funding and organization of services

The responsibility for health and social care provision in Norway is shared between three levels of government: central government, counties and municipalities. Central government retains overall responsibility for health care, including the task of regulating, monitoring and substantial block grant funding to local government. Funding for health and social services comes from a mixture of local and national taxation. Approximately one-third of the income of counties and municipalities derives from state grants from central government.

County services

Norway has 19 counties, the largest of which, Oslo and Akershus (which surrounds Oslo), have populations of over 400000 people. The two smallest counties by contrast have populations of less than 100000 and the average county population size is 200000. The counties are responsible for hospitals and specialized health services such as opthalmology. Hospitals do not provide long-term care, only medical treatment. The population of people aged 65 and over accounted for 50 per cent of the total days spent in hospital during 1993 to 1995 (Daatland, 1997a).

Municipality services

There are 435 municipalities, most of which are small. Just over half have populations of less than 5000, while 30 have a population of between 20000 and 49000, and only ten have more than 50000 residents. Municipalities are responsible for primary health care (GPs and nursing services). The majority of GPs are self-employed physicians who have a contract with the municipality which pays them a monthly grant in return for practising according to an agreement with stipulates location, working hours and public health duties. In addition to the monthly grant from the municipality, GPs are paid from fees raised through service reimbursement and patient co-payment (Elstad, 1997). Patients' fees for consultation with GPs are relatively low, while those for specialist physicians are higher. If approved medical costs, for example for domiciliary visits or essential prescribed medicines, exceed a certain level (€162) the whole cost is covered by the National Insurance Scheme.

The Health Service Act (1982) requires municipalities to provide 'essential medical services' to all inhabitants and the Social Services Act (1991) requires municipalities to provide 'essential practical help' for inhabitants who are not able to care for themselves. Municipalities are responsible for three main care services: home-based care (social and health), supported housing and nursing home care. None of the care is specifically for older people; however older people are clearly the main group of recipients. The services, taken together, are therefore considered to be 'care services for older people'. All municipalities have a large-scale home care service, the major elements of which are home help and home nursing, but other services provided include meals-on-wheels, alarm services, respite care, home counselling, heavy cleaning and occupational therapy. Services are increasingly available around the clock, especially nursing care, to reflect the gradual shift from institutional care to care at home. Legislative changes during the 1980s delegated to municipalities the responsibility for a wide range of services with the aim of encouraging an integrated approach to the delivery of care.

Supported housing is a comparatively new type of provision in Norway compared with Denmark and the UK and is seen as an intermediate care alternative to either nursing homes or ordinary retirement flats (Daatland, 1997a). Supported housing is designed especially for people with disabilities, enabling them to lead as independent a life as possible. Flats are rented or owned and there are usually facilities attached or close by, such as an alarm service, café, post office and chiropodist. There are no resident nursing staff and people receive home help or home nursing care according to their needs, as though living in an individual home in the community.

Nursing homes, which are regulated by the Health Service Act (1982) and are the responsibility of municipalities, provide medical and nursing care for frail and sick older people on a permanent basis and are designed to offer long-term care outside a hospital setting. About 70 per cent of residents have some degree of dementia. Nursing homes also offer short-term stays to people needing a period of rehabilitation or respite care, accounting for about 10 per cent of admissions (Lauvli, 1999). While institutional care has been reduced on a large scale in Denmark and Sweden, the reduction has been more modest in Norway (Daatland and Szebehely, 1997). However, the current *Action Plan for Care of the Elderly 1998–2001* targets substantial central government grants to municipalities to expand and improve local nursing and care services, including reiterating the aim that older people should be able to live in their own homes for as long as possible (Ministry of Health and Social Affairs, 1999). Institutional care is predominantly provided in nursing homes, but the number of beds is being reduced in parallel with an expansion of supported housing in the community.

Home care services are spread fairly thinly among older people: while there remains an intention to provide care for people with modest care needs, rather than concentrate on a smaller group of people with more severe needs, there has been a decline in service intensity. Denmark has so far invested substantially and comparatively more in community services than Norway and there is concern whether Norwegian services are able to provide sufficient care for the most needy (Daatland, 1997a).

Figures for 1998 show that there were seven institutional beds (nursing and residential combined) per 100 of the population aged 67 and over, and 23 per 100 of the population aged 80 and over. For home help and home nursing combined, 25 per 100 of the population aged 67 and over received either or both of these services, as did 82 per 100 of the population aged 80 and over. A total of 155 011 older people received home care services in 1998. User rates indicate that 60 per cent of people aged 80 and over are users of at least one of the services offered by the municipality, either institutional or home care (Daatland, 1997a).

Survey data from Norwegian surveys of living standards (SN, 1985, 1989, 1992, 1996) indicate that people are receiving fewer hours of home care now than they did ten years ago. In the surveys, people were asked how many hours per week of home help they received. In 1983, the average was 4.1, in 1987 it was 3.4, in 1991 it was 2.6 and in 1995 1.9 (Lingsom, 1997). The same surveys indicate that the number of home nursing visits per month declined during the 1980s and increased sharply between 1991 and 1995. In 1983, the average was 11.5 visits per month, in 1987 it was 9.5, in 1991 it was 7.4, but by 1995 the figure had increased to 12.1 (Lingsom, 1997). The increase in home nursing figures may be because of the increasing number of frail older people being cared for in the community as nursing home provision is reduced. The figures for home care may demonstrate a static budget to cover a rising number of older people requiring help, greater demand and an increase in the bureaucracy involved in the delivery of social care.

Decentralization of responsibilities to the municipalities, ostensibly to promote effective delivery of integrated care, may have generated local variations in the patterns of care delivery. Some municipalities have focused to a large extent on community care and special housing and not institutional care, which has tended to disadvantage older people with dementia. Critics of the decentralization policy point to the adverse effect which local policy setting can have on the more vulnerable sections of local communities, for example frail older people and people with mental health needs. Variations between municipalities reflect the availability of economic and human resources as well as the composition of the local population. The wealthiest municipalities offer services to more of the older population than do the less well-off municipalities. The size of the municipality also influences the service coverage: smaller municipalities (populations of less than 2000) tend to have better coverage of both institutional and home care than do larger municipalities (with populations of 50 000 or over). Smaller municipalities have more staff and a higher volume of services per inhabitant, while larger municipalities tend to offer a wider range of specialized services. Figures from 1995 show that smaller municipalities offered home services to 22.9 per cent of people aged 67 and over, while larger ones offered home services to 17.6 per cent of this age group (Næss and Wærness, 1996). Similarly, smaller municipalities had 32.5 institutional beds per 100 people aged 80 and over, while for the larger ones this figure was lower, at 24.7. There was also variation between municipalities in intensity of services delivered. On average a home helper spent 2 hours and 20 minutes per visit in small municipalities, 2 hours 6 minutes in medium ones and only 1 hour 52 minutes in the larger ones. Home nurses spent 54 minutes per visit in small ones, 69 in medium ones and 42 minutes in larger municipalities.

Local variations may reflect how different services have developed locally: this is mainly in the varied balance between institutional care and home care services. Each municipality, reflecting its historical legacy and political choices, can determine its own local policy for how to support independent living and allocate its funding accordingly.

However, a survey of 16 municipalities concluded that doubling the intensity of home care was not sufficient to compensate for a reduction in nursing home beds (Næss and Wærness, 1996). The authors stress the fact that municipalities have different care profiles, with some municipalities showing a traditional approach to care, with a large number of institutional beds and a moderate home care service for people with modest care needs, while others have a low number of institutional beds and more generous home services. But even when the amount of home help time is doubled in the latter municipalities, staff are more inclined to report that the time for each client is not sufficient. The authors argue that care in the community as an alternative to institutional care has not offered a satisfactory replacement level of care.

Charges

Care in hospitals is free for all residents of Norway. There are patient fees for consultations with GPs but these are relatively low, while fees for consultation with medical specialists are higher. There is a National Insurance Scheme which covers the costs, above a set level of €162, of approved medical items, for example essential prescribed medicines and physicians' visits. Home nursing is also free for the recipient, but for home help most municipalities charge a fee. A sliding scale of fees is graded according to income, with low income users receiving services either free or at low cost.

Payment arrangements for institutional care have remained relatively stable. A resident is charged a high fixed percentage of their basic pension (75 per cent) and supplementary income (85 per cent), but capital assets are not included.

Older people's incomes

All people aged 67 and over are entitled to the state old age pension, which consists of a basic pension, regardless of former income, and a supplementary pension which is granted as an additional source of income if the occupational pension is not available or is very low. In addition, many former employees are covered by occupational pension schemes and increasingly more people are subscribing to private pension schemes. Over the last ten to fifteen years, there has been a substantial increase in the number of pensioners who are home owners (currently 75 per cent) and who have capital savings (currently 60 per cent) (Gulbrandsen and Langsether, 1999).

The national old age pension is the major source of income for pensioners in Norway. The minimum (basic) weekly pension for single people was €193 and for married couples €332, as up to May 1999 (Rikstrygdeverket, 1998). These figures do not include housing costs and if these are high older people are entitled to a housing allowance.

The average weekly pension income in 1997 was €254, but other sources of income need to be taken into account to give a more realistic economic profile. The average income of Norwegian pensioners in 1997 was €303 (men €396; women €240). Pensioners who only received the minimum (basic) pension had an average income in 1997 of €179, compared to pensioners who had the supplementary pension, whose average income was €374. These figures demonstrate disparities between different groups of pensioners. Research by Koren and Aslaksen (1997) reveals that the majority of 'minimum pensioners' are women. About 50 per cent are married and live in a household with other income sources and are therefore a great deal better off than the other 50 per cent who are single and have no other income apart from the minimum pension. However, the same research study found that the majority of minimum pensioners have some savings. Most had a small amount (€3082 or less) but 20 per cent of even these minimum pensioners had between €12 330 and €24 660 in savings. Minimum pensioners represent less than one per cent of people receiving state benefits. Research into people's perceptions of their financial situation has revealed no difference between minimum pensioners and the general public on the feeling of having too little money (Gulbrandsen, 1997).

According to Koren and Aslaksen (1997), who base their figures on income statistics form 1990, 7.9 per cent of pensioners are below a poverty line, defined as half of median household income after tax. These are mainly women, commonly a widow with neither a supplementary income from earnings nor any financial savings. However, when asked, 'Do you have problems managing current expenses?' less than 4 per cent of older people reported that they did (Dahl and Vogt, 1995). There was a gender difference with 5 per cent of women and 3 per cent of men aged 67 to 79 saying that they had problems managing current expenses.

Access and entitlement

All residents of Norway are entitled to receive health and social care services on a universal basis, according to an assessment of their needs.

No applicants are excluded a priori on the basis that they should make their own provision or that their families are expected to provide for them. Social care, as described earlier, is subject to a sliding scale of fees. The main concern of national and local pricing policies has been to ensure that low income groups and high intensity users are not excluded from services. While the income-graded scale of fees limits 'unnecessary' demand associated with entirely free services, some evidence suggests there can be unintended consequences. More affluent people who pay the highest fees expect high standards and good value for money and can sometimes adopt an assertive, demanding and inflexible attitude towards care providers (Vabø, 1998). Meanwhile, less well-off users who pay minimum or no fees tend to be grateful for any care they are given, often regardless of poor standards, poor value or inconvenient delivery times.

Municipalities have a degree of local autonomy in how they choose to deliver care. The Ministry for Health and Social Affairs issues an annual circular to municipalities setting out national policy goals and priorities. The law does not specifically set out what kind of help or how much help a person is entitled to, or a clear definition of 'totally dependent' or 'unable to care for self'. Local interpretations are made by the municipalities according to political choices and the resources available, leading to variations between the different municipalities. Thus it may be difficult for individuals to form clear expectations about services to which they may be entitled.

Older people have certain procedural rights in Norway relating to decisions about the allocation of services. People have a legal right to an individual assessment of need made by competent authorities, to receive written decisions on the assessment and reasons given for a rejection of their request for services, and to complain. Substantive rights to municipal care services are limited, as eligibility criteria, service content and public sector obligation are not clearly specified in law and, as stated above, each municipality makes its own interpretation.

In the UK, the tension in care delivery is the divide between health and social care services, whereas in Norway that tension is between community and institutional services. Community services are comparatively well integrated as a result of the devolved responsibilities for home care and nursing care to municipalities. Now, however, the boundary between community and institutional care in Norway is becoming less rigid, giving older people more flexible solutions to their health and social care needs. If someone prefers to continue living at home rather than go into a residential or nursing home, they may now be offered technical aids, such as a hospital-style bed, wheelchair, alarm system and a range of home services. They may also receive respite breaks in a nursing home. But availability of provision may vary between municipalities.

Care and medical support should increase and decrease according to an older person's changing needs. The integration of local community services, which results in local teams of care providers, allows the needs of individuals to be regularly monitored and the necessary alterations or additions to services to be made. Municipalities have a statutory obligation to reassess needs every six months.

The community–institutional tension is also visible in a different way. Pressure on hospital beds continues to increase in Norway as elsewhere, with consequent reductions in average lengths of stay. It is often older people who lose out here since it is widely acknowledged that they need longer than younger people to recuperate after illness. Municipalities have a statutory obligation to provide rehabilitative care following discharge from hospital, but it is often difficult for local care providers to have arrangements in the community ready for older people being discharged. A recent legal ruling now means that hospitals have the right to charge municipalities for the cost of an extended stay in hospital if adequate arrangements are not in place in the community within 14 days of the patient being ready for discharge. This is similar to arrangements in Denmark.

As home care services take on responsibilities in the community for people with more complex nursing needs, the eligibility threshold for services has been raised to moderate levels of need, leaving lower-level needs ineligible for services. Home care staff are sometimes concerned that hospitals will unrealistically raise the expectations of older people about the services which can be delivered by home care providers. This may lead to disappointment and uneasy working relations between an older person, their family and care workers (Vabø, 1996).

Standards and quality

There are many national guidelines intended to influence standards of care in relation to institutions and home care agencies. These cover assignment of services, fee levels and quality. They aim to define more precisely what should be a legally required standard, and they reflect a move towards more formalized standards for care services and the setting of working practices. For example, guidelines recommend written procedures to ensure that services are holistic and flexible, that relatives are involved in making care plans and that services are delivered at times agreed with the user. There are definitions of 'basic needs' which include a sufficient, healthy and reasonable choice of food; sufficient assistance and time during meals; assistance in personal hygiene, dressing and undressing; the opportunity to have a normal diurnal rhythm including avoidance of unnecessary bed-rest; respect for privacy; opportunity for social contact and gatherings; opportunities for various activities indoors and outdoors; access to necessary medical investigations and treatment; rehabilitation and care appropriate to needs; necessary dental treatment; and a peaceful environment for those who are dying. Nursing homes are inspected by the county health authorities, whose inspection routines have altered recently and now include a greater emphasis on quality of care.

The recent government plan for older people's services includes commitments to maintaining and improving the quality of care services, providing uniform facilities nationwide and creating greater scope for user participation and choice in relation to service provision (Ministry of Health and Social Affairs, 1999). For example, all older people are to have the right to a single-occupant room from 2003, and the number of posts, specially adapted dwellings and 24-hour services are being expanded significantly over the period 1998–2001. Separate health and social services legislation is to be harmonized. Additional grants are being made available to municipalities, which are conditional on their achieving increased activity.

Norway was the first European country, closely followed by Denmark, to set up local councils for older people in the early 1970s. Guidelines and recommendations to form councils have existed since 1987, while the 1992 Act required all municipalities to establish a local council for older people with the aim of giving them some influence over issues which affected them. The councils have representatives from the Pensioners Association and charities, and function as consultative bodies with local government. All issues concerning older people have to be put before them and they may discuss other matters which they consider relevant. The councils are granted local government administrative support, although there is wide variation between different municipalities in the frequency of meetings, the issues debated, and the degree of influence on local issues (Daatland and Svorken, 1996). It appears that about half of the councils are satisfied with the arrangements in place and one-third say that their local councillors take heed of their opinions and advice. Since 1970 there has been a National Council for the Elderly, which functions as a pressure group in relation to central government and advocates for issues concerning older people. Representative organizations for older people, both national and local, are highly institutionalized and function on a cooperative rather than conflictual basis. This is the case for Scandinavian countries in general.

Choice and information

All people in Norway, if they have a legitimate need for care, are entitled to an assessment of health and social care needs, and applicants for home nursing and home help are assessed within a few days of referral. But there is little clarity about what constitutes 'legitimate need' and interpretation of need may change, especially when resources are constrained (Vabø, 1998). The gradual decline in resources, in proportion to the population requiring care, is putting pressure on municipalities to give priority to people with the most urgent needs. Increasingly and unofficially, there is an expectation that people should draw on their own and family resources for coping before approaching the public sector. There can also be differences of opinion over what are the substantial needs of someone requiring care. Front-line staff may regard support as adequate, but this may be contested by the user or their family (Vabø, 1998).

Since health and social care are mainly state responsibilities, this care is arranged for and delivered to older people by the local public sector, which has a virtual monopoly of provision. However in recent years this monopoly has broken down to some degree, creating opportunities for greater flexibility and choice. There is as yet a minimal market for private or independent agency provision in competition with the public sector, so that if people are not satisfied with the care provided for them by the public care providers there are few opportunities to choose care from an alternative provider at present.

Information about state-provided services is considered important in Norway to ensure that people who are entitled to care make use of it and benefit from the services available. However, some concern is expressed by recipients of care and their relatives about lack of information concerning the range of services available to them. For example, an older person who receives help with cleaning may be unaware that she is entitled to help with shopping or having her hair washed. Vabø (1996, 1998) suggests that there is a paradox here for care workers. Giving information to older people about services ensures that they receive whatever is most appropriate to meet their needs given the reality of what is available. But if too much information is given, it may create unrealistic or unnecessary expectations and wants among people who would otherwise have found their own way of coping with some of their needs. Care givers are likely to avoid giving too much information which might discourage family care (Vabø, 1996, 1998). More affluent older people are more likely to be better informed about services than the less well off, but it is likely to be the latter who are more in need of services.

Waits for non-emergency hospital treatment in Norway can be long, leading to continued discomfort and possible reliance on other community care services during the time of waiting. However, few older people opt to use private hospitals; these have traditionally been discouraged (there are three in Oslo) and many older people doubtless feel it would be too extravagant to use savings for a benefit they have already paid for through taxation.

There has traditionally been a free choice of GP, with patients being able to make an appointment with whichever doctor they chose. From 2001, everyone will be required to register with a specific GP on the grounds of ensuring continuity of care, but this does also restrict free choice. However, most people prefer to see a regular doctor and the vast majority of people aged 65 and over have a stable relationship with their GP or health centre. Therefore the new system is unlikely to represent radical change.

Whether people live in their own home or supported housing, or move to be near family and friends, there is no restriction in principle on access to home care services. Surveys indicate that the majority of people receiving home help and home nursing from their municipality are satisfied with the help they receive but would like to have more of it; likewise the majority of people surveyed describe their relations with the home helper as excellent but would like more time to talk with them. There is a widening gap between the help that the older person feels they need and the amount of help available from the municipality, with some people experiencing a reduction in the amount of help they receive despite deteriorating health (Helseth, 1998). A minority of people – those who are particularly dependent, or very demanding – are critical of the lack of alternatives. Public home care services are widely but thinly spread and, if not enough home care is available, an older person may have no option but to go into a residential or nursing home. Critics of care policy point to the gap between the high provision of care in an institution and the care available for an individual in their own home in the community. There is a need for expansion of supported housing and home care services to provide a real alternative to nursing home care for more dependent people. The current government plan for older people's care services is investing €4.5 billion over 1998 to 2001 to develop sheltered housing schemes and to improve nursing homes and domiciliary services (Ministry of Health and Social Affairs, 1999).

'Ageing at home' has been the official policy in Norway for many years. A government report in 1966 on home help for older people stressed that the traditional view of old age as a time of inactivity and dependency was outdated in the light of medical research demonstrating that a continued active lifestyle enables older people to remain healthy and continue to live independent lives in their own homes (Sosialdepartementet, 1966). The report argued that institutions encouraged decline and dependency, and therefore the home help system should be supported rather than making further investment in institutional care. While care in institutions is increasingly being confined to those older people who are most frail or sick, the local integrated home care system is designed to enable the majority of older people to continue to live independently in their accustomed lifestyle. This is laudable and generally appreciated. However, the emphasis of this culture is on rehabilitation and activity rather than maintenance. Resource constraints may contribute to a policy of not doing for the older person some tasks which it would be reasonable to expect an older person still to carry out, perhaps with some support and encouragement. There may be ethical concerns here: to what degree should self-help be encouraged if it creates pressure on older people to carry out tasks which they have never performed in their 'accustomed' lifestyle? Older people are encouraged to express their preferences, but some older people may find this autonomy difficult to handle (Vabø, 1998). Being asked for their preferences and priorities may be confusing or overwhelming for some people. They may prefer someone else to take responsibility for decisions about their care.

5
The United Kingdom

Sally Brodhurst and Caroline Glendinning

State, family and individual responsibilities

Over the last 20 years there has been a marked shift in responsibilities for the care of frail older people in the UK, with family members increasingly expected to provide (or pay for) social support and personal care, and with formal care services only stepping in when these informal sources are unavailable. Eighty per cent of older people who need help with domestic tasks rely exclusively on family and informal help (Wittenberg *et al.*, 1998). Indeed, family members are now increasingly involved in providing medical and nursing care as well as social support (Warner and Wexler, 1998). A 1995 national survey estimated that 4 per cent of all adults are providing substantial amounts of help to a relative or friend. It is important to note that 13 per cent of all older people (11 per cent of older men and 14 per cent of older women) are themselves family care givers to another frail or disabled person (Office for National Statistics, 1998).

The UK is relatively unusual in having a social security benefit, Invalid Care Allowance, which is paid directly to a family member who provides a substantial amount of care. However, entitlement is limited by strict age and employment conditions and it remains much lower than minimum adult social assistance payments (Schunk, 1998). In addition, older people with substantial personal care needs may themselves qualify for Attendance Allowance to meet extra costs. Although this could in principle be paid to a family member who provides care, in practice it is usually included in the means tested assessment of charges for local authority care services and is therefore likely to be used to meet these charges.

Legislation in 1995 gave family care givers the right to an assessment of their needs at the same time as an assessment of an older person's needs for local authority social welfare services. But there is no statutory obligation to provide services for carers following that assessment and little evidence so far that service support for carers has increased (Carers National Association, 1997). This is likely to change, however, as special funding was introduced from April 1999 to support an expansion of support services for carers as part of the National Carers Strategy. There are no statutory duties on health professionals to consider carers' needs for support in providing medical or nursing care to an elderly relative.

Structure, funding and organization of services

Health services

In the UK, in-patient and out-patient hospital services, family doctor/ general practitioner (GP) services, community nursing and allied rehabilitation services are all provided through the National Health Service (NHS). This is funded by central government from general taxation and managed by the NHS Executive which overseas local health authorities and is a national management structure providing clear lines of accountability to central government (Day and Klein, 1997; Klein and New, 1998). The main exception to this is GPs, who retain individual, independent contracts with their local health authority, despite increasing pressures to become incorporated into the mainstream management framework of the NHS (Glendinning, 1999). This has begun to occur with the creation in April 1999 of Primary Care Groups in England (with equivalent bodies in Scotland and Wales) responsible for the primary health care of populations of around 100 000 people. Run by boards largely composed of GPs, it is intended that all Primary Care Groups will develop into Primary Care Trusts, which will provide primary and community health services and commission hospital services. It is also expected that local authorities will delegate their social care services to these Trusts, achieving the integration of health and social care provision under one local body (Secretary of State for Health, 2000).

The universal availability of most NHS services, free at the point of use, remains a strong political principle in the UK (Department of Health, 1997a). Diagnosis, assessment and referrals by health professionals determine access to services; GPs are particularly important in gatekeeping access to specialist medical and nursing care.

Social care and housing services

Social care and housing services are currently planned and funded through local authorities (equivalent to Scandinavian municipalities and counties); services are funded from a mix of local and national taxation and charges, but are increasingly not provided directly by the local authority. There is considerable scrutiny from central government over performance management and levels of spending. Social care services include home help and personal care in the home, home meals services, day care services, and residential and nursing home care. More affluent older people must pay the full costs of nursing and residential home care themselves. Many care services, both domiciliary and institutional, are actually provided by private sector providers (both commercial and not for profit), under contracts with local authority purchasers. This is particularly true of nursing and residential care homes, in which a major private market has developed since the early 1980s; in North West England, for example, care homes funded *and* managed by local authorities themselves now constitute less than 20 per cent of all institutional provision (NWBMG, 1999).

Residential care homes provide care for people who need more intensive and/or frequent personal care than can be provided in their own homes, but who do not on the whole require on-going nursing care. Nursing homes provide both general and specialist (such as palliative) nursing as well as general personal care. However, because of the increasing dependency of residents in institutional care, growing numbers of homes are 'dual registered', providing both levels of care, albeit at different levels of charges. In total, about 480 000 people – 1 in 20 of people aged 65 and over – live in nursing or residential care homes (Royal Commission on Long Term Care, 1999a). These homes provide both short-term (such as for convalescence or respite) and permanent care.

Supported housing schemes with wardens have traditionally been a source of support for some older people – mainly those who are able to live relatively independently but who may need to call on someone nearby in case of an emergency. The number of public-sector sheltered housing schemes such as these has decreased, while a small number of specialist semi-public and private non-profit housing organizations now provide a range of 'housing with care' options, including very intensive domestic and personal care as residents become more frail. Responsibility for funding housing-related care and support has been very fragmented, and housing bodies have only been able to become substantial providers of care services if they engage in financial and service commissioning partnerships with other statutory agencies, especially social services departments (Audit Commission, 1998; Glendinning, 1998). However, from April 2003 funding for supported housing is to be brought together in a single budget under local authorities, with a more planned approach to how it is used (Department of Social Security, 1999).

The separate funding arrangements and organizational and professional structures of the NHS and local authorities have imposed major barriers on the provision of co-ordinated services for older people (Rummery and Glendinning, 1997; Department of Health, 1998b; House of Commons, 1999). One way in which the NHS has been able to maintain the principle of free health care has been for some former health services to be redefined as social care – particularly long-term residential home care, which is now almost entirely funded by local authorities or by older people themselves. Older people are now usually discharged from hospital immediately following treatment or surgery, with rehabilitation, recovery and long-term nursing care taking place in their own homes or in nursing and residential homes (Walker, 1995). From the mid 1980s the NHS increasingly narrowed its role in providing free services to medical treatment, including community nursing but not nursing homes. This was controversial and a recent court ruling established that continuous and intense nursing care in nursing homes must be provided free by the NHS, with only social care and incidental or ancillary nursing care subject to means testing under local authority arrangements (Loux, Kerrison and Pollock, 2000). In July 2000 the Government published plans to make all nursing care in nursing homes free from October 2001, and substantial new investment is to be made in intermediate care beds, rapid response teams, additional home care provision, adaptations and alarms, and carers respite services (Secretary of State for Health, 2000).

A number of new initiatives in England and Wales will reduce the current divisions between health (NHS) and local authority social care services, and the consequent fragmentation of services to which older people are particularly vulnerable. National priorities for developing services at the interface between health and social care have been set for the period 1999 to 2002, and local authorities and health authorities are urged to work together to review needs, current provision and priorities for investing in services for vulnerable people (Department of Health, 1997b). Since April 2000 it has been possible to pool budgets, transfer services across the health–social care boundary or create integrated provider organizations. Over the next few years it is likely that in England social care services for older people will be transferred to Care Trusts within the NHS, and it is planned that older people will access a single assessment process for both health and social care (Secretary of State for Health, 2000). In Northern Ireland, joint boards have been responsible for funding and providing both health and social services since the 1970s.

Coverage and variations in provision

Despite the proclaimed universality of the NHS there are wide local variations in the availability of services for older people and the conditions under which they receive them. These variations are particularly marked in relation to intensive home nursing services to prevent hospital admission or support early discharge, palliative care services for those with terminal illnesses, and community-based rehabilitation services (Robinson and Turnock, 1998). For example, in one area, round-the-clock home nursing may be available free of charge for a limited period after hospital discharge; in another, the hospital itself may provide an outreach rehabilitation service, again free of charge, in the home of a discharged patient; while in a third area an older person may be discharged to a nursing home for which she or he has to pay the full cost (see below). Major variations in the range and quality of GP and community health services also developed during the early 1990s (Department of Health, 1996).

Overall, 600 000 older people receive home care services provided through their local authority; about half of these contact hours are now purchased from private- and voluntary-sector agencies. Overall this represents 7 per cent of all older people and 20 per cent of those living in the community with some level of dependency. An even greater number – about 670 000 – purchase their own private home help services (Royal Commission on Long Term Care, 1999a). However, there are wide local variations in the availability of services and, therefore, the ease with which older people can obtain them. In some parts of England, only 20 per cent of all older people referred to social welfare services receive a full assessment of their needs, while in other parts 70 per cent of referrals are assessed. It is a legal requirement that all older people referred to the local authority receive an assessment, although this may only consist of a minimal screening interview by telephone. There are also variations in the maximum amounts which local authorities are willing to spend on domiciliary services for individual users, and in average levels of home care and home help services provided to individual households (Audit Commission, 1996). The result is that people with similar needs in different parts of the country, or sometimes within a single local area, experience very different forms of care, based on different assumptions, different sorts of providers and, crucially, different rights of access (Walker, 1995). In general, however, funding constraints mean that services tend to be restricted to older people with the greatest needs or at highest risk (Local Government Management Board, 1997a; Clark, Dyer and Horwood, 1998). Low-level services to prevent deterioration are now rare, although a specific government grant to local authorities is attempting to improve this situation (Department of Health, 1998a). The average level of home care service provision is low: older service users in England without an informal carer receive an average of three hours of home care services a week and those with an informal carer two and a half hours (Royal Commission on Long Term Care, 1999a).

It is possible that devolution between the different countries within the UK may in the long-term lead to greater regional variations (Rummery, 1998). On the other hand, the continuing strong emphasis on performance management and inspection of local authority and NHS services through national systems of inspection and accountability may reduce current variations in the level and quality of both health and local authority services throughout the UK (Department of Health, 1997a; 1998a). These management systems involve clear, outcome-focused service objectives, national service development priorities and close monitoring of change and routine performance (Department of Health, 1998a).

Charges

Because of the funding basis of NHS services, no charges are made or subsequently reclaimed from patients in respect of any GP, home nursing or hospital treatments. Older people are also exempt from most charges for drugs, eye care and dental care. Within the NHS, separate budgets for hospital and community health, family doctor services and pharmaceuticals have proved a major barrier to innovation and experimentation – for example, the substitution of physiotherapy for drug treatment or the use of nurses to provide services hitherto provided by doctors. From April 1999, there has been greater flexibility across these different health-related funding streams, although overall spending on mainstream health services will increasingly shift from being driven by demand to being 'capped'.

Levels of spending on local authority social care services have been tightly controlled since 1993 (Lewis and Glennerster, 1996). Moreover, since the early 1980s local authorities have introduced means tested charges for their domiciliary and day care services. In 1993, a standard means test (including the value of property owned by an older person) was introduced for all institutional care as well. Charges for home and day care services are highly variable, both between local authorities and between particular services within a local area, although the financial settlement negotiated between central and local government assumes that, overall, the latter will raise 9 per cent of its total budget from user charges (Baldwin and Lunt, 1996). In July 2000 the Government announced that it would take action to reduce the widely criticized variation in home care charges across local authorities (Secretary of State for Health, 2000).

The charges levied for residential and nursing home care (including short-term respite placements) and for domiciliary and day care services are based on an assessment of the income of the older person and spouse; no wider family means test is involved. However, there are many hidden care-related costs which can fall on individual older people and their families. For example, although local authorities fund residential and nursing home placements for older people, these will be at a set minimum fee and families may be asked to make additional contributions for extra services in the institution, such as hairdressing or chiropody. Older people who have to sell their houses to cover the cost of institutional care may deprive their children of anticipated inheritances; and there is plenty of evidence on the loss of earnings and pension entitlements of younger relatives who give up work to provide care for an older relative (Glendinning, 1992; McLaughlin, 1993).

Early in 1999, the Royal Commission on Long Term Care (1999a) recommended changes in the current balance of responsibilities for funding care between individual older people and the State. In particular, the Commission proposed that all nursing and personal care should be available free of charge, regardless of where it is provided, for those who are assessed as needing it. This recommendation would end the current situation, widely regarded as unjust, whereby older people in nursing and residential care homes contribute to the costs of this care according to their means, whereas older people living in their own homes receive nursing care free of charge. As noted above, the Government has responded with a commitment to make all nursing care free, whether in nursing homes or in the community, but social care services will remain means tested.

Older people's incomes

Although the average incomes of older people have increased in both absolute and relative terms over the past 40 years, very considerable income inequalities remain. Since the late 1970s, inequalities within the pensioner population have increased. In 1996–97 the poorest 20 per cent of single pensioners received an average income of €110 a week (before housing costs), compared with the richest fifth, who received €332 a week (Department of Social Security, 1998). Over one-third of single pensioners retired on incomes of €162 a week or less, and nearly one-third of pensioner couples had a joint income of €259 a week or less. The tenth of all pensioners with the highest incomes now have an average gross weekly income more than five and a half times higher than the average of the bottom 10 per cent (Falkingham, 1998). In 1996 over two million people aged 60 years or older were dependent on means tested social assistance benefits and a further 1 million were thought to have incomes low enough to be eligible for social assistance but were failing to claim it (Department of Social Security, 1997). Previous labour market experience and the opportunity to build up occupational pension entitlements and accumulate savings and investments are key determinants of higher incomes and financial security in later life – advantages which are all much more likely to be enjoyed by men than women and by younger retired people rather than older and very elderly people (Arber and Ginn, 1991). Variations in access to, and levels of, occupational pensions provided through employers have contributed substantially to the widening income inequalities among older people over the past 20 years. In future, inequalities in access to private, personal pensions are likely to widen further income disparities among older people (Ginn and Arber, 1999).

A recent analysis of inequality in the UK showed that nearly two-thirds of people aged over 70 were among the poorest 40 per cent of the population and were only half as likely as the average person in other age groups to be among the most well-off 40 per cent of the population (Goodman, Johnson and Webb, 1997). Under a major reform of the UK pension system, in April 1999 the Government introduced a new 'minimum income guarantee' for pensioners, based on means testing, which guarantees single pensioners incomes of at least €122 per week and couples approximately €189 per week, with slightly higher rates for those aged 75 or older (Department of Social Security, 1998). Low-income pensioners are also eligible for assistance with housing costs.

Access and entitlement

Almost all older people in the UK are registered with a family doctor. Any exceptions are likely to be homeless older people or those with particularly transient or chaotic lifestyles. Appointments can be made to see a doctor normally within a couple of days. Restrictions on choice may be experienced by older people in residential and nursing homes if local GPs identify one of their number to specialize in caring for the very high, and sometimes specialized, needs of this group (National Health Service Executive, 1999).

A range of other community health services is available through GPs. Patients will be able to access some of these directly, for example a nurse employed by the GP, for minor ailments or health checks. Other community health services, for instance more specialist services such as advice on continence management or palliative care, will only be accessible following a referral from the GP. GPs also play a crucial role in referring patients to specialist medical services such as psychogeriatric services for older people with mental health problems.

Since the Community Care Act of 1993, local authority social workers have been required to carry out detailed assessments, in collaboration with other professionals where appropriate, of all older people requesting residential, domiciliary and day care services. With increasing pressure on local authority budgets, these assessments are less of a comprehensive examination of the needs of an older person and more a means of rationing access by applying eligibility criteria that exclude older people with relatively low levels of dependency or risk (Lewis and Glennerster, 1996). Indeed, as already noted, many local authorities now ration access to assessment itself through a range of managerial and bureaucratic procedures which effectively delay or circumvent the full assessment process for all but those older people at the highest risk of harm (Davis, Ellis and Rummery, 1997; Rummery and Glendinning, 1999). By 2002 the Government intends that older people who are most vulnerable, such as those living alone or discharged from hospital, will be able to access both health and social care services through one assessment (Secretary of State for Health, 2000).

There is little hard evidence that the means tested charges imposed for local authority social care services deter older people from using them. However, there is evidence that social workers are themselves ill informed about charges and means testing and that the widely varying bases on which charges for domiciliary services are assessed can lead to confusion and anxiety, with older people reluctant to report any increased needs for services because they are uncertain about the likely financial consequences (Wright, 1998; National Consumer Council, 1995; Chetwynd *et al.*, 1996). There is also a marked lack of consistency across the country in levels of charges made, an issue which the Government has stated it will address (Department of Health, 1998a).

Standards and quality

During the early 1990s there was an attempt to improve the quality of public-sector services through the introduction of consumer charters – guarantees of minimum service standards. In the NHS these related to aspects of services such as waiting times for initial appointments, the identification of officials by name, and maximum waiting times for service responses. However, it is debatable whether these charters have contributed to any extension of rights in relation to access or the quality of services.

National Service Frameworks for health and social services are currently being developed (Department of Health, 1997a). These will set national standards and define service models for specific services or groups of people, including older people. They aim to develop and achieve greater consistency in the availability and quality of services provided by health and local authorities, reducing variations in care and standards of treatment. These frameworks are to be implemented and monitored by managers and health professionals, but it is unclear to what extent they will constitute 'rights' against which older people might make claims for particular services or treatments.

It is likely that substantial progress will be made during the next few years in regulating the quality of services in both the public and private social care sectors. At present, local authorities and health authorities are responsible for the registration and inspection of, respectively, residential and nursing homes. Neither the few remaining residential care homes run by local authorities themselves, nor public or private domiciliary care provider organizations, have been subject to independent registration or regulation. Moreover, registration of residential and nursing homes is currently largely restricted to the physical environment and staffing levels and does not cover many other aspects of quality of care. A Government policy paper in 1998 announced the introduction of new regional Commissions for Care Standards (CCS), independent statutory bodies with representatives from local and health authority purchasers, provider organizations and users (Department of Health, 1998a). These will regulate standards of all residential, nursing home and domiciliary social care provider organizations, register providers, carry out inspections and enforce improvements where necessary. In addition, at the time of writing new draft national quality standards for care homes are under consideration by the Government, and these will require all homes to conform to new quality standards, including levels of staff training (Green, 2000).

Within the UK, there are very few formal entitlements to health and social care services. Recent court cases have established that a local authority can reduce its provision of services to existing users because of financial pressures, regardless of whether there has been any change in the circumstances of individual users. However, such changes must be made as explicit policy decisions and be reflected in revised written eligibility criteria. They cannot be made *ad hoc* by frontline practitioners or managers.

The main formal entitlements are in relation to social security payments – pensions, Attendance Allowance for older people with considerable personal care needs, and Invalid Care Allowance for non-employed, informal carers of working age. Here conditions of entitlement are formally written in statutory regulations and there are rights of appeal to an independent tribunal if a claimant is dissatisfied with a decision about her or his entitlement.

Choice

In the UK the State plays a major role as a proxy purchaser of both health and social care services on behalf of older people. Health authorities and the new GP-led Primary Care Groups purchase health care on behalf of the patient. There are relatively few opportunities for patients (or potential patients) to express choices about the services which are purchased on their behalf (Chambers, 2000). Local authority social services departments also act as proxy purchasers of domiciliary and residential care services on behalf of older service users (Department of Health, 1989b). Each local authority social services department has been encouraged to purchase from a number of different providers. However, the degree of choice available to individual older people over which care home or home care provider they use is likely to be very limited in practice. Older people themselves tend to express a strong preference for local authority over private-sector home care provision (Sykes and Leather, 1997). Moreover, local authorities have quickly moved from individualized 'spot' purchasing to the 'block' purchase of large units of services. While this reduces transaction costs, it also reduces the range of choice for users (Lewis and Glennerster, 1996). In addition, the widespread introduction of care management during the 1990s did little to increase choice as one interpretation of the care manager's role is that she or he acts as a micro-purchaser of services on behalf of older people (Challis *et al.*, 1995).

Whether or not older people with care needs have any choices about how their needs are met depends on their own financial resources (whether they can afford to purchase domiciliary or residential services from a range of private providers); the financial and other resources of their families (whether their relatives can provide care or help with the purchase of services); the levels and range of services available in their area (whether, for example, intensive or round-the-clock home nursing services are available); and the liaison arrangements between local services and professionals (so that contact with one professional might lead to information about, or referral to, other services). In many areas, however, there may be little choice about whether to stay at home or enter institutional care, once care needs reach a certain threshold. The choice of care homes varies from area to area; there are particular shortages in London. Recent research has also confirmed the very limited choices available to older people about what home care services are provided, when and by whom (Hardy, Young and Wistow, 1999). This is partly because a comprehensive range of flexible and responsive domiciliary social care services has been very slow to develop (Audit Commission, 1997). It is also partly because it is often cheaper for local authorities to offer institutional care than intensive domiciliary support (Audit Commission, 1996).

Choices are likely to be particularly limited for those older people who need very intensive or expensive support services in order to remain in their own homes. Constraints on local authority funding mean that residential care may be the only option on offer, as local authorities may be unwilling to pay for often more expensive intensive home care services (Audit Commission, 1997). In some parts of the UK, particularly southern England, a labour shortage in the care market contributes to the lack of availability of sufficient home care. Choices are also likely to be limited for the growing numbers of people from other cultures and minority ethnic communities who are now growing old in the UK.

Since April 1997 some local authorities have provided cash payments to younger disabled people who then purchase their own domiciliary and personal care services. These direct payments will be extended to older people during the next few years, thereby offering at least some older people greater choice over how, when and by whom home care services are provided (Department of Health, 1998a).

There is little information on the extent to which more affluent older people use their own resources to choose and purchase services. One study found that older people discharged from hospital after a stroke were very reluctant to use their own money to purchase personal care or rehabilitation services, in contrast to the readiness with which they purchased larger cars or household equipment. This suggests that current generations of older people may be resistant to the transformation of health or social care into a consumer commodity (Baldock and Ungerson, 1994).

Information about services

The effective provision of information to older people is highly variable, particularly where decisions have to be made quickly or in a crisis. For example, pressures to expedite the discharge of older people from hospital may result in very little discussion of options or consultation about preferred arrangements (Clark, Dyer and Hartman, 1996). Even where such pressures are absent, information tends to be poor. Recent surveys of social services department users show that only 23 per cent of users and carers have any information on the services available to them before their first contact; 38 per cent receive no written information subsequently about the services they are to receive; and 57 per cent do not know how to make a complaint (Audit Commission, 1997). Voluntary organizations such as Age Concern may provide much of the information which is most useful to older people. The Government recently published plans to improve information provision through an initiative called Care Direct (Secretary of State for Health, 2000). Care Direct help-desks will be established in each local authority area to assist older people and carers negotiate and access services.

The timing at which information is given is also crucial if it is to promote informed choice. For example, it is debatable whether information provided prior to discharge from hospital offers a basis for informed decisions about long-term care options, given the context of managerial pressures to secure early hospital discharge and the length of time required for full rehabilitation and recovery (Audit Commission, 1997). A recent survey found that most older people discharged from hospital had not been given much advance warning; a few felt strongly they had been discharged too soon; and some reported not receiving any written information about their condition and care needs to pass on to health and social care professionals in the community (Dalley and Dennis, 1997). Recently, local authorities and health authorities have been required to develop together better rehabilitation and recovery services for older people. This should provide a greater opportunity for reassessing older people's needs in a more realistic time-scale, thus giving them a greater element of choice about the most appropriate setting for their future care (Department of Health, 1997b).

Health and social care services in the UK do not make provision for regular, multi-disciplinary reviews of older people's needs. Since 1990 family doctors (GPs) have been required to offer an annual 'health check' to all patients aged 75 and over. These checks are usually carried out by practice-based nursing staff. However, although older people receiving these checks appreciate them, they are not carried out systematically on all older people, they cover only a limited range of potential health problems and they do not necessarily lead to referrals for other, non-health services (Chew, Glendinning and Wilkin, 1994a,b).

Although local authorities have a statutory duty to assess social care needs following an initial referral, there is no corresponding duty to monitor and respond to changes in those needs over time. Older people whose residential or nursing home care is funded by the local authority are normally reviewed after six weeks and again after six months. However, the latter review may be too late to alter the care placement if, by this stage, the older person's home has already been sold to release funds for institutional care, or an older person's confidence in her or his ability to manage independently has been lost. There is no obligation on either health or social services professionals to review the care needs of older people who fund their own residential or nursing home placements.

Similarly, there is no statutory responsibility to monitor changing needs among older people receiving domiciliary or day care services. Alerting health or social services professionals to these needs may be particularly problematic when these services are provided by independent or private organizations, as formal referral and liaison mechanisms may be poorly developed. The lack of transparency in many local authorities over how charges for these services are calculated can also act as a deterrent to revealing new needs if the possible financial consequences are uncertain (Chetwynd *et al.*, 1996; Baldwin, 1997).

Major problems can arise in ensuring co-ordination and continuity, both between hospital and community services and between health and social care services (Audit Commission, 1997). A report of the experiences of older patients with hip fractures noted the problems which can arise in co-ordinating continuing complex needs for health and other services following discharge from hospital (Audit Commission, 1995). The extensive purchasing of domiciliary and day care services from voluntary and commercial provider organizations creates even greater challenges in ensuring continuity and co-ordination.

It is possible that these problems will diminish over the next few years. As already noted, health and social services organizations are to be permitted to pool their budgets to purchase integrated services, to delegate service purchasing or commissioning to a single lead organization, and to create integrated provider organizations (Department of Health, 1998b). Similar arrangements have already existed in Northern Ireland for some time; the proposals will allow their extension, in carefully monitored pilot schemes, to the rest of the UK (Rummery and Glendinning, 1997).

There are some major discrepancies between the provision of services and what older people themselves regard as important. Older people themselves prioritize services which maximize their autonomy and independence, adequate income, suitable housing, home help services, advice and information, transport, personal care and home maintenance and repairs (Sykes and Leather, 1997). In contrast, services are increasingly targeted at those with the highest levels of dependency (Local Government Management Board, 1997). Low-level preventive services are increasingly scarce (Clark, Dyer and Horwood, 1998), and the importance of housing and the environment to maintaining independence in old age is frequently neglected (Audit Commission, 1998).

On the other hand, there are some pioneering experiments in engaging older people in the development of community services in the UK and a new initiative, 'Better Government for Older People', is developing new ways in which older people can be involved in developing and monitoring the quality of local services generally (Benington *et al.*, 1998; Blunden, 1998). The new NHS Plan, published in July 2000, seeks to address many of the problems experienced with the co-ordination of care services for older people, the provision of intermediate and preventative services, and the scope and variation in charges, but it will be some time before the extent of improvements is evident (Secretary of State for Health, 2000).

6
Ireland

Janet Convery

State, family and individual responsibilities

Traditionally, the family has taken most responsibility for the care of frail older people in Ireland, and this is still the expectation. Although adults are not legally obliged to care for their parents or other elderly relatives, there is an implied moral obligation placed on them to do so, whenever possible. The evidence suggests that Irish families continue to show a willingness to look after dependent older people and the percentage of older people in institutional care has not changed much in the last century.

The specific nature or limits of the division of responsibility between the State and the family has never been spelled out in Irish public policy (Fahey, 1997). But the fact that even health services, apart from hospital care, are means tested, and the presence of family members and details of family circumstances are considered in means testing for social services, implies that central responsibility for care still falls to the individual and his or her family in the first instance. The gross underdevelopment of community services for older people living at home underlines this premise.

The State, the Church and voluntary organizations have played a residual role by comparison to the family, providing a basic level of health services but otherwise stepping in only when the older person has no family or when the need is greater than available family support. GP services, hospital services and public health (community) nursing are provided predominantly by the statutory sector, although many hospital services were originally developed by religious orders. Unlike the UK, the Irish State has never been a major direct provider of social services for older people at national or local authority level. This is unlikely to change. Historically, formal social care services, including institutional and domiciliary care, have been the responsibility of voluntary organizations, including religious organizations. The Roman Catholic Church, in particular, has exercised considerable influence in the development and provision of services for older people over time although, with a decline in vocations in the last 20 years, its influence has diminished considerably.

Organizations in the voluntary sector, including many comprising small groups of volunteers, still account for most formal social care service provision for older people at community level. State funding of voluntary services has increased dramatically over the years. Recently, the Irish Government, fearing a decline in voluntary participation in social service provision, has explored new ways to support local initiatives and even to expand the role of the voluntary sector, with private as well as traditional statutory financial support (Department of Social Welfare, 1997).

In the last few years, the need to support carers to look after dependent relatives has been acknowledged in Irish social policy (Department of Social Welfare, 1997). Carers who provide full-time care to dependent persons, including older people, may apply for a carer's allowance which is means tested. Although eligibility criteria have been extended in recent years, coverage remains limited, the rate of payment is set at a very low (social welfare allowance) level, and income of other family members in residence is considered. The carer's allowance is an income payment for those who have no other form of income, not payment for care services. As such, recipients are precluded from receiving any other form of social welfare benefit.

For carers with private income, full tax relief is given on payments for nursing home care of older people. Other forms of support to carers include information and advice from the National Social Service Board as well as from individual government departments; respite care, mainly in hospital; day centre services which may be provided by the health boards, voluntary groups or private nursing homes (with health board funding and available subject to means testing); and domiciliary care, provided in some areas by voluntary groups with support from state-supported employment schemes. These support services are poorly developed and unevenly distributed, availability varies greatly depending on geographical area, and older people and carers must take the initiative themselves to find out what is available where they live. In general, carers receive a low level of support.

The Irish Government is increasingly using the media to promote the idea that individuals should take personal responsibility for their own health and welfare. Generous tax relief is given for private health insurance and occupational pension payments, and workers are being encouraged to subscribe to both, with a view to increasing individual responsibility for future health care needs.

Structure, funding and organization of services

When the health boards were established in 1961 by the Health (Corporate Bodies) Act, there was no provision for the establishment of separate social services departments. As a result, health and social services in Ireland are organized and funded from within the same administrative department, the Department of Health (now the Department of Health and Children). While this should contribute to better integration of health and social services, it has also been at the expense of social service development because of domination by the medical and hospital sector in the eight regional health boards which plan and deliver services. Statutory personal social services continue to have low priority in a system dominated by the medical model and, as a result, they remain underdeveloped and under-resourced, with treatment the main focus and rehabilitation a poor second (Convery, 1998a; Giarchi, 1996).

When the health boards were established, there was an automatic assumption that social workers would work exclusively with children and families, and this has been the case with only a few exceptions. There are currently only two or three full-time social workers working in the community with older people and their families in the whole of the Republic of Ireland. Statutory psychological services for older people in the community are virtually non-existent. The development of occupational therapy, physiotherapy and speech therapy for older people is extremely limited. These services are referred to as 'paramedical' services and are typically defined with reference to the medical services (Convery, 1998b). The other factor inhibiting social service development in Ireland is the lack, up to now, of legislation obliging the health boards to provide community care services to maintain older people at home in the community (National Council on Ageing and Older People, 1998). In the absence of a community care act, the medical and health needs of older people continue to dominate, social services have low priority when resources are being allocated, and social service development and provision has been left to voluntary organizations which are funded on a discretionary basis.

Health services

Irish health services are centrally financed and mainly provided by regional health boards. Seventy-five per cent of health expenditure comes from general taxation and 25 per cent is funded by private health insurance and income (Leahy and Wiley, 1998). Until recently, health boards were typically divided into three or more programmes: hospital, special hospital (psychiatric) and community care. There are currently eleven health boards. The Eastern Health Board, which covers the Greater Dublin area and is the largest health authority in Ireland, was recently divided into three separate health authorities. Health board services for older people include hospitals, hospital day care, medical assessment, public health nursing, occupational therapy, physiotherapy and in-patient and out-patient psychiatric services. These statutory services are administered under different programmes or by more than one programme, depending on the health board. For example, in the Eastern Health Board, geriatric medicine, psychiatry of old age and residential units for older people formerly were administered under the Acute Hospitals and Elderly Programme, while community services, including public health nursing, occupational therapy and physiotherapy were administered by the Community Care Programme. GP services are administered separately by the General Medical Service.

There are moves taking place to devolve responsibility for health planning from regional level to local areas which will be expected to assess local needs and develop strategic plans for developing and providing services in each area. The division of the Eastern Health Board reflects this new direction. Local areas will have new responsibility for their own budgets and for establishing formal contractual arrangements with service providers. The framework for the allocation of national resources is to be 'measurable health and social gain' as spelled out in a 1994 health policy document (Department of Health, 1994).

Social care services

The health boards provide some social care services directly, but most day centre services, meals services and home help services (in the Eastern Health Board and some other health boards) are provided by voluntary organizations, with at least partial funding in the form of grants from the health boards. Until recently, funding arrangements between the health boards and voluntary organizations were informal, that is, unwritten and based largely on historical precedents and relationships between individuals in each sector. This inhibited voluntary groups from planning and developing new services. The lack of mechanisms for involving the voluntary sector in area planning and decision making contributed to serious problems regarding co-ordination and integration of services. Historically, there has been poor communication between voluntary organizations and the health boards, and very few joint projects have been initiated (Haslett, Ruddle and Hennessy, 1998). The proposed development of formalized contractual arrangements between the health authorities and voluntary service providers is calculated to improve accountability but also to put voluntary providers on a more secure financial footing which, it is hoped, will encourage new service development (Department of Social Welfare, 1997).

Against a background of unprecedented growth in the Irish economy, there is evidence of increasing use of private sector health and social care services, including private nursing home care, home nursing, home help services, and private meals services. Estimated figures suggest that the vast majority of people with dementia who are in residential care are in private nursing homes (O'Shea and O'Reilly, 1999). This is a function of increased demand for private services, which some feel are of better quality than state provision, and is also related to the decrease in public long-term beds and the dearth of statutory service alternatives, especially community home care services. Long waiting lists for statutory 'public' services and means tests with low income thresholds are other factors influencing the growth in the market for private health and social services.

Coverage and variation in provision

Health boards are obliged to provide basic health services but all are means tested, except in-patient public hospital care, assistance with the cost of prescribed drugs (above a minimum level each year) and some community services. Older people whose income is below a certain level are eligible for a medical card, which entitles them to further services including general practitioner services; dental, optical and aural services; drugs and medicines; and medical, surgical and technical appliances. Currently, income limits for medical card eligibility go from approximately €127 per week for a single person from 66–69 years up to €177 per week for a single person over age 80. For a couple, the income limits range from approximately €188 per week to €265 per week if one spouse is over 80 years. Seventy-five per cent of older people in Ireland qualify for the medical card and thus have free health services, where available. Fifteen per cent are covered by private health insurance and 10 per cent are covered by neither the medical card nor private insurance, which is a cause of some concern (Layte, Fahey and Whelan, 1999).

GP and basic hospital services are widely available to everyone in Ireland, including those living in rural areas. Public health nurses, working from local health centres in every part of Ireland, provide services to older people in need who are living in their geographical area, although priority is given to the terminally ill and to those in need of acute health care. Occupational therapy assessments are available in all health boards and medical, surgical and technical appliances are provided, although availability is limited and there may be waiting lists. Chiropody services are available to older people through private chiropodists with funding from the health boards, but provision is unevenly distributed and scarce in some areas (Ruddle, Donoghue and Mulvihill, 1997).

Home help services, providing personal care, home care and emotional support, exist in almost every area of Ireland, although coverage is low, with only 3 per cent of people over 65 in receipt of services. The majority of home help recipients live alone (Lundstrom and McKeown, 1994). Intensive but short-term personal care and domiciliary rehabilitation services are available to medical card holders in the Eastern Health Board region and only two other health boards through the District Care Units (or community wards) which target older people who are at risk of institutionalization, often following hospitalization. The District Care Units offer a multidisciplinary care management approach to assessment and development of care plans to this select group of older people, although there are no social workers on the team. Apart from this, formal care management is not employed at all in work with older people in Ireland unless they are in hospital.

Other services, including day centres, day hospitals, meals on wheels, respite care, rehabilitation, specialist consultant services and residential care services are, in general, scarce and very unevenly distributed, with some areas, including Dublin, much better served than other areas. People in isolated rural areas are particularly disadvantaged in this regard. There are only ten Psychiatry of Old Age services in Ireland, with six located in Dublin. There is a particular shortage of specialist dementia services, including day care, respite care and residential care throughout the country (O'Shea and O'Reilly, 1999).

Charges

Medical card holders get free health services although they may have to make a contribution towards social care services which receive health board funding. These contributions are typically very small, for example €1.2 per day for day care services, €1.2 per day for transport, €1.2 per day for meals, and €6 per week for home help services. Voluntary providers fix their own charges and practices vary between areas; some organizations do not charge at all although, due to rising costs, most groups are under some pressure to raise a proportion of costs from charges to service users. The desirability of educating consumers about the need to pay for services in future has been argued in the social policy literature in recent years (O'Shea and Hughes, 1994; O'Shea and O'Reilly, 1999).

Those who do not qualify for the medical card usually would not be considered to be eligible for social care services in the statutory or voluntary sector. They would expect to buy services in the private sector. Older people without medical cards also pay for all health services, including GP services, except for basic in-patient hospital care to which everyone is entitled. Hospital charges have been introduced for X-rays and hospital tests in hospital casualty departments, and non medical card holders are also charged a minimum daily charge for hospital care. Costs for all health services, including private domiciliary nursing, are rising; private health insurance will only pay a proportion of costs, and usually there is a time limit on services covered. The rising cost of private long-term nursing home care is of particular concern in the Irish context. In Dublin especially, costs may be five to six times the old age pension, which is the main source of income for over 80 per cent of older people living alone in Ireland (Layte, Fahey and Whelan, 1999). In contrast, the maximum statutory nursing home grant, with availability subject to a medical assessment and a means test, is roughly only one and a half times the amount of the pension. Social care costs are usually not covered by private insurance, so individuals or families must bear the entire cost.

Older people's incomes

All older people are entitled to a basic income in Ireland. There are two categories of social welfare payment: contributory and non-contributory. Eligibility for the contributory pension requires a certain number of deductions for social insurance payments during the person's working life. Additional payments are made for dependants. The contributory pension for a single person under age 80 is approximately €121 per week, €128 for a person over age 80, and €203 for a couple. The non-contributory pension, subject to a means test, is paid to people who were never employed or who did not make the minimum number of employee contributions. The current rate is approximately €108 per week for a single person under age 80, €114 per week for a person over 80, and approximately €174 per week for a couple. People aged 65 or older may receive other non-cash benefits which may increase their well-being. Everyone in this age group is eligible for free travel on public transport, including trains, at off-peak hours, although this is of no use to older people who live in areas without public transport or to those who cannot access it because of disability. An electricity allowance, solid fuel allowance, television licence, free telephone rental and living alone allowance (for those over age 80) may also be offered, depending on household circumstances.

The income situation of older people in Ireland has improved considerably over time, largely due to increases in the old age pension as well as increases in the number of people covered by occupational pensions. However, pension rates have not increased in line with incomes for the working population in recent years and this is a source of some concern because social welfare pensions are the main source of income for the majority of Irish households headed by an older person (Layte, Fahey and Whelan, 1999). Thirty per cent of households headed by older people have incomes that are less than 50 per cent of the national average, while almost 60 per cent have incomes below 60 per cent of the national average. Under 10 per cent of older people in Ireland are poor as defined by income plus material deprivation, which is the same as other population groups. But there are sub-groups in the population of Irish older people, including women, and rural women in particular, whose incomes are particularly low compared to the rest, and these are at a higher risk of poverty. Those on non-contributory pensions and widows pensions are also vulnerable. Certain groups of older people may also be disadvantaged because of poor physical housing standards and because of inadequate access to health services (Layte, Fahey and Whelan, 1999).

Access and entitlement

Older people's access to services in Ireland depends partly on their address. Because of the uneven development and distribution of services throughout the country, people with equal need do not receive the same services across counties or regions. Older people who live in rural areas without public transport have difficulty accessing services and must either rely on family or neighbours for lifts or pay for taxis where available. Those with mobility problems, although they may live near public transport, may also be unable to use it and thus are also disadvantaged regarding access to services. Income also determines access to services; those with incomes above the threshold for medical card eligibility must pay for services from their own income, or by private health insurance, or both. Those whose income is low enough to qualify for the medical card (75 per cent of older people) are entitled to the range of free health services described above and, assuming that need for medical services has been established, the principle barrier to access is availability of services.

There is no statutory entitlement to the comprehensive assessment of care needs in Ireland nor is there entitlement to social services based on need. Services are at the discretion of the health boards and voluntary providers. Carers do not have a statutory entitlement to assessment of their needs. Existing legislation empowers the health boards to provide services to older people in the community but does not require them to do so (National Council on Ageing and Older People, 1998). In hospitals, social workers, working in teams with occupational therapists, physiotherapists, nurses and consultants, may do an assessment of older people's care needs at the point when they are being discharged from hospital, but the priority is less on comprehensive assessment of individual need than on the pressure to free up hospital beds. At that stage, the hospital social worker or liaison nurse may refer the patient leaving hospital to community support services, but there are major problems with follow-up.

The medical card is often used by voluntary organizations to establish basic entitlement to social services, including home help, for example. But entitlement to a voluntary service does not mean that applicants will automatically be able to access it. Each organization providing services may determine its own eligibility criteria and these may differ from those of other comparable services, even in the same area. Day centre directors, home help organizers, meals-on-wheels coordinators and others may do their own assessment of individual need (based on interviews with the applicant, local knowledge about the applicant and her family, and information from professionals). They prioritize referrals accordingly. In the ordinary course of their work, public health nurses assess social as well as health need and refer older people to other services as appropriate. They act as gatekeepers to other community services in an informal care management capacity. To a lesser extent, GPs may also act as gatekeepers to social support services like day centres and home help services. In general, priority will be given to medical referrals for any community support service, and only doctors can refer people for hospital respite care.

Formal care management with respect to older people does not exist except in hospital settings in Ireland, apart from District Care Unit teams operating in three health boards, which do not typically target older people with chronic care needs. The lack of formal care management is seen as a weakness in the Irish social care system, and care management structures are now being recommended in policy documents (O'Shea and O'Reilly, 1999).

Standards and quality

Attempts to evaluate quality or to set quality standards for health and social services in Ireland have been isolated and individual up to now, although the formation of the multidisciplinary Irish Society for Quality in Health Care in 1994 is evidence that there is concern about standards in health care (Leahy, 1998). The lack of systematic methods of data collection and poor development of information systems in the health services is a factor that has inhibited the development of national standards (Keogh and Roche, 1996). This problem is beginning to be addressed. There is increasing emphasis in government policy statements on achieving cost effectiveness in the Irish health system. In the past ten years, service evaluation has been a condition of funding for local partnerships involving voluntary service providers in the community, mainly to ensure accountability for statutory funds, but quality assurance may also be part of the agenda. The issue of accessibility to health services is also beginning to be addressed at Department of Health level, in part driven by political pressure caused by media reports of long waiting lists. However, there are no national minimum service quality standards to date, apart from policy recommendations which often focus on professional staff/patient ratios rather than on quality of service. Private nursing homes are the only service where inspection is required by legislation under the Health (Nursing Homes) Act 1990. Senior public health nurses working in each health board area carry out the inspections. The emphasis is on health and safety more than quality of service, although there is a voluntary code of practice that has been developed from within the private sector. Voluntary and statutory residential care facilities are not subject to the same legislation.

For non-institutional services including day centres, home help and meals services, there are no standardized application procedures for services, no standard criteria for eligibility for services, no standard minimum service levels, and no quality standards across or even within health board regions in some cases. The proposed introduction of formal contracts for services between statutory funding agencies and voluntary service providers, and between providers and consumers in the case of private nursing homes, will improve service accountability and could help to formalize quality standards.

There has been recent research, and a focus in policy documents, on consumer views of services and consumer participation in health care planning and decision making. Health boards are beginning to develop consumer complaints services and even to solicit the views of service users. A major research project is currently being undertaken by the National Council on Ageing and Older People in two health boards, including the Eastern Health Board, to assess older people's views of community care services for older people which will influence future developments. Following a pilot project initiated by the Department of Health, committees have been set up in each health board to focus on women's health issues, with participation of service consumers, including older women in some cases. Age and Opportunity, a voluntary body committed to changing attitudes towards older people in Ireland, has been conducting workshops to make health professionals more aware of the way in which older people experience the health services. All of the above developments are contributing positively to the development of quality standards in Ireland.

Choice and information

Little is known about older people's access to, or use of, information about services. Because of the fragmented nature of health and social care provision, it is not easy for consumers to get a full picture of what services are most appropriate and what is available locally. The lack of a community social work service accentuates this problem. The National Social Services Board develops and distributes information leaflets and also trains volunteers who staff Citizens Advice Centres in towns all around the country. The Department of Social, Community and Family Affairs publishes very 'user-friendly' documents explaining its services to consumers. These and other information literature are found in local health centres, GP offices, social welfare offices and post offices. Sometimes social welfare entitlements for older people are publicized in the newspaper where there is thought to be low take-up. A national telephone helpline service for older people, which is also staffed by older people, has been developed recently by a voluntary organization in the Northeastern Health Board, and the service received 150 calls in a three-month period following its initiation. Service objectives include the dissemination of information and about 23 per cent of callers during that period used the helpline for that purpose (Morton, 1998). It is interesting to note that this service is modelled on a similar service in Italy. There are telephone helplines in three other boards and there are plans to develop similar services in the remaining four health boards using voluntary organizations to provide services, with financial support from the health boards.

Individual choice of services is not really an issue for older people in Ireland except perhaps for those living in Dublin who can afford to buy services from the private sector. Otherwise, services are spread so thinly that the only choice is whether or not to take up a service that is available. People in rural areas are confined to using the hospital and sometimes even the GP who is nearest to where they live. Other health services available to them are determined by the catchment area in which they live. If they are lucky enough to have a day centre in the vicinity, they can choose to attend or not, but because of difficulties around distance and transport, it is unlikely that there will be a practical alternative. Likewise, although they may refuse to accept home help from someone living in the locale, it may not be easy to offer an alternative. Even in Dublin, the relative scarcity of available social care services in the statutory and voluntary sectors, and the unevenness of distribution of services, often means that older people in need of services are offered no choice. People who have sufficient income can buy in home nursing, home help type services, prepared meals and other domiciliary supports, and they also have the option of paying privately for respite or long-term residential care. They may also have a choice of day care services in the private sector. Older people with low incomes do not.

The Irish Government is increasing public spending on care services for older people. Residential units with 20–50 places are being developed to provide long-term and short-term care, respite care and day services. With the growth of private nursing homes – over half of all long-stay beds are now in the private sector – the publicly-funded subvention for private nursing home care is being reviewed at the time of writing with a view to containing costs. District Care Units are being developed or extended in several health board areas, targeting short-term rehabilitation services at frail older people who are at risk of institutionalization. However, Ireland continues to have a shortage of long-term care provision, and current shortages of nurses and care staff have resulted in the closure of scarce public beds, inhibited private nursing home development in some areas and raise questions about quality of care in both sectors.

7
Italy

Janet Convery and Elisabetta Cioni

State, family and individual responsibilities

In Italy, family ties are very strong and it is assumed that families will take primary responsibility for providing care and support to older relatives. Considerably more is expected of daughters than sons, especially regarding the personal care of dependent family members. Table 7.1 presents survey data showing that, depending on level of disability, 80–85 per cent of older people needing help with care or mobility received this solely from family members, with most living with their children. At the highest level of disability, 20 per cent received help from public or voluntary services.

Although there is a subtle shift taking place from an acceptance of family duty to a notion of citizenship rights to public services, publicly provided services still carry stigma and are largely confined to individual older people who are without family and on low incomes (Cioni, 1999). People must ask for services; they are not offered, and a distinction is made between the 'deserving' and 'undeserving' poor. Better-off older people, on average or above-average incomes, would not approach the municipality for assistance. 'Deserving' generally means that the person has a recognized health need and entitlement to free health care, although services provided to meet any associated social care need may still have to be paid for on a means tested basis.

Disabled people, including older people, are entitled to receive an attendance allowance, regardless of their means, but the amount is so low that it must be interpreted principally as a token reward and an incentive for the family to take responsibility. Family obligations, and their gender specificity, are widely held expectations, supported more through the lack of provision of alternatives – non-policies – than

Table 7.1 Help received by older people in Italy from informal and formal sources, 1990

Level of disability	Help only from family		Help from public or voluntary services	Number of respondents (1000)
	In same household	Not in same household		
Bedfast/chairfast	45.1	34.8	20.1	237
Needs assistance with activities of daily living	48.5	37.8	13.7	277
Needs assistance with mobility outdoors	41.2	41.0	17.8	330

Source: ISTAT (1990).

through the provision of positive incentives encouraging this behaviour (Saraceno, 1998).

According to Italian law, an older person who cannot support him- or herself financially is expected to be supported by their relatives, in the order of spouse, children, grandchildren and siblings. Although this is of symbolic importance, in practice very few older people are supported financially by their families – an estimated 0.6 per cent of older men and 1.5 per cent of older women (ISTAT, 1997). The tacit acceptance of an intergenerational contract can also mean that older people with good pensions give financial help to their adult children. The financial contribution of older people to households is very high and amounts to more than 50 per cent of income in households of two or three people in some areas of Italy, especially the islands and the south (Mirabile, 1999).

When the decision to place an older person into residential care is made, the resources of the family are taken into account and family members may be called on to share the cost of care, even if they do not agree with the decision. Personal property, including home ownership, may be considered, but people cannot be compelled to sell their homes to cover the cost of institutional care. Some municipalities may try to recover the cost of care after the older person's death, but they seldom succeed.

Relatively standardized health services are available to all permanent or temporary citizens, including older people, through the National Health Service (Ferrara, 1996). This universalist system was established by legislation in 1978, replacing previous fragmentary occupational coverage. Universal coverage of health care has improved access to social care where there is an associated social care need, as noted above, but social care services are not provided as of right. All municipalities will include in their budgets provision for social care services, at least for residential care services for poor older people, and many now provide domicilliary services. Residential and nursing homes provide care at three levels: if an older person is eligible for full support, the municipality pays all the cost of the lowest level of care, while the cost is shared equally with the health service for the higher two levels. Private homes are used if places in public-sector homes are not available.

As in Ireland, voluntary organizations in Italy, heavily reliant on volunteer labour, have traditionally provided services which complement statutory services for older people, often with funding from the statutory sector. Not-for-profit Roman Catholic organizations are significant residential home providers. Domicilliary provision in any given locality for an older person without family help or the means to obtain private help will be a mix of direct municipal provision and – mostly – social co-operatives with which the municipality contracts for services. Social co-operatives started to develop from grassroots community initiatives in the mid 1970s. They saw strong growth during the 1980s, reaching an estimated 3800 in total by 1996 (Ranci, 1999). It is estimated that there are also 11 000 voluntary organizations providing social support for older people free of charge, mostly home help, transport, meals, educational and leisure activities, and help in hospitals and residential homes (Ranci, 1999). This 'third sector' is more developed in northern and central Italy than the south.

Those Italians who can afford to do so are taking out private health insurance and are choosing to purchase health and social care services in the private sector, which is growing rapidly (Jakubowski and Busse, 1998). This growth is encouraged by legislation that allows doctors in public hospitals to take private patients, a tax system which allows partial tax relief for costs paid for private health services, and a dearth of social care service provision in the public domain (Saraceno and Negri, 1994). Just over a half of residential homes for older people in Italy are in the private sector and 50 per cent of hospital admissions in some regions are to private hospitals (Hutten, 1996).

Structure, funding and organization of services

Both health care and social care services are administered through local authorities in a highly decentralized system and financed from a national fund for health care derived from general taxation and employer and employee contributions. Every year, the Health Ministry proposes a National Health Services Plan to Parliament in which general objectives and regulations are specified and financial resources distributed to the regions. The national government defines national health service standards and criteria for resource allocation based on regional differences in health service needs. It also retains responsibility for collecting workers' contributions and income taxes which finance the system (Saraceno and Negri, 1994). National and regional agreements determine the services that are provided by family doctors and the fees paid to them by the National Health Service. Family doctors dominate the primary health care system because of a large supply of GPs and a shortage of nurses (Hutten, 1996). They receive a higher annual amount from the NHS for patients who are over 60 years old.

The regional administrations have the main policy responsibility for shaping health and social care services. They determine the geographical boundaries of local health units (the Azienda Unita Sanitaria Locale or AUSL) which provide health and social services, and approve a Regional Health Plan, establishing objectives and fixing budgets for every local unit (Ferrara, 1996). The local units are headed by a manager responsible for budget and organizational decisions, under the control of a political organization composed of the mayors of the municipalities in each sub-regional area. Thus, the Italian health service is politically controlled at local level but operationally autonomous, in contrast to the more directly politically controlled municipalities. The territory of every AUSL is divided into smaller local organizational units, called districts.

Although practice varies between regions, the following example from Tuscancy is fairly typical. Requests for help will be directed to a social worker or GP who will make a referral to the district. If the request is for practical help only, such as domestic help, transport or laundry, the decision about service provision is made by a social worker. If there is a nursing or rehabilitation need, the GP makes the decision. If both types of need are involved, the case is referred for a multiprofessional assessment to a Geriatric Evaluation Unit (UVG). UVGs are multidisciplinary teams comprising the family doctor, the district specialist in geriatrics, the district nurse and the district social worker (De Gennaro, Palleschi and Zuccaro, 1997). So far, 12 of Italy's 20 regions have UVGs.

Historically, welfare services for older people in Italy consisted primarily of hospitalization (Mirabile, 1999). In the late 1970s, however,

there was a strong public reaction against the policy of institutionaliz-
ing the disabled and chronically ill, and powers of social service juris-
diction and organization were given to regions and municipalities to
develop non-institutional services for older people. Legislation in 1978
resulted in the establishment of local health centres and also set out
guidelines about the integration of social and health services (Mirabile,
1999). But without clear national guidelines, services developed very
unevenly, with innovations being introduced in the most socially
active regions and municipalities in north and central Italy but with
little development in other areas.

In 1992, Parliament approved the National Project for the Protection
of the Health of Older People which established new principles and
rights to services, including rights to financial benefits, home helps for
dependent older people and sheltered housing. Unfortunately these
rights have never been fully enforced. The project targeted older people
with disabilities who were at risk of becoming totally dependent and
was aimed at either preventing hospital admission or at the rehabilitation of older people to the point where they could continue to live at
home. Funds were made available to improve the availability and quality of residential care services and to develop non-institutional care
solutions including new domiciliary services. However, while financial
pressures have tended to reduce the use of hospital care for older people over time, the proposed range of alternative community services
has been slow to develop.

Coverage and variations in provision

Although the 1992 project aimed to provide home care to 2 per cent of
people over 74 in response to disability or risk of serious disability, and
to 10 per cent of older people needing medical care at home, the evidence suggests that the level of social service provision remains fairly
low. Costanzi (1991) sees a correlation between the general lack of cultural awareness in Italy of the need for domiciliary care and the lack of
legislation to dictate service development. Regions and municipalities,
influenced by different local political cultures, organizational capacities
and available resources, determine their own priorities regarding levels
of expenditure on social services, and they each decide which services
will be provided and to whom (Mirabile, 1999). Thus, local party politics has a considerable influence on the level and direction of social
service development and provision.

New service development in some areas may be hampered by local
municipalities having to find the funds for any services that are

provided above and beyond the nationally defined standard package of health services. Administrative inefficiency and funding nationally agreed wage agreements for public-sector employees have also constrained the development of health and social services. The relative political bargaining power of particular groups or geographical areas is another reason for uneven social services development and distribution (Saraceno and Negri, 1994). Other factors inhibiting domiciliary service development include conflicts between the health sector, which has a national remit to develop policy, and local community social service providers about their respective responsibilities, and the weakness of the nursing profession within the system (Hutten, 1996).

There are wide local variations in the availability of social services for older people and the circumstances in which they receive services. Specifically, there are notable differences in coverage of services between regions in north and central Italy where health service expenditure is higher than in southern Italy (Fargion, 1997; Saraceno, 1998). However, even though services are generally better and more widely available in the northern and central regions, there is still wide variation within these regions in the availability and quality of services, depending on different local policies. Overall, there is evidence of a serious general shortage of community support services and rehabilitation services for older people.

Typical of social services generally, home care services for older people vary considerably between areas and are not yet available at all in some parts of the country. As one moves south in Italy, home care service provision deteriorates and the proportion of older people receiving services falls dramatically (Hutten, 1996). The numbers receiving a service may be so small as to make provision insignificant in terms of the needs in a particular area. In addition, home care services in different municipalities are administered by widely differing organizational systems, and problems exist in co-ordination and integration with other services.

There is also a great shortage of residential care in Italy. In 1998 there were 3159 residential homes, with just under half being public (Prezidenza del Consiglio dei Ministri Departimento per gli Affari Sociali, 1998). Giarchi (1996) cites a shortage of long-term beds, especially for the 'non self-sufficient' elderly, including bedridden chronically ill older people and those with dementia. The closure of psychiatric institutions in 1978, the gradual fragmentation of family life, and a drop in religious vocations have also contributed to the problem and increased the demand for long-term residential care. In 1988 legislation was passed calling for the establishment of 'health care homes' for dependent older single people and for those who could no longer stay at home. A target was set of 140 000 beds but by 1998 only 17 per cent of this target had been achieved (Prezidenza del Consiglio dei Ministri Departimento per gli Affari Sociali, 1998).

Charges

Until the mid 1980s, all health services were free. Since then, the deteriorating public financial situation has forced the Government to start charging. Nowadays, only GP services and hospital care are still free in Italy. People are asked to pay for instrumental analysis, specialist services and prescriptions, depending on their income, age and disease. Drugs and instrumental analysis are free to people over age 65 in cases of chronic disease, or where annual income is very low, that is for an individual with an income of less than €10 000 and, for an elderly couple, €32 500. In 1994, only 38 per cent of older people who needed to visit a specialist paid for it, whereas 61 per cent of people under 65 paid (ISTAT, 1997).

Municipalities apply means tested charges for domiciliary and day care services as well as for institutional care. The social work assessment, which can be very intrusive, is not only based on the older person's income and assets, including home ownership, but also on the income of extended family members. Existing social service provision is not sufficient to meet the needs of the older population, so potential service clients are discouraged from asking for assistance. Scarce home care services are targeted first for older people who live alone and have low incomes; after that, services are allocated on the basis of local regulations and priorities and social workers' discretion.

In some cases, individuals who choose private health services or private specialist services in certain circumstances, such as when there is a lack of alternative public services or urgency, may have the costs partially reimbursed. Medical expenses may also be deducted from income tax with the greatest benefits going to those with higher incomes (Saraceno and Negri, 1994).

Older people's incomes

Most older people in Italy are owner occupiers – 79 per cent of males aged 65 plus and 70 per cent of females. Older households have incomes that are about 25 per cent below the national average in Italy. Monthly incomes average €775 to €1030, compared to €1030 to €1290 a month for other households (Mirabile, 1999). In 1995, households headed by a person over 65 were at a higher risk of poverty than other groups: 17 per cent were considered to be at risk of poverty, compared to 7.5 per cent of households headed by someone under 65. Among the poor, one in three is over 65 (ISTAT, 1997). The highest risks of poverty exist among the older elderly, who are mostly women, and for older people who live in the southern regions of Italy (Pace and Pisani, 1998).

The minimum social pension in Italy is one of the lowest in Europe, amounting to only 8 per cent of the average net earnings of manual workers in manufacturing and those uninsured people who are dependent on the social pension experience considerable hardship (Ferrara, 1996). Included in this group of the poorest in Italy are many older people, including ex-peasants and older women who have always been housewives or who had short and irregular working records (Trifiletti, 1999). On the other hand, those who have experienced job security and status in their working lives receive relatively high earnings-related pensions when they retire (Ferrara, 1996).

In 1995, 83 per cent of Italian men aged between 60 and 75 years, and 97 per cent of men over 75, lived principally on their pensions. The percentages are lower for women, 74 per cent and 90 per cent respectively. Among 60 to 75 year-old Italian women, one in five depends on her spouse's income (Cioni, 1999).

There are many different types of pension which, until recent alignments in benefits, showed great variation in pension levels. In general Italian pension levels based on employment are among the highest in Europe. There are three types of occupational pension. The first type, *di anzianita*, where the pensioner had been at work for a minimum number of years, differs according to occupation and whether he or she worked for the private or public sector. When a worker reaches pensionable age without reaching the minimum number of working years to be entitled to a pension, a second kind of pension, called *di vecchiaia*, is paid, proportionate to contributions. If this pension is under a minimum level, the State pays a supplement to bring the pension up to the minimum level, but only if the pensioner's spouse's income is less than three times the amount of the pension. Before 1992, the supplement was granted on the basis of the individual's income only and the *di vecchiaia* was considered to be a safety net for people, mainly women, who had worked in part-time, poorly paid occupations. A change in means testing criteria has negatively affected this group (Trifiletti, 1999).

The third type of occupational pension is called *ai superstiti* and is given to the spouse after the pensioner's death. It is equivalent to

60 per cent of the original pension. Those who have no other pension or source of income are entitled to receive a state pension called the social pension, provided that their spouse's income does not reach double the amount of this pension (Saraceno, 1998). Almost half of social pensions are below €515 per month (Ciocia, 1997).

Recent reforms to pensions have sought to control future expenditure, including a change in the way that contributory pensions are calculated, from calculations based solely on the pensioner's last working years to a system which takes into account an individual's entire working career. Other changes involve extending the retirement age to 60 years for women and 65 for men, and limiting early retirement on a full pension (Mirabile, 1999).

Access and entitlement

In Italy, every citizen has a right to free primary health care and has a choice of family doctor, although doctors cannot exceed maximum patient numbers. Most family doctors' surgeries are near where their patients live (ten minutes on average). But because it is unusual for them to give appointments except for home visits, patients may have long waits in the doctor's waiting room (Mapelli, 1994). Hospital care is also free and, except for emergencies, patients are admitted to hospital through the family doctor, who plays a crucial gatekeeper role in regulating access to hospital and to all other public health services, including specialists, diagnostic tests and drugs.

There is a problem regarding adequate assessment of older people's need for health services in Italy. In the first instance, many needs may be dismissed as being a normal part of old age, and older people may not be directed to health services even when they might improve their health and quality of life. If rehabilitation or recovery is possible, health services are more likely to be provided. If not, the person may be given social care services.

As noted above, there is no right to free social care services, which are available only to the very poor and, even then, people who apply for services are subject to very rigorous and intrusive means testing involving scrutiny of the finances of the older person's extended family. The main criteria of eligibility for home care services, which were set up in the 1970s in many municipalities in Italy, include the following: that the older person be resident in the area where the service is offered; that he or she be of a minimum age (which could be between 55 and 70 depending on the municipality); that the person's income does not exceed the minimum social pension; that he or she is in poor physical or mental health, including disability or invalidity; and that there is an absence or shortage of family help (Costanzi, 1991).

Social workers with university qualifications act as gatekeepers to all non-medical services at municipality level. Although they must conform to local authority regulations which may vary considerably between regions and municipalities, they do have some discretion over the allocation of services. There is pressure on social workers to ration services in an under-resourced system which cannot possibly meet the needs of the older population. Many social workers feel caught in a dilemma with their professional ethics on the one side and their loyalty to their employer (municipalities or AUSLs) on the other. Some express concern about what they see as a double mandate, and report tension between their roles as advocates for their clients who are in need of social care and as agents of the welfare state.

In the Italian context, more than charges, it is the lack of services or their scarcity that inhibits access. People with little money find it difficult to access free services. Others who have higher incomes may have doubts about the quality of public services, and so may choose to pay for private services. The well-off are ready to pay very high charges to be admitted to private long-term residential care or to access services. In general, education and income are linked with use of private health and social services (Mapelli, 1994).

The fragmented and decentralized nature of the Italian welfare state has inhibited the development of national service standards and quality assurance measures. In general, there is little evidence of any systematic effort at a national level to understand how health and social services work in Italy, to establish service standards or to evaluate formally service effectiveness. Many regions have not yet approved diagnostic and therapeutic standards and, in general, there is a lack of widespread practice of service evaluation (Turcio, 1997). Saraceno and Negri (1994) note that the State controls resources and regulation, but appears to disregard implementation at local level. They see attempts to diminish political clientelism by giving more power to professionals and managers at local and national levels as laudable but less effective than improving the co-ordination of existing organizations. Bureaucracy and party politics continue to be inhibiting factors in the implementation of care services for older people (Giarchi, 1996).

In the 1970s, regions in north and central Italy established standards regarding patient numbers, physical facilities and the provision and organization of services in the residential care sector. This was in response to the legacy of traditional institutional practices of the time. The regions funded municipalities and not-for-profit organizations to improve standards of care. Unfortunately, standards in residential care in the southern regions are still quite low.

There is a serious lack of regulation of the growing private sector which provides services for many older people, including nursing homes and other types of residential care, sometimes by contract with the local municipality. Service users have no access to information on standards and rights and are afforded little protection from malpractice or abuse. In the not-for-profit sector there is also an absence of monitoring and evaluation of services (Saraceno and Negri, 1994). A new Minister for the Family has been installed in the last few years and new national social services legislation, being debated in Italy at the time of writing, may legitimate and support the more advanced local initiatives taking place and provide national service standards.

Choice and information

Although information about social services in Italy tends to be very poor generally, Giarchi (1996) considers *patronati* offices located in some regions to be very helpful and supportive to older people and their families. The *patronati* have advisers and a lawyer who provide information regarding welfare rights, act as advocates and also assist with form filling. For health matters, the family doctor is the usual channel for information in the first instance. Social workers may also give information to their clients, who are mainly confined to the use of public services due to low income. A telephone helpline for older people operated by older volunteers in 130 centres in Italy under the auspices of AUSER, an association of retired trade union members, was the model for the development of a similar helpline service in County Westmeath in Ireland.

Informal networks are important to the dissemination of information about services in the private sector. A national survey conducted in 1991 revealed that 20 per cent of the sample surveyed had never heard about home help services, suggesting that lack of information is a serious problem and has inhibited service take-up by some older people (Giarchi, 1996).

Older people in Italy are still held in high esteem and may exert power in the family because of ownership of property and other assets. They may therefore have a strong voice within their own family in decision making about their care, although the ultimate choice of formal services depends upon family income. Since the mid 1980s, people with adequate incomes have increasingly been choosing to pay for private health and social care services, and the number of private, for-profit providers has increased commensurately (Saraceno, 1998). Individuals and families are choosing private services for themselves and for those who are dependent on them. Based on available evidence, older people themselves are likely to choose specialists and hospitals in the public sector, and this may reflect both lower educational levels and lower incomes among the elderly (Mapelli, 1994; Istat, 1997).

The local authorities have traditionally depended widely on non-governmental, charitable and other not-for-profit organizations to provide social services, and this fact is deeply rooted in the history of the Italian welfare state (Guimelli, 1994). During the last few years, the practice of contracting for services has been strengthened. In some cases, contracts with external organizations have been introduced for services that were previously directly provided by local authorities in an effort to increase flexibility and to reduce costs (De Leonardis, 1998). It is the local authority that chooses between prospective service providers; no choice is given either to the social workers who make referrals or to older people as users of the services. However, local associations of older people have spread in recent years and accessed funding and support from the municipality to run social activities and provide facilities. In this way, more than 600 Centri Sociali Anziani (older people's social centres) have been set up throughout Italy (Mirabile, 1999).

Currently, a system of payment for health and social care services is under debate, whereby individuals would be given vouchers which they can use to purchase services from the private or public sector or from social co-operatives. It is argued that this would enhance individuals' choice considerably, but to date there has been no political consensus on the issue. The past decade has also seen the spread of a new cash allowance, provided at local level by municipalities and sometimes local health units. This is targeted at very frail older people with low incomes, and is aimed at diverting these older people from institutionalized care. The allowance is paid directly to the older person, or sometimes their relatives, following an assessment. The money can be used as additional income or to hire care. Although the allowance is an attempt to contain the cost of caring for sharply rising numbers of older people in Italy, it is a popular measure (Gori, 2000).

8
Greece

Janet Convery and Anna Amera

State, family and individual responsibilities

Responsibility for health and social care services for older people in Greece is divided between the family, the State, local authorities, social security and mutual funds, the Greek Orthodox Church, non-profit organizations, and the private for-profit sector. Basic primary health care, as well as hospital care, is universal, provided through the National Health System and/or through the social security/social insurance system. Social support and social care services are discretionary and are developed mainly by the local authorities, the Church and other non-profit organizations. Provision is limited and there is little or no support for many carers, but there are signs of increasing state intervention in response to the needs of older people. The number of home help programmes offered by local authorities is growing rapidly and a new state-funded National Organization for Social Care, equivalent to the National Health System, emerged in 1998. There is a commitment to develop this area further. Residential care is offered by the State, the social insurance funds, the local authorities, the Church, non-governmental organizations and private companies, but availability is limited, and in most cases it is expensive.

Social security and insurance coverage is of utmost importance. Compulsory deductions are made from the wages of everyone in employment and this money is put into social insurance schemes which pay for services as needed. Employer and employee contributions totalling approximately one-third of workers' salaries throughout their working lives are paid in the expectation that if they need care or treatment, their social insurance scheme will cover the cost. The State acts as a safety net only in cases where people are either unable to work because of disability or where a person's employment record is short or broken, and even then state benefits are means tested and minimal. If an older person lives with other family members, then the financial situation of the household as a whole is taken into consideration before state benefits are allocated. If older people have social insurance or private insurance coverage for services, there is no means testing involved. Services or treatment are the right of the insured regardless of his or her financial situation.

The family plays a critical role in the care of dependent older family members in Greece and there is a legal duty imposed on adult children to care for their elderly parents under Article 1485 of the Greek Civil Code. Article 1485 assumes that parents and children have a mutual responsibility to care for each other. Failure to accept responsibility for one's parents may result in disinheritance. The shortage or lack of alternative statutory care provision makes family involvement essential, but there are also strong family values which continue to place the family at the nucleus of Greek society as its most supportive institution. Greeks are loyal to their family, expect to take responsibility for their family members, even in the extended family, and they also expect that the family will take care of them in times of need. They do not show a similar trust in the State or the Government, for historical reasons (Stathopoulos and Amera, 1992). Reduction in family size, internal migration to urban areas, changed expectations, participation of women in the workforce, low birth and death rates and high life expectancy have all contributed to change in the dynamics of family care in Greece in recent years. But the family network is still very important to the health and welfare of older people.

In spite of the predominance of the nuclear family unit in Greece in recent years, older people maintain close contact with family members and 30 per cent of older people live with their children. There is an important bond and sense of identification between generations that is unlikely to diminish in the future (Amera, 1990). Moussourou (1985) found that there was daily contact between grandparents and grandchildren in one out of three Greek families which increases if there is illness, and there is also a high level of residential proximity between older people and at least one of their children (Stathopoulos and Amera, 1992).

Reciprocity is a factor in the mutual support system that operates between the generations in Greek families. By their willingness to care for dependent children, many grandparents facilitate women to take paid employment outside the home, and the pensions of grandmothers living with their adult children often contribute significantly to household income (Amera and Maratou-Alibrandi, 1988). The close relationship that develops between the generations then leads to a commitment to care for older family members when they become dependent. 'Caring for the old is, thus, a way of life corresponding to that of raising children; a responsibility families are reluctant to give up' (Stathopoulos and Amera, 1992). However, Drew (1994, p. 56), in pointing out the gender aspect of Greek familism, notes that the lack of family policy to support the family in Greece reinforces 'the role of women as sole carers of children and the elderly by nurturing, reproducing and legitimising their dependency on men'. Greek women between the ages of 25 and 49 have the lowest employment participation rate in the EU, 40 per cent compared to the EU average of 60 per cent. The heavy reliance on family care can also impose a high price on relationships between carers and family members. The lack of part-time employment opportunities for carers in Greece contributes to tension in families whose members may be overstretched by the demands of full-time work as well as caring for dependent older relatives (Drew, 1994). Elder abuse and neglect is not unheard of, with verbal abuse being its most common form within the family. Spinellis and Pitsiou-Darrough (1990) report that Athens General Hospital had 225 cases of elder abandonment in a four-month period; almost 70 per cent involved families who either did not want to care for the older person any more or were not able to care for them.

There is little support for carers in Greece (Mestheneos and Triantafillou, 1993). The State offers tax deductions to any family caring for a person with more than 67 per cent disability and a monthly benefit to anyone who is declared by the appropriate state committee as 'totally disabled' and who is not insured by a social security fund. Social security funds vary in their benefits, but a number of them pay an allowance towards payment to a carer. Some accept a family member as a carer. However, the allowance is usually not substantial or even realistic in terms of the costs of care. The State's provision of tertiary or long-term institutional care of older people who are sick or disabled is minimal, with only an estimated 1 per cent of those aged 65 years and over in public or private residential homes (Mestheneos and Triantafillou, 1993). The vast majority of disabled and dependent elderly people are being cared for either by family members or by foreign and Greek care workers. Because the pension of many older people is sufficient to cover the cost of a live-in carer and because there are many immigrants, usually from Eastern Europe, willing to work for lower wages (including room and board) than Greeks would accept, it is possible for many families to employ others to provide care for older relatives in their own home. Greek home care workers demand higher wages than non-Greeks and are usually not willing to live in – which is very convenient for non-Greeks. If the person being cared for is more than 67 per cent disabled, the immigrant worker can obtain a work permit and this provides an incentive for some to seek out this type of work, to the advantage of everyone. So while families retain the responsibility for their elders, many are hiring others to actually provide the care.

Cultural values in Greece have also influenced the way that care services have developed over time. These include an approach to life that places more importance on resourcefulness than on long-term planning or systematic methods. Urban living is valued more highly than rural living because of the greater opportunities and access to education and health services available in cities. Belief in the importance of investment in education, in insurance for health and retirement, and in one's children is another value that has influenced Greek social policy up to the present (Stathopoulos and Amera, 1992).

Structure, funding and organization of services

National guidelines for the development and provision of health and welfare services are expressed through legislation and through the rules and regulations of the various organizations providing services. There is dialogue about these guidelines and rules between the interested parties, including social insurance organizations and unions, following assessment by experts of needs and options. The Ministry of Health and Welfare sets health policy in conjunction with the national Directorates of Public Health, Health Protection and Promotion, and Mental Health, which have responsibility over particular areas of health and welfare. The Central Health Council (KESY) which advises the minister on health policy and research is made up of professional service providers (mainly medical) and consumers (Jakubowski and Busse, 1998). Committees at prefectural level have some discretion in planning local services and administering means tests for services and benefits. They are also involved in administering services for social insurance organizations. Service providers must be registered at national and/or prefectural level. Health, welfare and residential care of older people comes under the Ministry of Health and Welfare. Social security, unemployment and public housing come under the Ministry of Labour and Social Security.

Health and welfare services are funded from taxation and compulsory employee contributions into a plethora of occupational pension schemes/social insurance funds which cover approximately 91 per cent of the population. Contribution levels are set by central government and contributions are supplemented by the central budget (Jakubowski and Busse, 1998). These schemes cover the cost of health and social services but there is great variation in the type and level of coverage. Access to all but very basic health care and treatment is determined by the occupational pension scheme to which a person belongs. Members of higher-status occupations have much better health insurance coverage than members of low-paid, low-status occupations. Those with no employment record, or who have a short or broken employment record, must rely on the public assistance network (Ferrara, 1996). At present, there is serious concern in Greece about the fact that some of the social insurance funds are going bankrupt as care costs increase. Many people have lost faith in the social insurance system and have taken out additional private medical, hospital and/or pension insurance. Increasingly, individuals are choosing to pay directly for private services as evidenced by the fact that Greece has one of the highest percentages of expenditure on private health services in the EU, despite the low per capita income of its inhabitants (Athens Medical Association, 1998).

National health services

With the introduction of Law 1397 in 1983, the National Health System came into being in Greece, giving the State the principal responsibility for the provision of health care services. The creation of new private hospitals or their expansion was prohibited, as was private practice by public doctors. Any state subsidy to private, non-profit hospitals was also stopped under the NHS legislation (Katrougalos, 1996). NHS goals included universal coverage of the needs of the population with equal access for all; the development of primary health care and general practice; and a welfare policy which allocates services to those most in need.

There are nine regions which encompass 53 prefectures with a total of 1033 municipalities in Greece. Services are delivered on a decentralized basis through the local municipalities which organize and provide them. Since its establishment, the NHS has achieved universal coverage for the entire Greek population, as well as for the more than 500 000 legal and illegal migrants living in the country. This is an impressive achievement, especially given the geographical features of the country and the spread of the population. Through the NHS, all communities, no matter how small, have the presence or weekly visit of a general practitioner. In rural areas, this service is often provided by medical graduates, who are all obliged to serve one year in a rural district of Greece after qualifying as doctors. A number of health centres, usually connected with a state hospital in the locale, are scattered all over the country. These health centres are usually staffed by a doctor, a registered nurse and possibly a registered midwife, both university trained. Some centres have various other medical specialists. There is heavy reliance on hospital care and hospitals are used to provide primary care as well as respite. The establishment of nearly 200 diagnostic centres since 1985 is an important feature of the Greek health care system.

The 53 prefectures have a total of 130 hospitals, with in-patient and out-patient departments. Big hospitals exist in the large urban centres or in cities where there is a university medical school. There is country-wide free ambulance service with motor vehicles and helicopters so that people who live in isolated communities can access hospital care in an emergency. All-weather helicopters have recently enhanced this service. Scattered around Greece are 20 state residential institutions for chronic illnesses. Dependent older people, especially those with dementia, are often placed in these institutions, although capacity is very limited and there are usually long waiting lists.

In spite of the achievements of the NHS system since its establishment in 1983, there continue to be serious problems in the Greek system of health and social care. It has not been given the attention and funds necessary to develop these services equitably throughout all parts of Greece. There is no community nurse service in Greece, there are no day care centres, no meals-on-wheels services or community chiropodists. These gaps in services have serious implications for dependent older people living at home, as well as their carers. Statutory home help services have only been available in a few areas in some municipalities: less than 1 per cent of the population is estimated to receive them (Giarchi, 1996). There is an overabundance of specialized doctors compared to the number of general practitioners, which is low, although there is considerable variation in the quality and availability of services. Specialist medical services are concentrated in the cities and there is a shortage in the numerous mountainous and small island communities. Sixty per cent of psychiatrists are in Athens, and psychiatric hospitals in Greece's two largest cities account for 60 per cent of total psychiatric beds in the country (Athens Medical Association, 1998). Best served are those who can afford to pay, either through their own funds or through good social or private insurance schemes.

The very serious shortage of nurses in Greece, even in big hospitals, private hospitals and nursing homes, means that those without family members to provide nursing support at their bedside are at a considerable disadvantage. In August 1999, the Minister of Labour and Social Security announced the employment of 4000 additional staff, including 800 doctors, to cover patient needs in hospitals, and this may lead to some improvement in nursing services in the short term. The level of satisfaction with the NHS is low and there is some feeling that older people are worse off than other groups since there are no geriatric beds and no places for older people to go once they leave hospital. Social workers experience distress continuously with cases of old, dependent people whose families are unable to care for them or who have nowhere to go. There is evidence that up to 50 per cent of Greeks voluntarily pay extra money to medical staff for NHS services which are technically free in the belief that they will receive better care or be shortlisted for an operation (Katrougalos, 1996). The NHS's failure to satisfy both the people served by it and those serving in it is, to some extent, related to Greece's application to join the European Monetary Unit, which dictates the lowering of public expenditure and which has resulted in increased privatization. The NHS's inability to manage health services efficiently and effectively in this decentralized system is another issue.

Municipalities' health and social services

In recent years, Greek social policy for older people has been aimed at providing care in the community for as long as possible and the provision of services to a broad segment of the older population, and not just to the destitute and seriously ill (Stathopoulos and Amera, 1992). To achieve these aims, KAPI centres (Open Care Centres for the Elderly) were set up to offer primary health services and social services for older people living in the community. These services are usually free of charge or have a token fee only, and all older people in their geographical area have access to membership. As such, KAPI centres, which now exist in the capital cities of all 53 prefectures, are a good example of a non-stigmatizing, universal service for older people where entitlement is based on residency and age (60 plus) alone. KAPI centres are staffed by a social worker, a visiting nurse or a registered nurse, a physiotherapist, an occupational therapist (all tertiary education trained) and a medical doctor (visiting or volunteer). They also employ home assistants. KAPI objectives include prevention of social, psychological and health problems; fostering co-operation and contact with other age groups;

promotion of social participation; and encouragement of social activity (Stathopoulos and Amera, 1992). They also aim to educate the wider public as to the problems and needs of older people and undertake research. KAPI centres are a model of the good integration of social and health services, with needs assessment and service delivery being offered from one central location. Services are local and personalized, and KAPI centres harness the participation of local volunteers (Karantinos, Ioannou and Cavounidis, 1992).

The range of health services offered to KAPI members is wide and includes medical care, physiotherapy, medical assessment and diagnosis, inoculations, advice and information, and counselling. Social activities include education programmes, excursions, dancing, arts and crafts, cooking, writing and many activities to promote Greek culture. On an informal basis, active members keep an eye on more dependent members who cannot attend KAPI centres. In recent years, some KAPIs have received funding to formally develop domiciliary home care/home help services for members who are confined to home. Some 300 home care schemes have been developed in conjunction with the KAPI centres, offering home care, home help and even home nursing in some cases. These projects employ social workers and nurses and depend extensively on volunteers from the community. The need for such services is great and this presents a major challenge to the municipalities.

Most of the 250-plus KAPI centres in Greece are located in the Greater Athens area. They are financed largely by central government and operated by the local authorities. Unfortunately, political pressure, party nepotism and clientelism are factors in their operation (Stathopoulos and Amera, 1992). Further development of the KAPI network has been slow and in many only recreational opportunities are on offer with few other health or welfare services available. While these services may be important to combating social isolation, availability and access to services remains a problem (Karantinos, Ioannou and Cavounidis, 1992). Hospitals are used for emergency respite care because of the absence of social support services for dependent older people and their carers. Social workers are employed in the public welfare department of each prefecture, including Athens, but in the rural, mountainous regions of Greece particularly they face special difficulties in delivering services to a population scattered over very large areas. Budget constraints in some local authorities may lead to a concentration on medical services at the expense of non-medical services to support chronic disabled people in the community. This will increase demand for residential services which are already scarce.

The Church and non-governmental organizations

The Church in Greece has traditionally played an important role in giving financial and material assistance to older people in institutions and at home. Volunteers provide services at local parish level and a proportion of welfare funds from donations and church collections go to older people. In Athens, a small number of social workers are employed by the Archdiocese and part of their work is with older people in the community. The Church runs community centres for the 'elderly and needy' and offers meals in these centres as well as in the homes of parishioners who are either temporarily or permanently in need of this service. The Church also gives financial assistance for the payment of bills, such as heating and electricity, and runs homes for the aged, including one for the chronically ill, where payment or property donation is normally necessary, although those without means may also be accepted.

Non-government organizations like the Red Cross, Volunteers' League, the Institute for Social Work and the Centre for the Care of the Family and the Child have researched and implemented new ideas about social care in Greece. New services initiated by NGOs have later been taken over by the State and the local authorities', including KAPIs', home help services and tele-alarm systems. In this way, they help to shape and direct statutory service development. Although the contribution of the Church and the NGOs has been very valuable, services provided have not been universal or consistent over time, and distribution has been very uneven.

The private sector

In recent years, the development of health and welfare services has escalated. In the Athens area, it is possible to access private services by telephone, including home help, nursing, medical tests, physiotherapy, general practitioners and even specialist medical services. The number of retired people moving to Greece from neighbouring EU countries to the north will undoubtedly stimulate the development of even more high-quality services in the private sector. But they may be out of reach for most Greek pensioners because of their cost (Stathopoulos and Amera, 1992).

Future trends

The development of a 'third sector' to provide not-for-profit services of high quality and lower cost to the State, under the direction and administration of local authorities, is a possible solution to weaknesses in the present system which is finding its way into new Greek legislation. Under local authority initiatives, funds from different sources, including state, private, social and private insurance funds, are administered by the local authorities to develop and synchronize services, including those provided by NGOs, which contribute to meeting social needs. The development of this sector is a major challenge for the immediate future (Yfantopoulos, 1999). The KAPI model offers hope but also suggests that developments in this direction must be approached with caution. Unless a formal commitment to services for older people, including social care as well as health care, is made, and standards regarding type, level and quality of services are established and safeguarded, services for older people may shrink in importance compared to services for other groups. Social service professionals may be considered to be non-essential, and services for older people may become medicalized again and the benefits of prevention and rehabilitation may be overlooked.

Coverage and variations in provision

As suggested above, there are very great variations in health and social services for older people in Greece. KAPI services are concentrated in the Athens area. Karantinos, Ioannou and Cavounidis (1992) estimate that only 6 per cent of the older population have access to KAPI services. The greatest variation exists between provision in the large cities and in the mountainous and small island communities where services are scarce, if they are available at all, and where service delivery remains a major challenge. The recent depopulation of rural areas, with the exodus of younger people to the cities or abroad, has contributed to increasing social as well as geographical isolation. This has a major impact on the 40 per cent of older people in the Greek population who live in rural areas (Giarchi, 1996).

Charges for services

Social services provided by the Ministry of Health and Welfare and delivered by the prefectural offices are free. Through these, citizens can get information about their rights to state and other benefits and can apply for such benefits. For the time being, existing services provided at the municipal level, including primary health care, vaccinations and social tourism in camps, are also free. Social tourism in hotels, off season, may involve small payments. KAPI membership costs between nothing and €5 per year, and members can enjoy all kinds of services, almost free, including recreation, physiotherapy and rehabilitation.

Home help and home care, where available, cost a small fee or are offered free to members.

Care for chronically ill or disabled older people is very expensive, regardless of whether the care is offered in hospital, in an institution or at home. In cases where a foreign care worker has been employed, the full amount of the elderly person's pension typically goes towards the care worker's wages (they would also receive free room and board). Because of the severe shortage of nurses in the Greek health system, untrained nurses must be employed by patients in hospital or at home unless someone in the family can directly provide this care. Private untrained nurses charge about €40 per seven-hour shift. Some social insurance funds do pay for nursing services, and individuals or families with money can afford to employ nurses where necessary. However, uninsured persons or those with the minimum social insurance, who are poor enough to receive totally free hospital care, are also expected to finance this service themselves, and obviously find this difficult if not impossible. This is the biggest problem in the Greek system of long-term care at present.

Charges for health care, including hospital, surgical and rehabilitation, vary with a patient's insurance fund and the agreement that each fund has with the State. For some funds, all services are free – for the patient but not necessarily for the fund – while for others the patient pays a proportion of costs. The following examples give an idea of how the system works. An ophthalmological examination may cost nothing at one's social insurance fund's out-patient clinic, €4 at a state hospital's out-patient clinic for a person without insurance but on low income, and €40 at a private hospital out-patient clinic. A home visit by a GP from one's insurance fund may cost nothing, but a private GP will charge about €35 per visit. Some funds may reimburse the patient for all or part of this amount. Open heart surgery may cost nothing or very little at a state hospital but may cost more than €28 000 at a private hospital, with the patient's insurance fund paying only about 5 per cent of that amount. Private insurance may pay the entire amount, depending on coverage.

Older people's incomes

Despite improvement in pensions during the 1980s, the fragmentation of the social protection system in Greece still perpetuates great inequalities in income (Stathopoulos and Amera, 1992). There are over 300 social insurance schemes with 95 organizations providing primary pensions or supplementary pension benefits. Pensions are determined by occupation. Many workers with high incomes are purchasing private pension insurance to complement their social insurance. Some groups of workers, insurance company employees and bank employees, have organized mutual funds into which they pay voluntarily towards an additional pension which is paid when they retire. Some of these funds are very strong, and the additional pension is substantial. For other occupational groups, however, pension levels are much below the estimated minimum cost of living for an elderly person (Katrougalos, 1996). The incidence of poverty in Greece increases greatly when the household head reaches 65 years and is even greater for those household heads over 75 years. Twenty-six per cent of households headed by the 65–74 age group are estimated to be in poverty. For the over 75s, 42 per cent are estimated to be in poverty (Karantinos, Ioannou and Cavounidis, 1992). In a 1990 National Statistical Services report, older people comprised one-third of the lowest income decile. Older people also fare badly in terms of housing facilities such as indoor toilets and heating (Karantinos, Ioannou and Cavounidis, 1992).

In 1999, the pension rate from the Farmers' Insurance Fund (OGA), which covers insured farmers and uninsured persons over age 68, was €90 per month, compared to approximately €350 per month from the IKA and TEBE social insurance funds, which cover employees in the private and public sector as well as small business owners. The OGA pension is below subsistence level for farmers living in rural areas and even more so for older people in urban areas where the cost of living is much higher. While family networks help to alleviate some of the financial pressure on older people, a high percentage still work at farming in rural areas because of financial need (Karantinos, Ioannou and Cavounidis, 1992).

The support given to people over 60 who have 67 per cent disablement or more in 1999 was €53 per month, provided the individual had no other insurance. Local Welfare Directorates of the Ministry of Health can give monetary aid between approximately €45–€300 once a year in emergency situations to individuals or families, including older people. Non-cash benefits include reduced train and bus fares from the Greek Railroad Organization (Karantinos, Ioannou and Cavounidis, 1992).

Access and entitlement

All Greeks are entitled to medical assessment by a GP and have a general entitlement to hospital services, although there are no beds specifically for geriatric patients. GPs make referrals to hospital or to specialist medical services where they exist. In the municipalities, the KAPI social worker is often the first point of contact that people have with services, although this is mostly in cases where there is no family, where the family has problems, or where the older person has no pension coverage through social security or private pension funds. In these cases, the social worker assesses the applicant's situation, including the financial situation of the family, and makes recommendations to the prefecture committees. Referrals are made to other services as appropriate. State committees determine eligibility for benefits for those who are 67 per cent disabled and without social insurance. There is no statutory entitlement to social services in Greece, although everyone is guaranteed a (very low) minimum income.

In general, access to services is determined by one's address and income. As noted earlier, there is a concentration of services in large urban areas and this is especially true of specialist medical and psychiatric services. There is a dearth of services in rural areas, except for GP services which are available to all and hospital care which is also generally accessible. In the cities, all older people are eligible to attend KAPI centres in the area in which they live. But in many rural areas, no such services exist. As noted earlier, many families can afford to pay immigrant workers to care for dependent older relations in their own home, if necessary. Older people with good pensions from well-endowed social insurance funds can access any of a growing number of private services. They can also afford to buy additional private insurance to cover service costs.

Standards, quality and choice

There is great variation in quality of services, and very often services in the statutory sector may be better than in the private sector. Recently two developments have been initiated with a view to making services accountable to consumers. The first is concerned with the protection of patients' rights and the other is that of the public ombudsman. The second appears to be more active than the first.

Choice regarding health and welfare services exists in Greece when there is money either through one's own means or family means, or through a good social security or private insurance fund. People in the best position to choose are those who can pay for private services, whether hospital care and treatment, specialist services, or residential or nursing homes. When it comes to long-term care, Greeks prefer to stay in their own homes with live-in help and, as discussed above, it is possible for many Greeks to make this choice. Those Greeks who have no family and very poor social security have no choice of services unless they live in an area where local services have been developed by voluntary organizations, including the Church, for people in poverty. Even then, their choice is whether or not to take what services exist. There is usually no question of choosing between alternative services or service types. For people living in isolated rural areas, the situation with regard to choice is even worse because so many services are concentrated in the big cities. Again, people in rural areas with financial means or good social insurance coverage do have the choice to go to the cities for treatment and care, especially if they have family living there, although sometimes this results in dislocation, increased dependence and death.

Information is not readily available, regulations often change, and older persons and even professionals have a hard time keeping well informed about services. Social workers find that KAPI members, especially female members who are illiterate and live alone, do not know their rights to state or other benefits and services. Most of these benefits have to do with financial assistance that may improve their standard of living. In every prefecture, even in very remote areas, social workers, nurses, GPs and priests do their best to inform people about what services might be available to them.

By March 2000, 49 of Greece's 53 prefectures had established home help programmes, operated by the local authorities under the authority of the Ministry of Health and Welfare and the Ministry of Labour and Social Security. More than 10 000 older people in Greece are benefiting from the programmes, which provide help with domestic tasks and personal care, meals-on-wheels, support from social workers, nursing care and, in some cases, physiotherapy. Services are offered on a daily basis if necessary. There is a commitment to develop these programmes to cover all municipalities in Greece (Amera and Stournara, 2000).

9
The Case Studies

Tim Blackman, Anna Amera, Sally Brodhurst, Elisabetta Cioni,
Janet Convery, Gunvor Erdal, Evangelos Paroussis, Merete Platz,
Bridget Robb and Mia Vabø

Chapters 3 to 8 have described the social care each of the six countries provides for older people at the 'system' level of family, public, voluntary and private institutions. This chapter turns to what this means for individual older people who need assistance with activities of daily living because of ill-health or disability.

The need to understand how the actual experience of social policy varies across countries has led to greater use of a 'micro' case study approach in comparative research (Mabbett and Bolderson, 1999). This is a difficult exercise with social care because there are no fixed entitlements and much depends on the availability of family and financial resources, and the judgements of care professionals. Data are not available that could be used to compare what older people receive in each country, given their needs and circumstances. The approach taken here, therefore, is to use informed judgement to demonstrate what an older person would typically receive.

Four contrasting cases of older people needing help with their care were selected, taken from actual case files held by the Social Services Department of Oxfordshire County Council in England, and selected by the department to be broadly representative of the variety of needs and circumstances which it encountered. More details are presented below but the four cases involved, respectively, chronic and terminal illness, moderate physical disability, mental health problems, and low-level physical disability. Family arrangements varied from living alone with no nearby relatives to living with a spouse or adult child. The contents of the files were presented as an anonymized statement for each case, giving the person's age, sex, ethnic group, language, health details, family details, key people involved, current support, a detailed description of their situation and any additional information which was relevant to the case. After agreeing that the case descriptions were also valid in the five other countries, a paper was drawn up for each country describing how each case's needs were likely to be addressed. Advice was also sought from practitioners known to the authors. The papers were circulated and discussed at a meeting of the group.

The assessments which were developed through this process are inevitably subjective. They are informed judgements of what care an older person would, in general, be likely to receive in given circumstances. Inevitably, this method is not totally reliable, both because of different individual judgements and because a feature of all countries is local differences – to varying degrees – in the services available. A further limitation is that this method does not enable the countries to be compared in terms of the extent of unmet need among older people who do not come to the attention of care services. The results, therefore, need to be considered as part of a wider picture, including the data presented in Table 1.1 in Chapter 1. The cases are presented here to illustrate the contrasts and similarities that emerge; each one is summarized in a table to facilitate comparison. They start with Mrs A, who has the highest level of need for care, and finish with Mrs D, whose needs are quite modest.

Mrs A: terminally ill with high-level needs

The first case, Mrs A, is an older person with multiple chronic health problems (see Table 9.1). She is 83 years old and terminally ill with only a short time to live. She was recently discharged from hospital after treatment for heart problems and wishes to remain at home. Mrs A cannot walk or cope with her own personal care and has occasional bladder accidents. She needs help over a 24-hour period, including toileting, drinking, feeding, changing position and dressing severe pressure sores. She lives with her husband in a small cottage with an upstairs bathroom. Her son and daughter live a 30-minute car journey away. Her husband is frail and unable to help his wife with physical tasks.

Denmark

In Denmark, Mrs A would be assessed in hospital as needing immediate intensive care services upon discharge. Three options would be discussed with her and her husband, and they would be able to choose which they preferred. The first option would be for Mrs A to move into a nursing home. Nursing and social care would be free of charge but

Table 9.1 Examples of social care services offered to Mrs A

	Denmark	Norway	England	Ireland	Italy	Greece
Mrs A: 83, chronically and terminally ill, with low income. Recently discharged following hospital care for heart problem. Wishes to remain at home, where lives with her husband. He can offer little practical help. Son and daughter live 30 minutes drive away.	Assessment in hospital by nurse. Three options: (1) free 24-hour nursing home care (charge for accommodation/ food); (2) free transport to nursing home for night stays plus meals (charged for) and daytime home care; (3) free round-the-clock home care plus daily district nurse visits and daily meals-on-wheels (charged for). Free loan of technical aids and alarm. Some municipalities would encourage (1) as cheapest option.	Assessment by nurse. Immediate offer of place in nursing home. Home care would not be regarded as satisfactory without family or voluntary help (husband would be identified as at risk from the burden of care). If she insists on remaining at home, would be offered aids and regular home nurse visits day and night.	Assessment by social worker. Home care 2½ hours per day, 7 days a week (means tested). District nurse visits 4–5 times a week plus night nurse, both free. Meals-on-wheels 7 days per week (means-tested). Alarm and telephone (means-tested). Possible hospice placement if available. If domiciliary package exceeds cost of nursing home, extra cost would have to be met by the family.	Unlikely to be discharged from hospital. If she and family very committed to returning home, in some areas home care, meals-on-wheels and night nursing would be available at no/minimal cost.	Assessment by District Geriatric Evaluation Unit. Social worker would manage case. Nurse visits at least 3 times a week (free). Home help visits for 2 hours every day to help with personal care and housework – children would be expected to pay for part or all of this depending on their income.	Son, daughter and families would organize care. Immigrant worker might be hired to live in. Nurse would have to be paid for, possibly partly met if insured. If nursing home is used, this has to be paid for, plus additional payment for exclusive nursing care (families often undertake this themselves).

Mrs A would pay for food and accommodation. The second option would be for her to stay at home during the day and go to a nursing home at night, with free transport from the local authority. She could have an evening meal and breakfast at the nursing home, for which she would pay. Nursing home staff would attend to her personal care. The third option would be for Mrs A to receive 24-hour services at home, with daily visits from a community nurse and frequent daily home help visits, at no charge, to assist with personal care and domestic tasks including weekly shopping, cleaning and laundry. Meals-on-wheels would be provided seven days a week, for which there would be a charge. Technical aids such as a toilet chair, hoist, hospital bed and continence pads would be provided free of charge, as well as a safety alarm. Of the three options, care in the home would be most costly to the local authority and some authorities would encourage Mrs A to choose the cheaper nursing home option. An alternative would be a hospice, but these are very rare in Denmark.

Norway

In Norway, Mrs A would be encouraged to move into a nursing home, although her wish to be at home would have to be respected if she insisted on it. The home care service would regard meeting her 24-hour needs for care to be excessively costly. An acceptable standard of care would only be possible if complemented by informal care, and this would only be an option if Mrs A received help from an adult child, a friend or a neighbour, a charity nurse or volunteers. In some Norwegian cities, religious organizations support people who are terminally ill and want to stay at home. If additional informal care is not available, the home care service would try to convince Mrs A and her husband that it is better for both of them that she moves to a nursing home to receive intensive nursing and personal care. Being terminally ill, she would be offered a bed immediately. The home care service would be concerned about the risk to Mr A of exhaustion and stress if he continues caring for his wife at home; they would want to prevent him becoming a new user. But Mrs A would have a legal right to remain at home and, if she insisted on this, the home care service would do what they could. An occupational therapist would assist with the provision of technical aids such as a wheelchair, lift and commode. Home nurses would visit every three hours round the clock to check on her condition and provide personal care. Up to seven hours of staff time each day would provide help with bathing, feeding, drinking and changing position. The house would be cleaned once a fortnight and, if close relatives were unable to help, home help staff would also assist with shopping and laundry.

England

In England, Mrs A's needs are likely to be addressed through a package of services jointly funded by the local authority's Social Services Department and the National Health Service. This would be based on a joint assessment of her needs. Some Social Services Departments might argue for full funding of her care by the NHS, especially if it is concluded that Mrs A will end her life with a short stay in a nursing home. But it is more likely that a jointly funded domiciliary package would be arranged. This would include daily visits by an NHS community nurse or Macmillan nurse (daily wash, toilet, commode, pressure sores and medication) and two home care workers, arranged by Social Services, visiting daily and during the night to undertake personal care, prepare meals, settle her for the night and turn her during the night. Help would be provided with shopping, laundry and cleaning (probably three hours per week). Meals-on-wheels, or frozen meals, and an alarm and telephone might also be offered. There may be daily visits by her family doctor. It is possible that Social Services would commission a private agency to provide home care because, compared with their own home care service, this is likely to be more flexible in providing care at the times required, and cheaper. Appropriate equipment such as a hoist would be installed in the cottage. Mrs A's husband would receive a carer's assessment and he is likely to be offered respite care, such as a sitting service, for perhaps three hours a week. Services are likely to be reviewed weekly.

An issue in this case is that the cost of a domiciliary package may be so high as to lead to a decision to offer Mrs A only a place in a nursing home because it is cheaper. Public funding of a domiciliary package is generally limited to the equivalent cost of a nursing home place; any expenditure above this 'cap' has to be met by the user or family. Some care managers may also have reservations about Mrs A being cared for at home at all. If she deteriorates quickly, she may be moved to a hospice if one is available, run by the voluntary sector.

Ireland

In Ireland it is unlikely that Mrs A would have been discharged from hospital unless she and her family were insistent about her going home. Given the heavy medical bias of Ireland's care system, and the dearth of services in the community to support someone in Mrs A's situation, it is more likely that hospital staff would recommend continuing hospital care, transfer to a geriatric unit in a general hospital or a move into a private nursing home. The GP and the public health nurse would be likely to agree that she should not be discharged from hospital. While hospital care is free, private nursing home care is not, although the family may be entitled to a subsidy in the form of a nursing home grant, subject to a geriatrician's assessment of need, which would pay a proportion of the cost. Mrs A's son and daughter would be expected to take some responsibility for both their parents but, given the extent of Mrs A's care needs, they would probably not be expected to meet her care needs themselves unless one of the children is single and without children themselves, in which case he or she might be expected to move in with their parents for Mrs A's final days. The daughter, especially if she has no family of her own, would be considered an obvious candidate; the son and any daughter-in-law would come under less pressure.

If the family are committed to Mrs A staying at home, domiciliary services exist in some areas of Ireland which could be provided at no or minimal cost for a short period until she died, including home help, care attendant services and night-time nursing. The public health nurse would be likely to call daily and act in a supervisory capacity. If there are no public or voluntary domiciliary services locally, private services would be the only option to complement family care. These would be expensive, especially in Dublin, and may not be available in rural areas. The public health nurse could arrange for equipment to be loaned, such as bedpans and mattress covers, at no cost. Meals-on-wheels could be organized for both Mr and Mrs A at very low cost. If hospice outreach services exist locally, Mrs A might receive palliative nursing care for a few hours a day. Mr A's future after his wife's death would be discussed between the family, the GP and perhaps the public health nurse. He would be perceived as needing help not only because of his frailty but also because he is a man. Options could include going to live with his son or daughter; continuing to live in their present house, in which case he would probably receive home help to assist with practical tasks; moving into supported housing, which however is rare in Ireland; moving into a welfare home for semi-independent older people if there is one in his area; or moving into a private nursing home if it is felt that he cannot care for himself and the family can afford it.

Italy

In Italy, Mrs A would be assessed by the district UVG (Geriatric Evaluation Unit), a multiprofessional team comprising geriatricians, social workers and nurses. Institutionalization is likely to be avoided, and Mrs A would receive care at home from her daughter, her son, a nurse and a home carer. Care services would be organized by a social worker, who would report back to the UVG periodically about Mrs A's condition. A nurse would visit at least three times a week which, as health care, would be free of charge. A non-professional home carer would visit for two hours every day to help with personal care and cleaning. The social worker in charge of the case would interview the children and, depending on their means, determine whether they should pay all or part of the cost of the home care service.

Greece

In Greece, family members would be very involved in the details of organizing all of Mrs A's day-to-day care, advised by the family doctor. Although her husband would not be expected to do more than he is able to do, it is not unusual for a husband to provide intensive personal care to a dependent partner (sons in Greece can also be involved in providing intimate personal care to mothers or mothers-in-law). The most likely solution for Mrs A would be that a woman is hired privately to provide care, possibly a nurse but quite likely an untrained foreign immigrant who would live with Mrs A. The cost is likely to be high (a Greek carer would be three to four times more expensive), but an insurance organization might pay towards the night-time care. If Mrs A enters a nursing home, the family would be expected to pay for exclusive nursing, which can be extremely expensive, especially if 24-hour care is needed. If this is unaffordable, she would be cared for at home or in a nursing home at a level covered by the insurance organization, probably a room shared with four or five other people, with family members visiting to share her personal care between them. If she lives in Athens, Salonika or several other large cities, a KAPI is likely to be accessible and could provide home care using volunteers. In Athens, Red Cross home care and home nursing are available in some areas. Very little help would be available in rural areas of Greece, where neighbours would be of heightened importance, although there are district nurses who provide some support.

Mr B: suffered a stroke, living alone

The second case, Mr B, is an 85-year-old widower (Table 9.2). Discharged from hospital following a stroke, he is recovering well but is weak on one side of his body, affecting his balance and confidence

Table 9.2 Examples of social care services offered to Mr B

	Denmark	Norway	England	Ireland	Italy	Greece
Mr B: 85, male. Discharged from hospital following stroke. Lacks confidence that he can cope. Lives alone with no regular support.	Assessment in hospital. Rehabilitation in hospital or day centre (free). Home help visits once a week or fortnight, plus technical aids and meals-on-wheels. May be rehoused into adapted accommodation (in situ adaptations generally reserved for younger disabled people). Can be delays in arranging care before discharge. Waiting lists for adapted dwellings.	Assessment in hospital. Daily visits to rehabilitation centre after discharge. Stairlift and alarm, help with housework once a fortnight, plus laundry and shopping if no other help available. Eligible for sheltered housing but likely to have to wait.	Assessment in hospital. Rehabilitation in a day centre (possibly at home) for 6 weeks. Grab rails, alarm, stairlift if needed, and frozen meals 7 days a week. Up to 2 hours a week home care for shopping and laundry.	Transfer from acute to community hospital where assessed for functional ability to return home. Intensive physiotherapy at the hospital (rarely at home). Adaptations to home (means tested). Home care plus possibly meals-on-wheels and day centre. Home care and hospital care might alternate. May be eligible for sheltered or welfare housing, but availability is patchy.	Assessment by Geriatric Evaluation Unit. Three months of rehabilitation in a day centre. Provision of meals. Re-examination after 3 months. May be referred for sheltered housing, but this is scarce.	Several possibilities: children organize return home; lives with relatives until ready to return home; KAPI social worker organizes help from volunteers and KAPI services (possibly with a charge; maybe including physiotherapy); remarriage; live-in helper or night nurse, possibly partly covered in short term by insurance. Other options are short-term hostel or rehabilitation centre.

(he was very anxious about returning home). He lives alone in a two-storey house with no family, although he has a son who lives in Canada. Mr B is worried about the stairs and does not feel able to shop, cook or do laundry and housework without assistance.

Denmark

In Denmark, Mr B would be assessed before leaving hospital to establish whether he would benefit from physiotherapy. Rehabilitation would take place in hospital or in a day centre, arranged and paid for by the local authority. Ideally, he would continue to receive physiotherapy at home to build up his confidence in managing for himself, but this is unlikely to be available. Arrangements would be made before discharge from hospital for a local authority community nurse to visit within a few days of Mr B arriving home to assess his need for home help. It is likely that he would receive one to two hours once a week or once a fortnight. Laundry would be arranged but at his own expense, and shops could deliver daily. He would also be assessed for any technical aids needed either in the home or to assist with mobility outside. Meals-on-wheels would be provided, for which there would be a charge. It is possible that not all services would be in place before Mr B arrives home from hospital. If he is unable to cope with the stairs, it is likely that he would be recommended for a more appropriate dwelling with no steps and stairs, and a large bathroom. This would be in preference to carrying out costly adaptations to his existing home, which in Denmark are normally restricted to younger disabled people. An insufficient supply of suitable housing means that he may have to wait quite a long time, and his situation would probably not give him a high priority. The rent level would depend on his income.

Norway

As in Denmark, in Norway if Mr B's chances of recovery are considered good he would be referred to a rehabilitation centre for daily visits. He would have been informed about local authority care services by hospital staff before discharge and the home care service would pay particular attention to him during his first week home. He would receive a daily visit by a home nurse to check on his situation. The home help service would clean the house fortnightly and help with laundry and shopping if no other assistance were available, perhaps providing some extra help because of his 'masculine helplessness'. An occupational therapist would visit him at home to assess needs for technical aids and adaptations to increase his security and comfort. He may receive a stairlift and a safety alarm. An important philosophy of Norwegian home care services is to promote the autonomy and activity of users and to avoid passivity, and Mr B would be encouraged to support himself. He may be offered a flat in a sheltered housing scheme, although he might have to join a waiting list as expansion of this type of housing has been quite slow in many areas, and other older people are likely to be assessed as having a higher priority than Mr B. His case would be reviewed after six months, which is standard practice in Norway.

England

In England, Mr B would receive an assessment from a hospital social worker. An occupational therapist may be requested to assess the need for adaptations to the stairs and kitchen (grab rails are likely to be installed, and a stairlift if his ability deteriorates further). He may be offered physiotherapy at home for a maximum of six weeks, after which his condition would be reviewed, but if not he would be able to attend the day hospital for rehabilitation once a week. He is likely to receive one to two and a half hours per week of home care to help with shopping and laundry, and to be provided with frozen meals daily (with possibly a couple of days of meals-on-wheels instead, or meal preparation by home care workers). An alarm might be installed. Day care once a week might be provided. Help with housework would probably have to be obtained privately. Services may be reviewed after one to four weeks to see if daily visits are still required. Some care managers may provide just day care once a week, with no home care. A key task will be to build up his confidence and ability to cope (home care workers would try to work with him, not for him). There may have been pressure from the hospital to discharge him because his treatment had finished, even though not all services are in place at home.

Ireland

In Ireland, it is likely that Mr B would be transferred from an acute hospital to a community hospital to allow time for a more thorough assessment of his functional ability and to build up his confidence. The public health nurse, who might already know him, would be notified when he was discharged home. He would be considered deserving of help because of his medical condition and lack of family, and because a man would not be expected to cope as well as a woman in his situation. Many – but not all – hospitals have social workers and, if Mr B was referred to a hospital social worker before discharge, he or she would do some work with him to improve his confidence and reduce his anxiety about moving back home. The nursing staff, hospital occupational therapist or physiotherapist might do likewise.

Once home, Mr B would be visited by the public health nurse in his area and would probably be allocated home help for four to ten hours per week to help with shopping, cooking, laundry and housework. He would also get meals-on-wheels if available. After Mr B has been home for a few weeks, he might be readmitted to hospital for a short period for respite care, further medical monitoring and rehabilitation. Continued short periods of hospital care alternating with time spent at home might be organized until his confidence returns and it is felt that he can manage at home full time. Home help would continue indefinitely and the GP and public health nurse would monitor his health. He might receive ambulance transport to the nearest hospital for physiotherapy.

If Mr B lives in one of the health boards that have District Care Units (DCUs), on discharge from hospital he would receive intensive domiciliary rehabilitation services, supplemented by day hospital services aimed at restoring some level of independence. DCU staff, including an occupational therapist, physiotherapist, and personal care assistant would stay involved with him for eight weeks or more. If his income is low, he could apply for a grant from the local authority for adaptations to his home, although the application process is slow and the grant fund very limited. A move to sheltered housing would be a possibility depending on local availability and waiting lists.

Italy

In Italy, Mr B would be assessed by the district Geriatric Evaluation Unit. They would be likely to recommend that he is given a place in a day centre for three months where he would receive meals and occupational therapy. The case would be re-examined after this period. He may be referred for sheltered housing which, however, is scarce.

Greece

In Greece, it would be quite unusual for Mr B to live alone after being widowed; it is likely that he would have remarried, usually to a younger woman. This contrasts with widows, who tend to live on their own or close to the family of a child. Many factors would influence what happens to Mr B: his personality, his contacts with other relatives, friends and neighbours, his social insurance coverage, the services available in his area, and his income and savings. If a son or daughter lives abroad, they would be likely to return to make arrangements for his care at home (the Greek International Social Service would make contact with an overseas relative). If there are no close relatives, then distant relatives, friends or even neighbours would be likely to make these arrangements. Mr B might also be invited to live with relatives in another city until he is ready to return home. If there is an Open Care Centre for the Elderly (KAPI) nearby, a social worker from the centre would arrange for help and company to be provided through its services and volunteers, enabling him to remain at home. Physiotherapy and medical care are also provided through KAPIs, and there may be help with arranging for installation of a ground-floor toilet, possibly through the local authority technical service. Other options that might be available are a safety alarm; a nurse during the night, either paid by himself or for a short period of time by his insurance organization; a live-in carer, hired privately and probably foreign; a short-term stay in a hostel (only in Athens); a short-term stay in a rehabilitation centre. If Mr B has a difficult personality he may well end up in a residential home. On the other hand, one case is known to the authors of a 75-year-old widowed man who was discharged from hospital with a physical disability and looked after for a while by a KAPI members' mutual support committee. They decided that he needed a more stable situation and found him a marriage partner: a woman in her fifties who was not Greek and wanted Greek citizenship, and who welcomed the prospect of a residence permit, a home and the possibility of inheriting a pension.

Miss C: living alone, with mild confusion

Miss C is a 73-year-old German woman with mild confusion, living alone (Table 9.3). Although she copes reasonably well on a day-to-day basis, her doctor is concerned about self-neglect and the risk to herself and others when she drives (which she does on occasions to shop). There are reports of her being at the shops or the doctor's surgery but unclear where she is going or why. Her nutrition appears to be poor and there is evidence of some lack of personal hygiene. She is very frugal and is reluctant to buy food, believing that she does not have the money, although she has significant savings at home and in Germany. When agitated she lapses into German. Miss C is a very private person, suspicious of professional staff and with no insight into her difficulties. She used to be a professional musician and taught music. Her only family is a nephew who lives in Germany, with whom she has only occasional contact.

Table 9.3 Examples of social care services offered to Miss C

	Denmark	Norway	England	Ireland	Italy	Greece
Miss C: 73, German. Evidence of confusion and self-neglect. Suspicious of professional staff. Comparatively well off financially, lives alone and drives occasionally. Nephew in Germany.	Psychogeriatric assessment. Ward of court is unlikely because only moderate risk. GP can withdraw driving licence. Meals-on-wheels and probably short daily home help visits. Direct debit can be arranged to pay for meals and other expenses.	Specialist assessment. Home care service would take things step-by-step, first offering help with housework and shopping, and a meals service. Charges can be waived. Aim would be to increase self-awareness of her difficulties. Occupational therapy assessment. Safety switch on stove.	Assessment by community mental health team. Day centre place once a week, home care one hour a day, frozen meals and alarm. Would have to pay. Some social services departments might refer her to NHS for monitoring and not allocate any services.	Assessment by psychogeriatrician. Intervention only if serious incidents reported. Community psychiatric nurse would try to organize voluntary services. Occupational therapy assessment. Nephew would be contacted. Possible ward of court if immediate serious risk – likely to lead to residential care (for which she would have to pay).	No formal services. May get a visitor from the parish church or from other volunteers. If GP or her neighbours refer, a social worker would visit but only intervene if the situation is dangerous. Courts can appoint a guardian who would decide on nursing home or domicilliary care paid for from her assets.	No district psychiatric nurse. Intervention is only likely in a crisis. Nephew may be contacted, and neighbours, friends or volunteers may help out.

Denmark

In Denmark, a geriatric medical examination would be undertaken following referral by her doctor or community psychiatric nurse to determine whether Miss C's confusion is linked to a physical illness or whether there is a psychiatric problem. If the latter, a case conference would be held to determine whether she should be made a ward of court. This is a rigorous process and it is unlikely that a decision to this effect would be made for Miss C as there does not, as yet, appear to be a serious risk of danger to her or anyone else. Her nephew would be asked to visit to encourage her to accept assistance. The community psychiatric nurse would contact the local home care service which would assess her with the nurse, if Miss C agrees to the visit.

There would be no doubt that Miss C needs help. She would be strongly encouraged to accept meals-on-wheels every day; the cost can be deducted directly from her pension so that she does not have to concern herself about paying. She would be encouraged to attend a day centre once or twice a week. She is likely to be encouraged to accept a home help for a half to one hour daily to ensure that she has breakfast, washes and dresses in clean clothing, that dirty clothing is sent to the laundry (at her expense) and to help with shopping. However, some local authorities would be more reluctant to offer home help for this case. If Miss C refuses services, the psychiatric nurse would stay in close contact and if her condition deteriorated the question of her becoming a ward of court would be reconsidered. If her GP is worried about her driving a car, he or she can arrange for Miss C's licence to be withdrawn.

Norway

In Norway, Miss C is likely to be regarded as a difficult borderline case. If, as seems likely, the home care service is contacted by a concerned neighbour, relative or doctor, the home care organizer will make an informal telephone call to contact her. Given Miss C's suspicion of professional staff, the home care service will seek to establish her trust and focus initially on neutral practical matters such as housework. She may be offered a home help to assist with cleaning and shopping, free of charge. The home care service would try to match Miss C with a suitable worker, probably mature, cheerful and easy to get on with. Her doctor would be likely to recommend that she applies for meals-on-wheels, which may be offered three days a week. If considered appropriate, charges can be waived. The home care service would seek to encourage Miss C to realize that she needs help because of her confusion, but it would be vital to make a correct diagnosis (possibly dementia, but possibly also another mental or physical health problem). Some local authorities have a specialized team trained for diagnosing dementia, and Miss C would be encouraged by the home help worker to appreciate that an assessment would benefit her. An occupational therapist would also visit to install a safety switch on the stove.

England

In England, Miss C is likely to have been referred to the Social Services Department by a community psychiatric nurse, who would have been involved in her case by her GP, or possibly by a concerned neighbour or friend. The referral is likely to go to a community team specializing in older people's mental health. They would offer Miss C an assessment. Alternatively, the social worker allocated the case might request a report from the psychogeriatric service (part of the National Health Service). These assessments would focus on the level of risk presented by her situation and inform an overall assessment made by the social worker. Monitoring will be seen as important, although Social Services may regard this to be entirely a health service responsibility and, indeed, may limit their involvement to making a referral to the NHS psychogeriatric service. It is more likely, however, that Miss C's social worker would offer home care services for half to one hour a day to assist with personal care, preparing meals and to monitor her condition. She is also likely to be offered meals-on-wheels or frozen meals each day, and might be offered an hour a week of home care for shopping and attendance at a day centre once a week, and a safety alarm. If Miss C agreed to these services, the social worker – as her 'care manager' – would make the necessary arrangements. Opportunities to converse in German, music therapy and safety at home (such as a smoke alarm) are needs that may be addressed by some care managers, drawing on voluntary services if they are available.

Miss C's care manager will be concerned about balancing her rights to control her own life with the level of risk to her and others. All practicable steps would be taken to meet her needs without recourse to a guardianship order, which would only be pursued in the event of serious risk and a medical assessment that Miss C is 'mentally incapacitated'. Services may be introduced slowly as the care manager seeks to get to know Miss C and gain her trust. Given her assets, she would normally have to pay for the social care services provided. This would vary depending on the local authority area in which she lives. For example, a few local authorities do not make any charge for home care, but the vast majority do and Miss C could be charged up to €14 to €15 per hour. Given her concern about spending money, charges may be waived pending arrangements about the management of her finances.

Ireland

In Ireland, Miss C is likely to be seen by a psychiatrist or psychogeriatrician for an assessment if her GP is concerned about her. A community psychiatric nurse would be involved and monitor her situation. Miss C would probably be allowed to continue as she is for some time unless a crisis arises, such as an accident or deterioration in her health which leads to hospitalization. There will be great reluctance from professionals to step in, partly because of her middle-class background and partly out of respect for her privacy. There could, nevertheless, be considerable discussion between Miss C's neighbours and the community psychiatric nurse, GP and possibly the psychiatrist, but no action taken unless there is an emergency. It would be left to the community psychiatric nurse to organize support for Miss C, probably from concerned neighbours, and to convince her that she should accept help. The nurse might be able to arrange home help, meals-on-wheels and whatever other support from voluntary or parish groups is available locally, or do this through the public health nurse.

If there is serious concern about Miss C's health and safety, such as continuing to refuse help despite reports of serious incidents, injury or physical illness, a case conference would be called to determine the level of risk and the action to be taken. This would ideally involve representatives from psychiatric services, care services and her GP. Strategies might be developed to help Miss C accept services that would lessen risk, such as home help, day hospital or day centre visits, meals-on-wheels and financial advice. Attempts would be made to contact her nephew so that he would talk to Miss C about her need for help, or provide direct support. The occupational therapy service would assess how her home could be made safer for her. In rural towns and villages it would be much easier than in urban areas to co-ordinate informally different services for Miss C. In urban areas the formal co-ordination that would be needed is often lacking.

If Miss C is considered to be at very serious risk, her GP or psychiatrist would act directly to commit her to hospital. If there is an immediate risk and she cannot be persuaded to accept services, Miss C might be made a ward of court. She might then be able to continue living at home if someone with the necessary skills could spend time introducing her to services. Home help services would work flexibly with her. The court could take control of her assets and use them to pay for her care. Some areas of Ireland have specialized Alzheimer's day centres where, if Miss C could be persuaded, she could go. However, if she is made a ward of court it is most likely that she would be committed to residential care, probably a private nursing home given her means, which would include money from the sale of her house. Few private homes specialize in dementia care although most accept people with confusion problems. If she deteriorates to become unmanageable in this setting, hospital care in a private or public psychiatric hospital or ward might be considered necessary, although there are few long-term beds in the public sector for people with dementia and policy has discouraged hospitalization for dementia in recent years. The Eastern Health Board is establishing small community residential units which might be an option, and similar developments are taking place elsewhere in the statutory sector, but the most likely result is that Miss C would stay in a private nursing home until she needs acute hospital care or dies.

Italy

In Italy, Miss C is unlikely to receive any services. Someone from the parish Church or other volunteer or friend may visit her. If neighbours or a GP contact the district social worker, he or she would make contact with Miss C, but action would only be taken in an extreme situation where the social worker's assessment is that Miss C is in danger or is a danger to others. This action would be an application to appoint a guardian to decide on her behalf what Miss C needs, paid for from her savings. The guardian may request that Miss C is admitted to a nursing home or arrange for home care, possibly hiring someone – maybe a migrant worker – to live in with her. The guardian can request help with making these decisions from the local authority social services, but is not obliged to do so.

Greece

In Greece, Mrs C's suspicion of professional staff and lack of awareness of her own situation also make it unlikely she would receive any help. There are no community psychiatric services. Intervention is likely only if there is a major crisis, proving that she is dangerous to herself or others. International Social Service might contact her nephew. If she can be persuaded to accept assistance she might receive home help or enter a home for the aged, finances permitting. If she comes to the attention of the prefectural social worker, the Church she belongs to, or the community of Germans living in Greece, it is possible that volunteers or professionals would contact her and keep an eye on her.

Mrs D: recently widowed and discharged from hospital after a heart attack

Mrs D is a 75-year-old widow with severe osteoarthritis (Table 9.4). She has been discharged from hospital after a heart attack which followed the sudden death of her frail husband, for whom she had cared for 16 years. She has been advised not to do anything strenuous, walks with the aid of a stick and finds it difficult to do housework and bath herself. Mrs D lives in low-income housing with her son, who is a long-distance truck driver and often works away from home. Her sister lives nearby and neighbours visit daily. She has lost confidence in going out alone, feels low and is physically weak.

Denmark

In Denmark, help would be arranged for Mrs D at home, unless there was a problem with the accessibility of her dwelling, in which case moving to more suitable housing would be considered. Her doctor, a hospital case worker or Mrs D herself would have been likely to contact the home care service before discharge from hospital. A supervisor, usually a nurse, would visit her at home and assess her needs for home help, a community nurse, day care and technical aids. The supervisor would arrange home care if necessary. If technical aids are assessed as likely to be beneficial, a visit by an occupational therapist would be arranged. There would be no reason to offer day centre visits as she has a good social network and would be regarded as capable of administering any medicine herself, without help from a community nurse. Home help would be considered necessary to assist with housework once a fortnight (excluding her son's rooms) and bathing once a week. Help with shopping would not be offered if there were alternative options. A nurse would visit once a week if necessary.

Some local authorities may decide that Mrs D's needs for housework can be met by her sister, but only if Mrs D and her sister agree; otherwise, housework would be undertaken by the home help service – the preferred option among older Danes. As a member of her household rather than living elsewhere, Mrs D's adult son would be expected to give practical assistance to his mother, but only when he is able to be at home. If this is on a regular basis, he would be expected to do the

Table 9.4 Examples of social care services offered to Mrs D

	Denmark	Norway	England	Ireland	Italy	Greece
Mrs D: 75, with severe osteoarthritis. Discharged from hospital after heart attack following sudden death of husband. Lives in low-income housing with son who is often working away. Sister lives nearby and helps with housework.	Assessment at home by community nurse. Free home help for housework once a fortnight and bathing once a week (but not shopping). Free loan of walking frame and alarm. Nurse visits weekly if necessary. Son expected to offer some practical help.	Assessment at home by community nurse. Home help for housework once a fortnight (small charge). Bathing assistance only if very frail. Safety alarm (small charge). Free bereave-ment coun-selling. Nurse visits weekly for 4–6 weeks. Son and sister encouraged to continue their help.	Assessment by hospital social worker. Minimum, if informal support judged adequate, is alarm and telephone. If not adequate, possibly 2 hours a week home care and day care once a week. Occupational therapy assessment for aids. Help may be available from a voluntary bereavement counsellor.	Assessment in hospital by doctor. GP and a public health nurse notified of discharge. Nurse would manage the case. Son, sister and neighbours likely to provide home care supplemented by health board or voluntary home help/care attendant. Day centre place, meals-on-wheels, aids and adaptations may be available from local voluntary services.	Situation considered by doctors and nurses in hospital. Meeting with a district social worker would follow to explore whether needs are health or social, why she cannot afford private help and why sister and son cannot help. If poor, will get a little home help but depends on social worker's discretion. Possibly minor help from health services such as some rehabilitation.	Sister and neighbours very involved. Privately hired carer, probably foreign, coming daily to help out (possibly live-in) paid for by family. If 67% plus disabled, financial assistance is available. In Athens, would receive Greek Red Cross home care and alarm. If near a KAPI, likely to have wide range of support.

laundry and shopping. Shops will also make home deliveries. It would be regarded as important for her quality of life that she regains the confidence to get out and about, but home care services in Denmark do not provide for this and the need would probably only be addressed by offering a walking frame. It is also possible that she would be offered an alarm call device which she can keep on her person, improving her security and confidence indoors and out. Because Mrs D's sister would not be required to do housework, she might have more time to take her out for a walk and do a little shopping. Neighbours may also help in this way.

Norway

In Norway, Mrs D would be given general information about the local authority home care service by a social worker or nurse while she is in hospital. She would be visited within a few days of being discharged by a registered nurse who would assess her home care needs. Her son, sister and neighbours would be taken into account in considering these needs and how they might help with them. Given the fact that her son is frequently away working, she would probably receive a home help visit once a fortnight to clean the house (although not her son's rooms). Her son's help with laundry and shopping means that these would not be provided. The home care service would be careful not to replace family care or discourage Mrs D's capacity for looking after herself. Assistance would probably not be offered for a bath as long as she can manage on her own while her son is in the house. If she comes to need help with bathing, this would be offered. Her son would not be expected to help his mother with intimate personal care tasks. She would probably have to pay for her home help because user fees are based on household income and her son is in employment. This would not exceed more than about €165 a month. She would also probably be offered installation of a safety alarm, which in Norway is linked to the fire service and would cost a further €16.50 per month. To ease her grief, Mrs D would be offered counselling once a week for four to six weeks. A nurse would also visit during this period to check on medication. She may also receive help from a physiotherapist, following a doctor's referral, to improve her confidence moving about outdoors.

After a period of time, if Mrs D feels lonely she may be encouraged to attend a senior service centre. These centres provide leisure activities for all older people, with a leader funded by the local authority and active older people working as volunteers. Transport is sometimes provided, and there is a scheme for reduced taxi fares.

England

In England, a social services assessment is likely to conclude that Mrs D has adequate current support from her son, sister and neighbours (especially for emergency contact). It is unlikely that more than a minor input of services would be provided, probably a safety alarm and, if she does not already have one, a telephone. This would, however, depend on her informal support being stable and consistent. Her carers are also entitled to an assessment of their needs, and this would include their willingness to continue caring.

Although some social workers might decide not to offer Mrs D any services, others might offer more, most probably a half to one hour of home care each day to help with personal care (including bathing), and an hour a week for shopping together with perhaps an hour for housework. Housework is a low priority for Social Services in the UK so it is likely that only help with shopping would be offered, and this only when the son is away. Mrs D would be expected to manage housework herself or pay privately. She may also be allocated one or two days a week at a day centre to address her social isolation, and possibly either frozen meals or meals-on-wheels. The social worker might ask an occupational therapist to assess her needs for technical aids and adaptations such as handrails. Bereavement counselling is very unlikely to be offered unless a voluntary organization provides this service in her area. If Mrs D is not offered any home care, she is in any case likely to be entitled to Attendance Allowance (a cash benefit) which would assist with buying one or two hours of private help. Given her low income she will receive any services provided by Social Services either free or for a small weekly charge (perhaps €3.30 a week). These services are likely to be reviewed after one to four weeks.

Ireland

In Ireland, the decision to send Mrs D home from hospital would be made by her doctors in consultation with Mrs D and her son. Discharge would be likely to happen speedily given the existence of family care. If there is a social worker at the hospital, he or she would be called in to assess Mrs D's situation at home, whether she needs services, and whether these are in fact available locally, including making referrals to voluntary services. Responsibility for Mrs D's care would lie with her family and friends, with monitoring by the GP and the public health nurse in her area, who would automatically be notified of her discharge from hospital. The nurse would assume a case management role and, with Mrs D's GP, be involved in any decisions about health interventions while Mrs D continues to live at home. Home help or care attendant services would probably be considered necessary given Mrs D's physical weakness and that she lives alone much of the time. The hospital social worker or public health nurse would contact the local home help organizer to arrange a visit, or these arrangements might be left to the family. A health board care attendant might be allocated for a short period. Mrs D might also be referred to a day hospital or to a day centre. Transport to the day hospital would be provided, but might not be available at a day centre. Consultants make referrals to day hospital while eligibility for day centre services is often determined informally, largely depending on whether there are places. A private day care centre might also be an option. Meals-on-wheels, from two to five days a week, might be another option depending on availability. The public health nurse might make a referral to the occupational therapist to assess needs for adaptations and technical aids.

Mrs D would be considered well-supported by her social network, although her son's absences would mean she would be regarded as deserving of additional help. Her family care would be expected to continue, including the son's help with bathing. Emotional support to help with her bereavement is not provided by statutory services and would come from the voluntary or private sector, if available, and be arranged by family or friends.

Italy

In Italy, Mrs D's case would be considered in hospital where it is likely to be decided that she does not need help if she is upper or middle class. However, if she is in poorer circumstances she would be referred to the local authority and be visited by a social worker. The social worker would explore what help her son is not able to provide, and her sister would be regarded as having a duty to care unless she had family difficulties herself. It is the responsibility of the older person to request services in Italy. A GP would not do so, but might suggest that the son sees a social worker. The social worker's assessment is intrusive and is essentially 'detective work'. The social worker would determine whether Mrs D's needs are for social or health care, why she cannot afford private help and why her family are unable to assist her. Her son would be expected to help and only if Mrs D is poor, and the economic circumstances of her son and sister are also poor, would she receive, at best, a little assistance. If she has already received assistance, such as with social housing, the social worker may well decide that she has already received enough help and it is her turn to pay. It is possible that she would receive some help from health services, such as free rehabilitation, although this would be little more than a gesture. A social worker can recommend to a multiprofessional team meeting that she receives health care. Her sister might receive a care allowance, but it would be very small.

Greece

In Greece, Mrs D's sister is likely to be extensively involved in providing care for her. A Greek or foreign carer might be hired to live in or visit during the day, providing company and help with personal care and domestic tasks. Often such carers would not speak Greek, but many Greeks would be able to communicate at some level in, for example, Albanian or Russian. Greek speakers cost more: overall, paid carers who live in earn anything from the wage of an unskilled labourer to a college lecturer. Cash benefits would be available for Mrs D from the State or her insurance organization if she is certified as 67 per cent or more disabled. If she lives in Athens, she might have access to Greek Red Cross home care and home nursing, as well as a safety alarm. If she lives in the vicinity of an Open Care Centre for the Elderly (KAPI) she is likely to have been a long-standing member well-known to health and social care workers at the centre. They are likely to have made contact with the hospital and to have planned her care on discharge (some KAPI centres can also connect members with a long-distance electrocardiograph). A members' mutual help committee may be involved in helping with shopping and providing company, possibly also providing help with laundry and bathing, although her sister is more likely to be involved with the latter. Most KAPIs now have a home care/home help scheme to which she would have access. All organize social activities and excursions.

Summary

Mrs A has the highest level of need among the four cases, and would receive an intensive package of nursing and social care in Denmark, Norway and England. Despite wanting to stay at home, she is likely to be persuaded to enter a nursing home in Norway out of concern for both her quality of care and the cost to the local authority of a domiciliary package. The latter factor would also be a strong influence in Denmark and the UK, and in the UK it would be likely that the excess cost of a domiciliary package compared to nursing home care would have to be met by Mrs A's family if she insisted on this option.

In Ireland's more medicalized system, Mrs A is unlikely to be discharged from hospital and would probably be denied her wish to end her life looked after at home. In Italy, she is likely to go home because of a lack of alternative options. She would receive a reasonable level of support from services, for which her family may have to pay. Finally, in Greece there are several possibilities for Mrs A, including a live-in carer, but all of these options would cost a lot of money, and her family would carry the responsibility for organizing her care.

In all six countries, some level of rehabilitation services would be available to Mr B, but only in Denmark, Norway, England and Ireland could he expect to receive home care for domestic tasks, an alarm and technical aids to assist with mobility. His 'male helplessness' is a factor; in Ireland in particular it is likely he would receive quite a lot of help with domestic tasks. Although in short supply, a move to suitably adapted housing is a possibility in all countries except Greece. In Greece, Mr B would have to depend on his family or volunteers from a KAPI; remarriage or hiring someone to live with him would also be regarded as possible care solutions.

It is Miss C, with possible dementia, who meets with most variety in how her needs would be addressed across the six countries. In Italy, Greece and Ireland she is not likely to receive any formal services unless a crisis erupts. She would receive a specialist assessment in Denmark, Norway, England and Ireland. In Denmark, Norway and probably England, a modest input of care services would follow.

Mrs D's needs are quite modest, and she also receives help from her son and sister. In Denmark and Norway she would receive some home care and technical aids; in Norway she is also likely to be offered bereavement counselling. In England the response to Mrs D's needs is likely to be very variable, with some care managers matching the Scandinavian response and others offering only a safety alarm. She is likely to receive home care for domestic tasks in Ireland. In Italy, she is unlikely to receive any formal services after discharge and to rely on her family. In Greece, the main responsibility will also be with her family, who may hire some help for her, or she may have access to a KAPI.

Discussion and conclusions

All four cases, following referral, would receive a formal assessment of their needs in Denmark, Norway and the UK, undertaken by a community nurse in Denmark and Norway and, most likely, by a social worker (now often called a 'care manager') in the UK. These assessments should be comprehensive and may involve further specialist assessment by, for example, an occupational therapist or a housing officer, and negotiation with home care and other services about appropriate provision. They would also consider the needs of any informal carers. In the UK, where social workers do not receive training in health care, more complex cases may involve further assessment by a health professional, such as a community nurse, at the social worker's request.

These three countries have a system of care management whereby formal services work with the user and any family carers under the co-ordination of a single professional, the care manager. The allocation of formal services is guided by written eligibility criteria which match spending to the resources available in a way that attempts to achieve a degree of equity between cases. As is apparent from this and earlier chapters, however, significant variability can occur in what older people with similar needs receive. Although assessments are in principle 'needs led', the response depends on the level of resources available. The level of provision of social care services is higher in Denmark than Norway, and higher in Norway than the UK. This is reflected in the services the four cases receive, but variability also exists at an individual level. This is especially the case in the UK with the low to moderate needs cases of Miss C and Mrs D. They might receive no home care at all or they might receive anything from seven to 14 hours a week, depending on judgements made in their assessment, particularly concerning risk and the availability of informal care.

The absence of comprehensive assessment and care management arrangements in Greece, Italy and Ireland reflects the lack of development of formal care services for older people in these countries. However, this does not mean that there is no responsibility or supervision exercised by the public sector. In Greece, the local doctor or a social worker may help the family with advice and organizing care. The public health nurse in Ireland plays an important assessment and supervisory role in the care of older people who are considered to be vulnerable, responding to requests for help, working with family carers and putting the older person in touch with what formal services exist locally. Hospital social workers may perform this role at the point of discharge from hospital, and GPs also make referrals to social care services. But intervention normally only occurs when needs cannot be met by the family and a crisis point is reached, often an emergency hospitalization or an extreme situation arising from chronic ill health, disability or dementia. Case management does not exist, other than occasionally and in the short term for older people needing rehabilitation when it is delivered through a District Care Unit, as with Mr B. Ireland's 'last resort' system of formal social care provision places relatively little priority on support in the community and still tends to be dominated by a protective risk-adverse medical model. This leads to an undue emphasis of residential care, and protective and disempowering practice within residential homes.

In Italy, social work intervention is typically for older people with below average incomes; social care services are discretionary, with no attempt to establish universal coverage or minimum standards. The social worker's assessment seeks to find the support an older person needs from the caring and financial resources of their own family. If health care is appropriate this will be provided via a GP or UVG, unless the person's problems are dismissed as 'old age', and social care may be included. Residential care and supported housing are scarce, and following a policy of closing Italy's psychiatric hospitals there is a serious problem of families coping with older people with dementia. More positively, Geriatric Evaluation Units (UVGs) are a new model being established mainly in areas of northern and central Italy, providing joint assessment of health and social care needs, with regular reviews.

There is an absence of formal eligibility criteria governing access to mostly voluntary organized social care services in Italy, Ireland and Greece. Entitlement is based on public perceptions and traditions. However, this can work in favour of older people, who are widely seen as 'deserving', especially if they have no family carers. In Ireland, where services do exist they are often personal, responsive to local needs and very flexible. If an older person, or a member of their family, refuses to pay towards a service it is likely to be provided anyway if the doctor or public health nurse thinks the need is there.

In Greece, Italy and Ireland, a strong sense of family obligation and duty still prevails. Older people can have a strong voice within their families because they own property and younger members of the family may depend on their pension. But this is changing. The picture is less true of urban Ireland than rural, and of the north of Italy compared with the south. There are signs of a shift in social attitudes from family obligation and responsibility to individual responsibility and citizenship rights, and this is influencing social workers' decisions about eligibility and access to services. In Greece, the dominance of professional opinion evident in some other countries is not so marked, and the extent of care in the family – even with a hired live-in care worker – maintains older people's place within the family structure. With Miss C, families in all three countries would be likely to take responsibility for someone in her condition and determine what level of risk is acceptable; ward of court proceedings would only occur in extreme cases, perhaps after the police have been called in a crisis. This lack of professionalization is also apparent in the extent of volunteering and community-based activities associated with the KAPIs, which are open-access community facilities, although also accommodating small multiprofessional care teams.

The down side of this informality, however, is the great potential for inequities in how individual older people (and their families) are treated, and of course the threat of large financial bills. An Italian social worker, for example, might deny Mrs D services because it is felt that she has already received enough help from the State. There is no single assessment procedure and different assessments may be made by care professionals, with eligibility often decided informally by care services themselves. Although in all these countries an older person or their family can turn to the local authority to request help, what they receive depends on both the judgement of the professional they contact, or the service provider, and what is available locally. Family members have a lead role in providing or paying for social care, supplemented by formal services depending on their local availability, which is low and varies greatly.

In Ireland, the lack of publicly funded social care services means that the focus of care policy for older people tends to be on pathology. Unless an older person has the money to buy the care they need, they can find themselves patronized by doctors and nurses in a medicalized system which defines old age as an illness. Medical services predominate and rehabilitation services are few and far between.

The centrality of the family is apparent in all these case studies. There is no country where a member of the family cannot choose to provide social care, including intimate personal care, which is of course not the case with much medical care. Publicly funded social care services complement rather than substitute for family care and in no country are they subsidized to the extent of health care services. Sipilä and Anttonen (1999, p. 2) comment that formal social services are quite marginal issues when considering the social care of older people in Europe:

> Even in the countries of most developed social policy the responsibility of care has primarily rested with the family and the kin, which both are called informal actors in social service research. Without rules on paper the family and the kin have defined who takes care

of whom, how and to what extent. In this sense we might say that there is only one regime of care – all the world belongs to the informal regime. Differences in the ways of care concern the margin: what happens when the informal network does not provide the care needed.

Thus, the major context of care is the work and emotional support of family members, although much of this work is undertaken by paid care staff in Norway and Denmark. Even in Denmark spouses, particularly spouses of people with dementia living in the community, undertake much of the care of older partners needing support. Rostgaard and Fridberg (1998) report Danish survey data which show that among people aged 70 years and older, most of their personal care and domestic tasks are undertaken by themselves, with the next highest proportion undertaken by the spouse, followed by the home help service. Only a few older people receive help from children and this is generally with practical tasks such as laundry or minor repairs. Formal care services are thus interventions in this wider context of self-help and family care among older people, and conditional upon need being demonstrated in an assessment.

While Norway and Denmark's extensive public provision has displaced private sector providers to a marginal role, and reduced the cost of care services for the user to a minor consideration, in Greece the needs of an older person for substantial help may face the family with a large financial burden, relieved only by rather inadequate insurance coverage and the availability of immigrants from Eastern Europe, Albania or another Asian or African country for hire as care workers. In Ireland and Italy, the provision of social care is normally contingent on the older person having needs for health care as well: the idea of taxpayers funding social care for its own sake, to contribute to older people's quality of life, has little saliency. In the UK, the organization of social care in Social Services Departments separate from the NHS has often been justified because of a 'quality of life' role distinct from health care and its treatment focus. But provision has been cut back and increasingly the priority is for social care to be 'targeted' as a preventative arm of health policy in an attempt to reduce costs. Help with housework has been a prominent victim of this reorientation. While similar pressures are evident in Norway and Denmark, there is no institutionalized divide between social and health care, and the strength of a social model of health in these societies means that it is accepted that social care should be as universally available as health care. The Greek

KAPIs demonstrate the same commitment in principle, but within a very underfunded public sector in which the extent of formal care provision depends greatly on volunteering.

As already noted, in Greece, Ireland and Italy the role of the family extends to providing often substantial financial support for an older dependent relative needing care. In Greece, money can come from family businesses or family members in civil service jobs, working overseas or in the merchant navy. Paying for a live-in carer, normally foreign, is an option that would be financially possible for a majority of Greek families. It is a popular option because it keeps the older person out of an institution and the family in control; such carers become part of the extended family and if they leave they will often find someone to replace them from within their own family. Social insurance can also be an important source of financial help in Greece, but in the case of nursing will be limited to a short period of time. KAPIs also emerge from the case studies as a significant part of social care provision in Greece. They bring several health, social care and recreational services together and make them available either free or for a small charge to all older people in their area, drawing substantially on volunteers among more active older residents. Their expansion is critical in Greece's attempts to meet the needs of its ageing population. Community based, they emphasize prevention, activity and ageing well. However, while there are plans to develop small residential units, the major issue for Greece is still older people who are poor, frail and living alone. KAPIs have problems in finding solutions in these circumstances. Home nursing is not provided and the coverage of home helps, provided by the municipality through the KAPI, or by volunteers, is not universal, although it has increased tremendously in importance and availability since the middle of 1999 (see Chapter 8).

In Italy family care, based on strong family ties and a generational contract which can see older people helping out their children from a relatively good pension income, is the norm. Social care competes with other services for funding and many local authorities have made large cuts to social services budgets in recent times. There are very few places in institutions and they are unpopular. A church influence in Italian society encourages separating 'deserving' from 'undeserving', and this is combined with a sociological emphasis on providing only temporary help after which people should be able to manage for themselves. Public services carry a stigma in this climate.

While Denmark is a model of universalist principles by comparison, its provision is by no means comprehensive. It is low-level needs that are most likely to remain unmet. An example is Mrs D's need for someone to accompany her so that she can develop the confidence to get out and about; but it is important to note that by relieving her sister of any 'duty' to do housework, the Danish care system creates the potential for family carers to have the time to attend to this type of need for emotional and social support. Even with Denmark's generally high level of services for older people, with all local authorities required to provide community nursing and home help services free of charge, it is not the case that older people in the same situation will receive the same level of services. Different local authorities may address the same needs in different ways, and the level of provision – especially home help – differs across authorities. Denmark is, however, unique in having a formal system of preventative home visits by a nurse or social worker to all people aged 75 or older, at least twice a year, to detect unmet needs for social and health care, as well as housing, income and leisure needs. Despite being at the other end of the spectrum, only Greece has a similar approach in the form of KAPIs which undertake visits and surveys of older people in their area for the same purpose.

The organized home care services of Denmark, Norway and the UK are all under pressure from rising demand and tightening budgets. All three countries now give less priority to housework, especially in the UK. Growing use is made in the UK of private home care providers which are less costly than in-house home care services. The growth of private and voluntary sector services, stimulated by the reforms made in the early 1990s, has expanded choice of provider compared with the local authority monopoly in Norway and Denmark, but the extent to which this actually increases user satisfaction is unclear: certainly it has helped to improve the flexibility and reduce the cost of both private and public sector services. Some Norwegian authorities have begun to contract out in an effort to reduce costs, and home care services generally are much busier and staff are under more pressure.

10
Social Exclusion and Social Care

Tim Blackman

So far in this book we have explored how older people are cared for in six European countries, discussing similarities and differences at the level of both care systems and individuals. Each of the countries presents a different national context. Formal care services are interventions in these different contexts: in Ireland, Italy and Greece, interventions are quite rare – usually to avoid, or in response to, a crisis arising from inadequacies in family care, income or insurance which leave an older person at risk. In these countries, the vast majority of older people depend on the context of family and community life for their care. Day care in Greek KAPIs is perhaps an exception because it is open access and aims to improve the general quality of life for older people, but its success owes much to the way KAPIs are part of their communities, drawing on substantial voluntary help. In other countries, notably Denmark and Norway, services are likely to be provided to any older person needing assistance, rather than being provided as a last resort. In the UK, services aim to provide assistance beyond a basic level of responding only to crises, but they are frequently criticized for being inadequate and means tested (Royal Commission on Long Term Care, 1999a).

This chapter takes the analysis a step further by using the concept of social exclusion as a means of evaluating the adequacy of arrangements in each country, especially the quality of care in different care settings. The idea of 'welfare culture' is introduced to take account of national differences in the role of the family, and the chapter considers whether social exclusion can be applied as an evaluative concept across different welfare cultures. This is done by focusing on issues of *access* and *entitlement*, including variations in the provision of services, the roles of assessment and discretion, and the balance between informal family care and formal, organized services. The chapter ends with some observations about where particular weaknesses lie in the different care systems.

Ageing and social exclusion

Social exclusion has different meanings in different national discourses. Rene Lenoir has been credited with inventing the term in the early 1970s, and it gained in popularity in France during the 1980s, spreading through European Commission channels to be introduced into other national debates (Haan, 1997). In the UK, until recently, more attention has been paid to poverty and its measurement than to social exclusion, which has been regarded as a broad concept that is difficult to measure. Inequality captures some of its meaning in operational terms, but not those aspects of social exclusion that relate to the solidarity and status of shared citizenship and common opportunities to participate in society. Tiemann (1993) comments that, 'Social exclusion can be seen, not just in levels of income, but also matters such as health, education, access to services, housing and debt' (quoted in Spicker, 1997, p. 134). A European Commission (1993, p. 43) commentary states:

> When we talk about social exclusion we are acknowledging that the problem is no longer simply one of inequity between the top and the bottom of the social scale (up/down) but also one of the distance within society between those who are active members and those who are forced towards the fringes (in/out). We are also highlighting the effects of the way society is developing and the concomitant risk of social disintegration and, finally, we are affirming that, for both the persons concerned and the society itself, this is a process of change and not a set of fixed and static situations.

The idea of social exclusion in France arose from the French concept of solidarity and the role of the state in furthering social integration. According to this view, social exclusion entails a rupturing of the social bond between an individual and his or her society, culturally and morally. It is a multifaceted idea and the policy responses have been equally multidimensional, although focusing on the concept of 'reinserting' individuals, families or groups. This is perhaps easier to understand in terms of reconnecting unemployed people with labour markets through training and job subsidies than with regard to older people who cannot, or do not wish to, take up employment. Indeed, the integration of all people of working age into the labour market is now a dominant theme in social policy across Europe, both to reduce dependency on welfare spending and to promote economic growth (Cousins, 1999b). Levitas (1996, p. 5) argues that this has overshadowed other aspects of social exclusion as a policy issue:

> the concept of social exclusion ... has become embedded as a crucial element within a new hegemonic discourse. Within this discourse, terms such as social cohesion and solidarity abound, and social exclusion is contrasted not with inclusion but with integration, construed as integration into the labour market ... Within this discourse, the concept of social exclusion operates both to devalue unpaid work and to obscure the inequalities between paid workers.

Marginality in relation to the formal labour market, however, is a general feature of social exclusion, underlying its manifestation among diverse social groups (Corden and Duffy, 1998). This is because of the central importance of paid work as a distributional mechanism in market economies. But while being unemployed or unwaged is an important cause of social exclusion, the condition cannot be reduced to economic disadvantage. This is in part because social exclusion is multidimensional, but also because it is not a distributional concept (Room, 1996).

The main dimensions of social exclusion are relational. Corden and Duffy (1998) summarize these dimensions as discrimination in relation to rights; marginalization in relation to economic production; and a catastrophic break from the rest of society (Corden and Duffy, 1998). Older people – vulnerable to age discrimination and dependency on others, often regarded as 'non-productive', and often isolated from the rest of society by immobility and a decline in social networks – are clearly at risk of the multidimensional impact of social exclusion.

The difficulties of old age are conventionally attributed to biological ageing – the process by which the body's adaptive mechanisms are impaired, contributing to the increasing incidence and prevalence of most diseases and disabilities with age. The ageing process, however, is not purely a genetic process: it is a consequence of an interaction of genetic, environmental and social factors. Although the influences of extrinsic environmental factors, such as the design of buildings, neighbourhoods and household appliances increases with age, they are often modifiable or preventable. Old age is also socially constructed by wider values and attitudes about ageing, and by economic exclusion such as compulsory retirement from the labour market, so that the experience of old age can have relatively little to do with biological ageing.

Those older people who have to cope with chronic illness or disability can find that their quality of life greatly depends on a wide range of these extrinsic environmental, economic and social factors. They include, for example, support from family members and friends; environmental obstacles and availability of public transport; income and the ability to pay for services; and the availability, accessibility and quality of organized social care services. Older people with chronic illnesses or disabilities are dependent on suitably adapted environments, practical help with activities of daily living, and appropriate medical, nursing and personal care. But they occupy different positions of power in relation to these resources (Gibson, 1998).

The extent to which an older person is empowered in relation to the resources needed for their care has ideological as well as material dimensions. Ideologically, disempowerment can occur because older people are not regarded as having legitimate needs as individual citizens because they are unproductive and at the end of their lives. The 'burden of ageing' still dominates both popular and policy discourses. For example, an OECD Policy Brief published in 1998 states:

> Population ageing in OECD countries over the coming decades could threaten future growth in prosperity … Countries could finance future social spending obligations by raising payroll taxes to whatever level was necessary, but these would be so high as to discourage work effort and would cut deeply into working people's living standards. These considerations point to the overriding importance of curbing the growth of spending on public pensions, health and long-term care. (OECD, 1998b, pp. 1–2)

This view is contested by other economists and the argument is essentially political rather than economic: it is about the allocation of resources rather than the sustainability of expenditure (Atkinson, 1995). In ageing societies, assuring the living standards of all those in retirement while protecting the quality of life of those with particular health and social care needs does call for debate about the balance between private and public income and expenditure, and the targeting of public resources. However, the continuing currency of the 'burden of ageing' in these debates contrasts with the relative success of the disability rights movement which has made much progress in reframing disability as a social and political issue, concerning discrimination and the distribution of resources, rather than a personal issue of individual functioning and burden (Oliver, 1998). The idea of ageing as a burden on society stigmatizes older people as well as the services they receive, both of which become devalued and associated with negative dependency (Spicker, 1984).

While physical and mental disabilities are causes of dependency, most older people are not disabled. The major cause of dependency for older people as a group is low income arising from compulsory retirement. Although many older people in Europe enjoy a relatively comfortable retirement, many do not and the extent of inequality both within and between countries is a growing issue. The trend in many countries is towards income polarization as older people divide between pension-poor and pension-rich groups depending on whether they have a good second pension, especially an occupational pension. Among the six countries discussed in this book, only Denmark is seeing a trend towards greater equality in pensioner incomes (Ministry of Finance, 1999). There is little evidence that many older people want to remain dependent on waged employment, and where early retirement pay has been relatively generous, as in Denmark, it has been a very popular option and much more so than partial retirement schemes (Platz and Freiberg Petersen, 1992). The issue is instead one of securing adequate living standards for older people in retirement, including enabling older people's continuing involvement in productive activities.

Because formal health and social care can be very costly for those who need it, no income support scheme can incorporate these needs, and special arrangements for funding care services are necessary. As noted in Chapter 1, arrangements for securing access to health care through universal health insurance or service coverage are reasonably comprehensive across Europe, although the level of public expenditure on health varies greatly. In 1995, spending per capita ranged from about €1600 in Denmark and Norway; to about €700–800 in the UK, Italy and Ireland; to only €350 in Greece – although Greece increased its spending eight-fold between 1975 and 1995, compared with increases of about five times among the other five countries (OECD, 1999). This range in spending per capita, however, is smaller in terms of purchasing power parity – from €545 in Greece to around €1300 in Norway and Denmark (OECD, 1999).

These differences are much more pronounced with regard to social care, largely because there is no policy commitment to universal coverage in Greece, Ireland or Italy. The southern Europe, family-based welfare regimes are characterized by a preference for direct monetary benefits rather than services. In Italy, children are legally obliged to provide financial support to their parents, including paying for care, so older people may be placed in a position of negative dependency on their children. Mirabile (1999, pp. 112–13) comments that:

> this arrangement penalizes older people because they are forced to look for care services on the market. These services are costly and often older people cannot afford them, in spite of 'high' pensions. From this point of view, the wide variations in the economic and social circumstances of older people in Italy should be mentioned... within this spectrum, there is a particular predominance of women receiving social pensions (about 80 per cent of total beneficiaries). This kind of benefit is so low that it is often an indication of poverty or hardship.

Pension policy is often considered in terms of the prevention of poverty. Greece, the UK and Italy fare badly in this respect, with 20–30 per cent of their older people (65 years plus) classified as poor in terms of incomes at or below minimum social security standards (Tsakloglou and Panopoulou, 1998; Walker and Maltby, 1997). Poverty is a particular issue in Ireland among a significant minority of older women who never married and lack sufficient contributions to obtain a full pension. In Greece, all employees and their dependants are obliged by law to join a contributory social insurance scheme which provides health care, holiday and pension benefits; unemployed people receive a state retirement pension and free medical services (see Chapter 8). But Stathopoulos and Amera (1992, p. 184) observe that although insurance coverage for medical needs and retirement benefits is effectively universal, 'there are great differences in both benefits and contributions, and there are some pensioners who have 10 or 20 times the amount of the minimum pension'. There is a marked lack of trust in the social insurance system and inadequate benefits, leading those who can to opt for 'top-up' private insurance. In the UK, the poorest 20 per cent of single pensioners in 1996/97 received an average income some three times lower than the richest fifth (Department of Social Security, 1998). The state pension is below the minimum social security threshold, with the result that pensioners with no other source of income must claim a means tested benefit, Income Support, to bring their income up to this threshold. It is estimated that about one million eligible pensioners in the UK do not claim this entitlement (Pension Provision Group, 1998).

In understanding the effect of low income on quality of life, it is inequality rather than poverty alone which is important because in unequal societies low income excludes people from a wider general prosperity (Atkinson, 1995). Thus, the European Commission defines people who face exclusion as those who have an income below 50 per cent of median household income after tax (European Commission, 1993). Exclusion defined in this way is least prevalent in the citizenship-based welfare states of Scandinavia, but not absent. In Norway, although no more than 1 per cent of older people have to resort to means tested social assistance payments, in 1990 7.9 per cent of people aged 67 or older were poor by the EC definition (Koren and Aslaksen, 1997). Surveys have also revealed a gender difference. Fifteen per cent of women and 6 per cent of men aged 67 or older reported that they would have problems paying an unforeseen bill of NOK 2000 (about €255), while 5 per cent of men and 3 per cent of women aged between 67 and 79 reported problems managing current expenses (Daatland, 1997a; Dahl and Vogt, 1995).

In both Denmark and Norway, state pensions are a right of citizenship. They are universal and set at a level that secures the participation of older people in the country's general prosperity. Norway's state pension is structured rather differently from Denmark's and is not as egalitarian (Daatland, 1997a). The level of pensions in both countries is such that family members will normally not feel any obligation to give financial support and in Norway surveys indicate that older people often support their children with financial help (Gulbrandsen and Langsether, 1999). Social inclusion is a general principle in these welfare systems and extends beyond pensions to universal social care coverage and the extensive provision of disabled access housing. While all is certainly not perfect, the social policy debate in Denmark and Norway is framed by a particular welfare culture in which social inclusion is a public issue and state responsibility (Chamberlayne *et al.*, 1999). Romøren (1996, p. 70) comments that despite experiments with private provision

> the principle of equal access for every citizen to almost total public financing of formal care has not changed. Today it is reasonable to consider this model more as a cultural pattern in the small and homogeneous Scandinavian populations than as a view held by one or other political wing.

The welfare culture of southern Europe is quite different. Social inclusion is not evident as a strong public policy objective. But as a set of norms and values the concept is manifest in these societies, although in the private realm of family responsibility. The Greek family has been described as a type of 'clearing house' for the provision and receipt of financial and social support, mediating between individuals and the country's fragmented employment and income maintenance structures. Without this clearing house role, these structures would fail to provide security and welfare for many individual Greeks. Papadopoulos (1998, pp. 54–5) states that

> One could argue that the Greek nuclear family functions internally as a cooperative while competing with other families in a society dominated by the idea of social mobility. Solidarity remains firmly within the private sphere, as an inter-generational responsibility towards the family unit. In this context, the development of notions of social responsibility or social solidarity, essential for the creation and functioning of a civil society, encounter enormous obstacles. Thus, the possibility of creating a sustainable ideological base for expanding the residual welfare state in Greece is limited.

Although the inclusion of older people within families in countries such as Greece appears to be high, the perception of older people themselves may be different. Giarchi's (1996) description quoted in Chapter 1 of older Italians living within a type of closed institutional care within the family questions any necessary connection between family care and social inclusion. Karantinos, Ioannou and Cavounidis (1992, p. 82) comment about the Greek situation that

> the fact that recourse to family networks is often if not usually a matter of necessity for elderly people rather than a matter of choice means that older people are often forced to compromise their dignity and become dependent on their kin. Tensions and strain in relations with kin are often the result, and while the necessary economic or physical aid may be forthcoming, it is often at the cost of satisfactory emotional relationships … (T)he burdens placed on members of informal networks, whether kin, friends, or neighbours, are numerous and severe. Among these burdens are the strain on economic resources, and the time and effort that must be devoted to care of the elderly. There are particularly serious implications for women, as it is they who bear the brunt of the latter burden.

Hugman (1994) reports recent studies that have found high levels of self-reported loneliness among older people in Greece and Poland, both countries with an apparently high degree of family centredness (see also Chapter 2). He suggests that this is due to the greater expectations that older people have in these cultures about the range and frequency of contacts they should have, compared with the more individualistic Anglo-Saxon world.

Just as familism is not synonymous with inclusion, individualism does not imply that older people are excluded in terms of their family relationships. There is plenty of evidence from the UK, Denmark and Norway that older people generally prefer to live apart from their adult children, but that close kin remain important in their lives through 'intimacy at a distance' (McRae, 1999; Jakobsson, 1998). There is no necessary relationship between the apparent 'closeness' of family relationships and the social inclusion of older people. Indeed, Platz (1989) found in Denmark that while it is single older people in particular who feel lonely, frequent contact with children and others does not compensate for this feeling.

McRae (1999, p. 23) comments that in Britain co-residence of older people with their children was more common in the past because of necessity rather than choice:

> What we are seeing in Britain today are increased opportunities for older people to realize their wish to live independently: they are healthier and live longer, so there are more close friends with whom to socialize; there is better state support and more facilities (both state and private) to support independent living; and there is a significantly larger housing stock, so older people have somewhere to live. Had these conditions existed fifty or sixty years ago, it seems likely that many more older people would have chosen to live apart from their adult children.

Does the extent of familism in some countries reflect economic underdevelopment rather than cultural preference? Within Italy, 60 per cent of disabled older people in the less-developed south of the country live with their children, compared with 20 per cent in the more developed north, suggesting a relationship between the level of development and opportunities for independent living (Cioni, 1999). The cultural distinctiveness of southern Europe has been used as a basis for identifying a separate type of welfare regime. However, Katrougalos (1996) contests this, arguing that in the case of the Greek welfare state it is essentially a less developed version of a Continental 'state-corporate' welfare regime like Germany or France, a model not represented among the six countries in the present book (Esping-Andersen, 1990). It is less developed because of economic underdevelopment.

The type of care dependent older people receive is likely to reflect wider social attitudes towards old age, a point made at the conclusion of Chapter 1. Kitwood (1997) develops the idea of 'personhood' as a relational term in the care of people with dementia, using it to describe a type of interaction with older people that validates and empathizes with the experiences of ageing, rather than regarding these experiences as undesirable, either denying them or treating them as problems to be managed. Kitwood (1997, p. 12) makes a connection between the micro level of how older people are cared for, and the macro level of social norms and policies. Writing from a UK perspective, he describes the 'psychodynamics of exclusion' in the following terms: 'Many societies, including our own, are permeated by an ageism which categorizes older people as incompetent, ugly and burdensome, and which discriminates against them at both a personal and structural level.'

The care setting itself can exclude rather than promote the inclusion of older people; Kitwood (1997, p. 116) criticizes the 'warehousing' of older people with dementia, but notes that smaller, more homely residential units are still no guarantee against isolation:

> Huge benefits are to be gained when the doors of formal care settings are opened, giving access in both directions. The clients can maintain their links with the community, and more readily maintain a sense of their own history: doing some shopping, going to the pub, to the theatre, to church, taking a walk in the local park. People from the community – not merely relatives and close friends – can become regular visitors. In some instances a local school has established a strong contact with a day centre or residential home. Some organizations are making provision for people to become fully-fledged volunteer helpers, providing the necessary preparation and training … When volunteers are fully drawn into dementia care there is even the possibility of having 'staff' to client rations of 1 : 1.

If social exclusion is to be used as an evaluative concept for comparing arrangements for the social care of older people across different countries, it is necessary to take account of both cultural and socio-economic differences. For example, what may seem to be a high degree of segregation of many older people living alone in small apartments in, say, Copenhagen, actually reflects the extent to which suitable housing is available to enable older people to make this choice to live independently. What may seem to be the impressive integration of older people in their families and communities in Athens exists alongside quite the opposite degree of opportunity. Similarly, an apparently stigmatizing process of assessing and means testing older people in need of help from care services in the UK may appear to a Greek or Italian older person as an extensive procedural right to assessment and a gateway to care services targeted at those who really need them.

A definition of social exclusion is needed which takes account of cross-national diversity. Taking into account the above discussion of family care, retirement and formal services, the following seems to meet this criterion, defining social exclusion as 'a process of interaction of the dynamics of the family and personal networks, the labour market and the welfare state that results in a chronic and structured inability by individuals and groups to participate in social life' (Duffy, 1996, p. 13). This definition captures the dimensions of family and personal relationships, the unwaged ex-worker role and dependency on the welfare state that are so important to the experience of old age. The extent to which each dimension is significant depends on the welfare regime in each country. The prime focus of this book is on the role of organized social care services that support older people's activities of daily living. Exclusion occurs when an older person does not control the resources he or she needs in order to undertake everyday activities with the degree of autonomy most other people would take for granted. This is partly a question of whether the necessary care resources exist and can be drawn on, but it is also about how care is provided and by whom. An absence of rights, marginalization from economic and political power, and isolation from the mainstream of society tend to compound each other for the most vulnerable older people.

Welfare culture and social exclusion

It is difficult to avoid the significance of the level of economic development in explaining cross-national variation in the provision of formal care services. Even the link between women's labour market participation and publicly funded services for older people noted in Chapter 1 reflects the higher demand for labour in the stronger economies of northern Europe. Referring back to Table 1.1, there is indeed a relationship between the gross domestic product of each country and the level of publicly funded social care services for older people. There is, though, also evidence pointing the other way – towards the significance of welfare cultures. For example, from Table 1.1 it seems that Italy and

Ireland should be able to afford a level of social care provision closer to that of the UK than Greece, but there is little evidence of this being a significant policy priority for their governments, even in Ireland where GDP growth has been the highest of all OECD countries during the 1990s. Given its low GDP, it is perhaps surprising that Greece even achieves the low level of social care provision which it does. It seems plausible that it is lack of funds rather than familism which holds back provision in this country although, as suggested by Katrougalos, this may not be evidence that welfare culture is of little importance in explaining cross-national differences because the basic welfare principles of the Greek system are closer to the Continental 'state-corporate' regime than to the more Catholic-influenced southern European model.

The Nordic countries provide an interesting test of the influence of welfare culture. Eydal (1999) discusses the anomalous position of Iceland among these countries with regard to the state provision of child care. Despite having the highest level of female labour market participation of all the Nordic countries, Iceland has the lowest level of day care provision. Eydal suggests that Iceland's particular history and culture have created an attitude that problems such as reconciling paid work and child care should be solved privately, reinforced by a common view that too much adult supervision of children is undesirable. Among the Nordic countries, Iceland also has the highest proportion of older people living with their children – about 20 per cent, compared with 5 per cent in Denmark. Iceland's public expenditure on older and disabled people is also lower at 8 per cent of GDP compared with 15 to 20 per cent in the other Nordic countries, and it has the highest proportion of older people in institutions (Jakobsson, 1998).

Returning to the Greek welfare state, however, Cousins (1999a) questions whether its distinctiveness can just be explained in terms of economic underdevelopment. There are similarities with the Continental state-corporate welfare regime because of the high degree of fragmentation in social insurance arrangements along occupational lines and an emphasis on cash benefits rather than welfare services. But Greece differs from countries such as Germany and France in fundamental ways, notably the extent of clientelism and patronage in its welfare state, and the gulf between workers in core sectors of the labour market who have good social protection and others in weak labour market positions who have meagre or no benefits. As already noted, even with economic growth the role of the family in this wider context militates against political demands for a more developed welfare state because the family is already meeting many needs, a situation also applying in Italy and generally in southern Europe.

> The family meets a whole range of needs of members, for example, provision of housing and financial support for those who are unemployed or in precarious jobs, education expenses, as well as caring for ill, disabled, and elderly people and for young children...The family therefore takes much of the strain of high unemployment, precarious work or inadequate social protection. (Cousins, 1999a, pp. 17–18)

Echoing Papadopoulos (1998) on the Greek family, Trifiletti (1999) describes the Italian family strategy as a 'synthesis of breadcrumbs', involving the pooling of a range of partial incomes from different sources such as agriculture, self-employment and benefits. The duty to care falls mainly on women in the absence of extended formal provision for child or elderly care, but Cousins (1999a) observes that support among women across generations means that the lack of formal services is not the constraint on women's participation in paid work which it is in northern Europe, as carers can still be found within the family.

Welfare culture is clearly important in determining whether needs become expressed as political demands on the State. High employment levels have been a product not just of strong economies in Scandinavia but also of deliberate policy measures (although increasingly challenged by globalization and competitive market pressures). State intervention is an independent factor, with effects on society separate from wider economic forces, and either reinforcing or moderating their influence, especially with regard to the distribution of income and services (Musterd and Ostendorf, 1998). The extent and nature of such intervention is greatly influenced by the value systems prevalent in a given welfare culture, especially the centrality of social exclusion in political debate. Social exclusion exists because access to a resource – including both material and social resources – is prevented by economic, political or social barriers. These barriers are constructed by mechanisms of exclusion controlled by people with more power than those who are excluded. Exclusion for some is created by the actions, words and beliefs of others, and although economic power is a key factor, exclusion is also created ideologically through the social construction of marginality and vulnerability in both political and everyday discourses.

As considered above, social exclusion is a wider concept than income inequality. It focuses analysis on 'exclusion mechanisms': the structures and processes which marginalize older people and their needs within a given welfare culture. It might appear that the welfare cultures of Norway and Denmark are more successful than those of the other countries in achieving the social inclusion of older people because of the existence of well-funded welfare states. But in other countries social inclusion is achieved in different ways, such as the provision of care and sharing of resources within families in which older people occupy a position of relative power. Although there is evidence of loneliness in familist welfare cultures, there is also evidence of dissatisfaction with services in well-funded welfare states where older people may feel less empowered because of professional dominance. Even bringing the situation of the family carer into consideration, it is not necessarily the case that familist care systems exclude women from wider opportunities because of their 'duty' to care. There is evidence of women taking up new opportunities for education and employment because of cross-generational support within their families, and extensive volunteering in familist welfare cultures gives many older people a productive role in their societies. This is not to deny the extent of burden that can exist for female carers and the loss of dignity that can be involved when, for example, a son has to attend to the intimate personal care needs of his mother, but it is to argue that whole systems of care cannot be rejected as exclusionary because they do not conform to, say, the traditional Scandinavian welfare model. All systems have strengths and weaknesses, and the possibilities for reform lie in building on the strengths and tackling the weaknesses.

Social exclusion therefore involves looking at the overall situation: it is perhaps most extreme in the economically depressed and depopulated rural areas of Greece or Italy where there are few informal or formal supports, but it can also exist in much more developed care systems. For instance, the well-being of many older women is bound up with their sense of self as competent adults able to maintain socially acceptable standards such as a clean house. In the UK, Norway and Denmark, the withdrawal of housework from the services provided by a local authority for older people, because funding and providing personal care is a higher priority than help with 'non-essential' practical tasks, has been criticized for impairing this sense of competency and undermining the person's motivation and ability to stay independent (Clark, Dyer and Horwood, 1998). Even in Denmark, the rising cost of care services for an increasing number of ageing older people has seen a tightening of eligibility criteria for services. Some local authorities, for example, no longer offer help with shopping and cleaning unless the older person has mental health problems. The number of home care users has increased but services are more sharply targeted. There has been a reduction in hours per user, largely due to less help with housework and other practical tasks, and a focus on personal care and security. Sixty-five per cent of Danish home help users receive less than three hours help per week (Leeson, 1997). The same trend is evident in the UK, although the situation is not comparable given that about 20 per cent of older people receive some sort of local authority help in their homes in Denmark, compared with about 10 per cent in the UK.

Social exclusion is about how older people feel as well as structures and processes that deny material resources to older people in the interests of other more powerful groups in a society. The issue of how accessing the services that are available is experienced is crucial in this respect; in particular, the effects on an older person's dignity which follow from the experience of referral and assessment. 'Gatekeeping' is an inevitable feature of resource allocation, but this can take place either within a framework of rights or within a culture of disempowerment and discretion. Variations – or inequalities – between countries in the care services available for older people raise difficult political issues about the large-scale cross-national transfers of resources which would be needed to reduce them. However, there are also aspects of practice and policy within each care system which involve unnecessary exclusionary mechanisms that create inequities and stigma within the system. Variations in the allocation of resources and decisions about access and entitlement are particularly problematic issues in this regard.

Allocation of resources

None of the six countries provides substantive rights to social care services for older citizens, although the insurance-based system in Greece defines certain rights to financial assistance towards hiring care if a person is assessed as more than 67 per cent disabled. Generally, social security systems tend to define legal rights to cash benefits, but rights to social care *services* are not defined in law. While legal rights to care could be regarded to be an ideal situation, this would be likely to encourage a mechanistic approach, removing the capacity of assessors to make sensitive judgements about complex individual circumstances because of fixed rules about entitlement (Blackman, 1998).

Norway, Denmark and the UK have legislation requiring all local authorities to provide social care services. Types and levels of provision are not prescribed in Norway and the UK, but are for home help and community nursing services in Denmark, including one or both of these services being available round the clock. These three countries also have a procedural right to assessment whereby an older person who appears to be having difficulty with his or her care must be professionally assessed. These rights extend to the older person being informed about the reasons behind the subsequent decision whether to provide services, which is *guided* by eligibility criteria. As described in earlier chapters, however, older people may not understand what their rights are, and practitioners may not apply them as rigorously as they should, often due to workload and budgetary pressures.

The selective and discretionary nature of social care provision is evident to different extents in all six counties. This should in theory be moderated in Denmark, Norway and the UK by the routine use of standard assessment and eligibility criteria, which are publicly available and guide decisions on the basis of consistency and proportionality in the treatment of different cases depending on their needs. But even if selectivity is undertaken systematically according to objective criteria, there is still plenty of room for professional discretion. This was investigated in detail by research in the UK which used case study exercises in assessment and care planning to explore the consistency with which social care professionals responded to each case (Blackman, Durbin and Robb, 1998). The study was undertaken in two local authority areas, involving 160 practitioners. Marked variation was found in the number of hours of home care allocated to the same case, especially for older people with low or moderate needs. For one case with a low level of need as suggested by the local authority's own eligibility criteria, just under half of the 160 practitioners allocated no home care, about 40 per cent allocated up to four hours per week, just under 20 per cent allocated four to ten hours per week, and a few allocated ten or more hours per week. Another case with a high level of need revealed more consistency, probably because there are fewer options at this level and a greater focus would be expected. Over two-thirds of practitioners allocated this case ten or more hours per week, although over 10 per cent opted instead for long-term institutional care. About 10 per cent allocated between five and ten hours of home care per week, and a few allocated less than five hours.

Variations are also evident across local authorities in the UK in levels of service provision. It is difficult to make like-with-like comparisons because of social and geographical differences between local authority areas, which influence the level of central government grant paid towards funding local services. But taking the 'big city' metropolitan district councils in England, in 1998/99 the proportion of people aged 65 or older receiving social care services in their own home ranged from 5.5 to 17.1 per cent, with 80 per cent of authorities within the range 5.7 to 12.4 per cent (Department of Health, 1999). The proportion of older people receiving an intensive domiciliary package of ten or more hours of home care per week varied from 0.3 to 3.4 per cent, with 80 per cent of authorities within the range 0.5 to 1.9 per cent. The number of publicly funded admissions to a residential or nursing home as a proportion of all older people varied from 0.9 to 5.5 per cent, with 80 per cent of authorities in the range of 1.1 to 2.2 per cent. There was no relationship between the level of home care services provided and the level of residential and nursing home care.

Similar variations are apparent with regard to the 'shire' county councils in England. The proportion of older people receiving social care services in their own home ranged from 2.2 to 14.4 per cent, with 80 per cent of authorities within the range 4.1 to 8.6 per cent. The proportion of older people receiving an intensive domiciliary package varied from 0.2 to 2.8 per cent, with 80 per cent of authorities within the range 0.3 to 1.1 per cent. The proportion of older people admitted with public funding to a residential or nursing home varied from 0.2 to 3.4 per cent, with 80 per cent of authorities in the range of 0.8 to 1.8 per cent. There was also no relationship between the level of home care services provided and residential and nursing home care provision.

There is also evidence of geographical variation in Norway, as discussed in Chapter 4. Næss and Wærness (1996) report variations in receipt of home care services across local authorities from a high of 22.9 per cent to a low of 17.6 per cent of people aged 67 plus – not a considerable difference. Home help visits ranged from an average of 140 minutes to an average of 126 minutes. More marked were differences in the number of institutional beds for people aged 80 or older, which varied from 16 to 39 per 100 people in this age group. These local variations reflect the different care profiles of local authorities in Norway: some have 'traditional' profiles with a relatively large number of institutional beds and moderate provision of home care services catering for people with more modest needs. Others have a low number of institutional beds and more generous provision of home care services, with more frequent visits and longer hours.

In Denmark, receipt of home help services has been found to vary from 40 per cent below the national average in the local authority with the lowest coverage to 40 per cent above in the authority with the highest coverage (see Chapter 3). These variations cannot be explained by either geographical or demographic factors. While the size of the local authority is the key factor with regard to differences in levels of provision, other differences reflect local decisions about the service mix. In the quarter of local authorities with the lowest coverage of nursing homes, 9 per cent of older people receive evening help and 4.7 per cent night-time help, compared with 5.7 per cent and 2.1 per cent respectively in the quarter of municipalities with the highest coverage of nursing homes. Fewer nursing homes places are thus compensated to a degree by more home care services. In both Norway and Denmark, there is an inverse relationship between the number of older people in a local authority area and the number of nursing home places and care workers, so that the volume of services in smaller local authorities is proportionately higher than in the large local authorities. Thus, the State having a responsibility for the social care of older people is not the same as people having substantive rights to services that are equitably allocated.

However, it is in those countries where the State has little responsibility for the general population of older people who need social care that inequities are most evident due to patchy provision and no formal allocation criteria. Italy has very marked geographical variations in provision, with the southern regions having significantly lower standards of living, and scarcer and poorer quality social and health care services (Giarchi, 1996). In all regions there are also significant local variations, with extensive decentralization following the principle of subsidiarity leading to a coverage of services that is determined by local political factors rather than by any national framework or needs-led allocation of resources. Levels of provision reflect the political make-up of municipalities, with left-wing administrations of north and central Italy far more likely than those on the political right to have developed social care services. Extensive bureaucratization is also a feature of Italy's care system.

Greece is attempting to develop its social care services beyond a traditional residual focus on the destitute and seriously ill to achieve a broader coverage of the older population. Older people with very low incomes who are chronically disabled receive cash help with the cost of care through the social security system. For other older people, Greece is seeking cost-effective ways of providing services, such as the open-access KAPI centres which now form a key part of the country's health and social services provision for older people, combining public sector and voluntary resources (see Chapter 8). A significant expansion of home help programmes operated by local authorities is underway. Services provided by religious and non-governmental organizations and the private sector contribute to the patchy and uneven coverage of services rather than help to improve equity of access. The Church and large charities such as the Red Cross work autonomously. A range of private-sector organizations meet gaps in provision such as residential homes, nursing, home help and befriending, but only for those who can afford to pay.

In Ireland, the formal social care services that are provided are absorbed within a health service run by large area health boards and are often fragmented, with poor co-ordination between health and social care planning and delivery. In the largest of these, the Eastern Health Board, services for older people were, until recently, grouped together with acute hospital services. A relatively large voluntary sector, including many organizations associated with the Catholic Church, provides services that vary substantially in geographical coverage and the types of assistance they provide (see Chapter 6). The recent expansion of short-term services by health boards is not addressing Ireland's lack of universal long-term care provision.

Assessment

The right to a formal assessment of need is not a feature of care services in Italy, Ireland or Greece, where there is no legal duty on local authorities to provide social care services. Assessments in these countries are *ad hoc* and decisions about responding to need are discretionary, unregulated and strongly influenced by whether a local authority or, in particular, a voluntary organization happens to be providing a service in the locality. In Italy, Giarchi (1996) reports that discretion about what help is provided entails judgements about an older person's health and disability and whether they live alone. Provision of services is often limited to people with incomes below the official poverty line – about one-fifth of older people in Italy – with others expected to make their own arrangements privately. There are also long waiting lists for assessment.

In Ireland, the assessment of an older person's needs can be made by a community nurse who will also provide limited help with organizing services such as home help and meals-on-wheels. An older person may also receive assessments by particular service providers in the voluntary sector which each have their own criteria for eligibility, and these assessments are often informal and judgemental. General practitioners can take a lead role in assessment and organizing services, as can hospital social workers with discharge cases.

The formality of the assessment process in the UK, Norway and Denmark is important because it represents a single access point to services and is linked to decisions about eligibility, and these have become increasingly explicit and standardized. It is also linked to the practice of care management, with one professional taking responsibility for organizing services for an individual older person. This system of formal assessment and care management makes older people very dependent on professional power, but efforts are made to include users and carers in decisions. Unlike Greece, Italy and Ireland, the system can in theory make professionals accountable for their decisions because of the existence of bureaucratic guidelines. For example, many local authorities in Norway use a dependency scale as part of the individual needs assessment, both as a check-list and as a means of making decisions transparent. The need assessment is provided in writing to the user, but it is very general. It is recognized that there must be room for frontline staff to make informal judgements and adjustments with time, especially as it is not always possible to obtain a clear picture of needs at the beginning. Needs, however, are formally reassessed every six months. In Denmark, a similar type of written statement is used, but it is more tightly worded. A home helper must sign after each visit to the effect that she or he has provided the help defined in the statement. While protecting both the care worker and the user, the system discourages flexibility about what is done for the user from day to day.

There is a difficult balance to strike between formally defined entitlements and day-to-day flexibility, especially as a user's condition and social context may change over short periods of time. Without formal entitlements, however, discretion may occur on subjective grounds that cannot be justified objectively and remain hidden: for example, discriminating between 'deserving' and 'undeserving' older people on grounds other than need, such as personality, apparent material circumstances or family context. There is a growing number of examples of successful legal action to establish rights to social care. In the UK these have concerned mainly procedural rather than substantive rights, with the important exception of a recent case that established a right to free nursing care (see Chapter 5). In Norway legal action has established a right to care services in an older person's own home rather than their transfering to a residential or nursing home. But it is much more difficult to establish rights to particular amounts of help or, frequently, the type of help provided.

A significant issue with access which exists in the UK is that the procedural right to an assessment of need is combined with a financial assessment in the form of a means test. This is different from the systems of co-payment which exist for some services in Norway, including visits to family doctors, which are quite low and do not generate significant income for the local authority. In some UK local authorities, means testing can involve even older people on a very low income having to contribute something to the cost of their services, while users on middle or high incomes have to contribute a substantial proportion of the cost of any services they receive.

Intrusive means testing and judgements about ability to pay increase the stigma many older people feel about publicly funded services. In Greece and Italy, the older person's children are included in assessments of ability to pay, reflecting their wider duty to care. In Ireland, this was also the case until 1999 for private nursing home grants but was abandoned because of difficulty with enforcement. In the UK, means testing is restricted to members of the person's immediate household, although there is no provision in law to *demand* a contribution towards the cost of services from a liable relative (Schwehr, 1999). The means test is normally undertaken by a social worker, who will require the older person to provide evidence about their income and savings. Liability to pay towards the cost of a placement in a residential or nursing home is also assessed against the value of the person's original home, unless it cannot be sold because a partner continues to live there (although from April 2001 no sale will be required for the first three months of such a placement, and the alternative of a new loan system is to be introduced). In Ireland, where property has greater legal protection, the State does not have a claim on the value of a home vacated by a person who moves into subsidized nursing home care. Private nursing home beds are helping to free up hospital beds, although the cost of this strategy is escalating.

Older people in Ireland who hold medical cards are eligible for, although not entitled to, services such as home help, day centres and meals-on-wheels. This is normally for a small charge and although both home help and meals-on-wheels exist almost everywhere, their availability may be limited. With social care services in the community predominantly provided by voluntary organizations, means testing can be rough and ready. Even if someone refuses to pay, a service is unlikely to be denied if a doctor or public health nurse considers it is needed. Some 25 per cent of older people do not have medical cards, of whom two-thirds have health insurance; others are faced with the full cost of buying health or social care services. An older person without a medical card would normally not expect free services and would be likely to pay for private services in an increasingly buoyant private care market. Access to public funding for nursing home care is means tested and requires a medical assessment of dependency, but the grant provided, added to the older person's pension, can often be less than the fees charged. Families are therefore under pressure to pay the difference. In very exceptional cases, where the person is very dependent and has no family, the health board will pay the full cost. The escalating cost of Ireland's private nursing home subvention system has led to a major national review being undertaken at the time of writing, including exploring non-residential care options.

Charging is least prevalent in Denmark. Charges for home care for more affluent users were introduced in 1992 but later removed. Users of residential and nursing home care must pay for their board and lodgings, but this is not a particular financial burden given the relatively generous level of Denmark's universal and earnings-linked state pensions. Charging is more extensive in Norway, but it avoids some of the worst features of the UK's approach and is largely aimed at limiting 'unnecessary' demand while ensuring that low income and high-intensity users are not excluded from services. Charges for home care are low and cover only 5 per cent of the service's budget; local authorities have direct access to tax records which enables the financial assessment to be done without a personal means test. As in Denmark, there is a flat-rate, cost-price charge for meals-on-wheels, and nursing home care is directly subsidized so that users pay 75–85 per cent of their pensions in charges. These arrangements in Norway and Denmark reflect their relatively high pensions and avoid confronting older people with the full cost of their care and then requiring a means test before a decision is made about providing services.

In Italy social workers explore in detail why an older person cannot afford to buy the services they need and only provide publicly funded services if it is clear the person has no alternative. Older Italians are therefore very dependent on their pensions to buy care. With state provision being cut back in many localities, the private sector and – for poorer older Italians – the voluntary sector are increasing their role. Social co-operatives have grown substantially in importance, originating from grassroots action but often contracting with the local authority to provide services.

In the UK, a 'mixed economy' of publicly funded care services was introduced during the 1990s to extend choice of provider and contain costs through competition. Privatization is most extensive in the residential and nursing homes sector where a huge growth in the number of private homes during the 1980s was a largely unplanned consequence of demand-led funding of places through the social security system (see Chapter 2). Particular criticism was made of the lack of flexibility of local authority services, such as few 24-hour services and little multitasking, as well as their cost of unionized workforces. While the UK has gone much further down the privatization route than Norway or Denmark, there are trends in the same direction in these two countries. Some Norwegian local authorities have contracted out the provision of care services and separated the need assessment function from service provision – reforms which have been budget driven. Such pressures have stirred up debate in Denmark about whether there should be a charge for help with domestic tasks. Local authorities increasingly contract out the delivery of domestic help to private and non-profit organizations, and some give the option to older people of a cash payment to purchase their own services rather than use local authority domestic services – a practice that is likely to become more common and includes the possibility of employing a family member. The absence of any significant private care market in Denmark, however, makes users dependent on local authority gate keeping because the only access to services is through a local authority assessment. In contrast to the UK and Ireland, where it is quite common for better-off older people to purchase a place in a residential or nursing home without any local authority involvement, in Denmark and Norway a state monopoly means that access is via a professional assessment of need, with the possibility of a long wait or that access will be denied if need is not established.

Care settings

Although developments are taking place that are extending formal social care services in the familist social care systems of Ireland, Greece and Italy, there is as yet no national coverage equivalent in philosophy or scope to Denmark, Norway or the UK. Greece has recently established a National Organization for Social Care equivalent to the National Health System, but services are still very limited in availability. The formal sector in these countries still consists largely of services provided by private or voluntary organizations, and access depends on ability to pay in cash or through insurance schemes or, for a minority, on charitable benevolence. The nature of social care provision in the

UK is much closer to that of Denmark and Norway than to these three other countries. This is because there is a universal entitlement to assessment, a national system of funding local authorities to provide social care services for older people, and a legal duty that they make appropriate provision for their areas. Crucial issues, however, are the equity of these arrangements and the adequacy of their funding. All three countries have now moved towards national 'frameworks' which set out general standards regarding what should be available in all localities, a development that is new for the UK but is in fact a shift away from earlier and stricter national norms and standards in Scandinavia (Jakobsson, 1998). The expansion of devolved budgets and devolved policy implementation is creating variation in patterns of services within municipalities as well as between them. The question of how national norms can be reconciled with local discretion remains unresolved; it is a particular concern in the UK where local decision making in the NHS is already unaccountable to local government (there are, however, proposals for this to change, with elected local authorities having the right to carry out formal scrutinies of local NHS services and refer major planned changes to central government (Secretary of State for Health, 2000)).

All the countries are entering the twenty-first century from different situations. Norway has high levels of both institutional and home care provision while Denmark, with a higher overall level of spending, has had a stronger policy of home care and 'ageing in place'. Thus Denmark has only 4 per cent of older people living in residential and nursing homes compared with over 7 per cent in Norway (Leeson, 1997; Daatland, 1997a). However, Denmark has been an important influence on the ideology of the Norwegian long-term care system, which is shifting its emphasis from a traditional medical orientation towards a social model, including a rebalancing of resources towards community care and supported housing. Denmark's number of nursing homes has fallen and access is more selective, with the result that their residents are severely disabled, often with dementia, and older. Indeed, it is also the case that most residents in Norwegian nursing homes – some 70 per cent – are people with dementia. Overall, about 16 per cent of those aged 80-plus live in nursing homes in Denmark, compared with Norway's figure for this age group of 23 per cent. Even special housing for older people in Denmark is now largely confined to older people who are very disabled or ill. Small communal schemes for older people with dementia have been built since 1988, justified by their contribution to the quality of life of people with dementia and the protection of neighbours from disruptive behaviour (Platz and Petersen, 1992). Dementia is one of the last challenges to the philosophy of deinstitionalized care for older people.

The UK's social care services are as deinstitutionalized as those of Denmark, with 4 per cent of older people living in residential and nursing homes. During the 1980s there was a rapid expansion of private homes funded by demand-led social security payments but reforms implemented in 1993 capped expenditure on social care and transferred responsibility for managing budgets and rationing provision to local authorities. This budget-driven scenario continues to encourage diverting older people from care in residential and nursing homes. In recent years the number of older and physically disabled people living in residential care settings has fallen and this is projected to continue (Hirst, 1999). Largely as a result of this, domiciliary services such as home care are being concentrated on relatively fewer, more dependent older people. Residential care is increasingly reserved for older people with dementia.

In Denmark, Norway and the UK, the role of residential and nursing homes is largely an issue of how to achieve a high quality of life for very dependent older people in these type of settings. In contrast to the UK, both Denmark and Norway have come to see residential homes as compromising the quality of life of older people. In Denmark, there are no residential homes and nursing homes have a much smaller role than in the past, and in Norway most residential homes have become nursing homes, with improved staffing and equipment, or have been converted into supported housing with independent small flats. In Italy, Greece and Ireland, however, the issue is still one of underprovision of affordable institutional care outside the hospital. Italy has relatively few nursing or residential homes, the tradition having been for the family to care for very frail older people within their household. In recent years this lack of provision has been recognized as a national shortage of suitable care, and attempts are being made to increase the number of homes. In Ireland, until recently, there was heavy reliance on non-acute hospital care of older people when family caring arrangements were either inadequate or broke down altogether. However, in the last decade there has been a huge increase in the number of older people going into private nursing homes, some health boards have developed purpose-built residential units based on a nursing model, and there has been an increase in respite and day care services. Nevertheless, there is a severe shortage of places in statutory residential units where the cost for the resident is low and limited to their pension minus a 'comfort allowance'.

Supported housing in the community remains a very underdeveloped type of provision in Ireland, Italy and Greece. In Ireland, 'welfare homes' were set up in the 1970s for fairly mobile older people who could no longer stay at home, with a view to residents moving on when they became more dependent. The closure of long-term hospital wards, however, has meant that there is often nowhere to move on to. The homes, either run directly by health boards or by voluntary organizations, and financed mostly by health boards, now accommodate very dependent populations, needing more support than originally intended. Sheltered housing schemes for older people provided by local authorities or voluntary organizations are relatively scarce and often lack the resources necessary to provide in-house social care services.

Greece has the lowest level of provision of residential care, with less than one per cent of older people living in residential or nursing homes (Stathopoulos and Amera, 1992). This represents a very substantial underprovision and those few homes that do exist – run by voluntary groups, religious orders or sometimes local authorities – usually have long waiting lists. Sometimes an older person needing nursing care receives this in a series of consecutive stays in 'short-term' clinics. Residential and nursing homes are very expensive to build and staff, but attempts are being made to expand this type of care so that each prefecture has at least one home, also offering day care services. However, it is not unusual for family members to provide the nursing care themselves for an older relative who is in a home.

In all six countries an important policy priority is to find the most cost-effective care setting for older people with care needs. With the exception of Denmark, there is a general trend towards developing services that support and complement family care in the hope that gravitation towards more expensive care settings can be prevented or delayed. In the UK, as noted above, it is relatively common for residential homes to be used by local authorities as a cheaper option than a domiciliary package of support for very dependent older people. The responsibility of the NHS for paying for nursing care in a nursing home, rather than this cost being met as part of a means tested local authority 'social care' placement, has been ill-defined; the recent Government decision that all nursing care in nursing homes will be free of charge should help to resolve this although activities defined as social care will remain means tested (see Chapter 5). In Norway, supported housing is a cheaper option than nursing home care for local authorities. While local authorities fund both types of provision, residents in supported housing must pay rent and, because this is sometimes

Table 10.1 In-patient hospital care: beds and length of stay

	Beds per 1000 of population		Average length of stay in days	
	1986	1996	1986	1996
Denmark	6.9	4.9	10.2	7.3
Norway	16.1	15.0	11.3	9.9
Greece	5.3	5.0	12.0	8.2
Ireland	8.0	4.9	8.0	7.2
Italy	8.1	6.2	12.1	9.8
UK	7.2	4.7	15.2	9.9

Source: OECD (1998c).

quite high, many residents receive a housing allowance which is paid by central government.

There is a marked trend towards shorter stays in expensive hospital settings, enabling the number of hospital beds to be reduced, although to a lesser extent in Italy (see Table 10.1). While this has, in part, been a welcome move away from a medical orientation that tended to construct older people with social care needs in a dependent sick role, it has given rise to concerns about the adequacy of services in the community, both health and social care. Italy and Ireland have lagged behind northern European countries in shifting from hospital care to community support, although in Italy polyclinics have been successful in providing local access to health care for older people (Giarchi, 1996). Denmark has the strongest commitment to reducing unnecessary hospitalization among older people but, even with its generous provision of community care services, delays in hospital discharge can occur because of a shortage of services and suitable housing in the community. This situation shows marked variation between local authorities but overall has improved in recent years, although many municipalities believe that counties discharge hospital patients too early – the situation reflecting an organizational and financial divide between community and hospital services (Platz and Freiberg Petersen, 1992). This issue is also evident in Norway, and among attempts at solving it in both countries is the power of hospital authorities to charge local authorities for the cost of each day that discharge is delayed by lack of community provision.

Despite their established publicly funded social care services, defined quality standards are a recent innovation in the UK, Norway and Denmark. The UK adopted quality standards for nursing and residential homes in 2000, backed up by regional inspection arrangements

(Department of Health, 1998a). Denmark's local authorities started introducing standards in 1998, but progress has been slow. In Norway, by 2000 all local authorities are expected to have established comprehensive quality control systems based on professional standards. Ireland, Italy and Greece are well behind in setting and regulating quality standards. In Ireland the lack of mandatory quality control over a growing private care sector – with a trend towards building large private nursing homes of 100 beds or more in some cases – is currently causing concern. Grants towards the cost of private nursing home care are only available if the home is registered by the health board, requiring conformity with minimum health and safety standards but not quality of care standards. In Greece conditions within the small number of public nursing homes are poor and 'such that many of those admitted soon lose the self-serving capacities they had upon entry … Evidence suggests that approximately 30–50 per cent of the residents of these homes become bed-ridden within a few years of entry' (Karantinos, Ioannou and Cavounidis, 1992, pp. 89–90).

Conclusion

Social care in Europe sits uneasily between the policy priorities of governments seeking to contain public expenditure and the needs and rights of growing numbers of older people. Older people and their carers want practical help and other support when and where it is needed. The low coverage of publicly funded provision to address these needs in Greece, Italy and Ireland does not necessarily mean that older people are less likely to have these needs met at some level, but that responsibility falls on the family. In the UK, Norway and Denmark it is the State that has a legal responsibility to ensure that social care needs are met when there is no alternative, but services are subject to increasing rationing and targeting of 'legitimate' needs only. This is most marked in the UK, where there is a marked trend towards more intensive services for fewer, more frail, older people. The result is that older people with needs for less intensive support are often failing to receive any services because provision is being skewed towards higher levels of need: for example, between 1993 and 1997 the number of users who received one home care visit of less than two hours fell from 37 per cent to 23 per cent (*Community Care*, 1999). Even in Norway's relatively generously funded system, Vabø (1998) found that family members may be undertaking care work out of a feeling that public services are inadequate, although not intimate personal care.

This chapter has sought to bring together the range of material from earlier chapters and discuss its different aspects from the perspective of a concern with social exclusion. The results are multifaceted, from issues of variations in coverage of services to the effects on older people of assessment and care practices. The next chapter concludes the book by discussing some of the positive lessons that can be drawn from this analysis.

11
Conclusion: Issues and Solutions

Tim Blackman

This concluding chapter reviews a number of issues that arise from the material presented and discussed in previous chapters. It points to some possible solutions to the problems encountered with the social care of older people, identifying the various strengths that exist in both policy and practice, especially where these help to prevent the types of exclusion discussed in Chapter 10.

The chapter first considers the extent to which it is possible to generalize about welfare regimes and care systems, and whether such generalization helps us to understand why countries have different approaches to the social care of older people. This is followed by a short discussion of Denmark as a possible exemplar of social care provision, and a wider discussion about cross-national policy transfer. Issues and solutions are then explored, drawing on the experiences of all six countries considered in the book and, where appropriate, other research evidence. This starts with the decentralization and integration of social and health care services, and then moves on to the assessment of need, supporting informal care, the relevance of a social model, and the empowerment of older people. A final section draws together the main themes and conclusions.

Welfare regimes, care systems and cross-national policy transfer

We opened the book by asking whether the values and structures of Europe's diverse welfare regimes predispose countries towards particular configurations of social care provision for older people. We asked whether welfare regimes, and the systems of care that exist within them, determine particular patterns of responsibility, provision, access and entitlement for older people needing social care; and we posed the question as to what extent these configurations or systems of care could be regarded as successful in tackling social exclusion. What answers might be suggested to these questions?

First, can we distinguish separate welfare regimes? Broadly speaking, Denmark and Norway are two representatives of the Scandinavian social democratic regime of high public spending on a welfare state, including social care. The liberal welfare regime, with a high degree of selective provision and extensive means testing, captures many of the features of the UK and Ireland. Italy and Greece generally accord with the south European 'familism' model of very limited state-funded social care services (Castles, 1995; Daly, 1996; Ferrera, 1996; Katrougalos, 1996; Leibfried, 1993; Rhodes, 1997).

The difficulty with these general models is that features of welfare provision differ by the type of provision as well as by country. This is apparent if we compare health care with social care provision. The UK, Norway and Denmark have universal health care systems that are used by all sections of the population and have substantially displaced private-sector providers. In Norway and Denmark, but not the UK, this is also the case with regard to social care for older people. Ireland, Italy and Greece have established universal coverage of health services but with arrangements that allow considerable scope for private health care. Social care services are largely informal or private, and publicly funded or voluntary services are unevenly provided and very discretionary. In Ireland, hospital care in public wards is free (except for small token charges to non-medical card holders) and there is a free community nursing service. Greece achieves universal medical care coverage by requiring employees and their dependants to join social insurance schemes and providing subsidized state care for people aged over 67 years. But the Greek National Health Service has serious shortcomings, including a major shortage of nurses, and, despite one of the lowest per capita incomes in the EU, a high proportion of health care spending in Greece is on expensive private care (OECD, 1998).

The Scandinavian and liberal welfare models derive from Esping-Andersen's (1990) early classification of welfare regimes. This classification has been criticized for being based on a male breadwinner model of society, marginalizing the experience of women, and for being core-centric, thus marginalizing the experience of peripheral countries in the world economic system such as Greece (Lewis, 1992; Cousins, 1997). The core-centric criticism has led to the addition of the southern European welfare regime as a separate model distinguished by its dominant ideology of familism, a model with which Ireland has much in common (Cousins, 1997; Ferrera, 1996; Papadopoulos, 1998). The feminist critique of the male breadwinner model, on the other hand, has turned attention to the gender-based analysis of welfare. This does not focus on the extent to which welfare states free wage earners from dependence on the market, as with Esping-Andersen's (1990) concept of the 'decommodification' of labour power, but on the extent to which women are freed from gendered caring roles and can participate on equal terms with men in the labour market (Sainsbury, 1994).

Thus, it is possible in general terms to group the countries according to regime types, but there are important differences not captured by these broad classifications. Ireland, for example, shares some features of its welfare state with Britain, has comparable if not slightly better pension provision but considerably worse social care provision, making it similar in these respects to Italy (Anttonen and Sipilä, 1996). Britain organizes many aspects of its social care services in the same way as Norway and Denmark, but provides less extensive coverage and has a much more poorly trained social care workforce. Norway and Denmark still conform to the classic Scandinavian model, but Norway has a higher proportion of older people living in nursing and residential homes compared with Denmark's more deinstitutionalized system. Although Italy's social care provision is typically southern European in nature, many of its pensioners enjoy incomes comparable to those of the Scandinavian countries; the patchy provision of social care services is compensated to some extent by the ability of a large majority of older people to purchase services, as long as their needs are fairly modest. Similarly, Greece is often included in the southern European model, but is now making significant investments, as resources allow, in developing home help and home nursing services.

The Scandinavian countries have pursued policies aimed at the optimal mobilization of both men and women for paid labour. The model which has informed this strategy is individualist, based on the right of both men and women to economic independence, despite the collectivist arrangements developed to realize this right. There is a general consensus about the State's role as a source of security for the individual; Daatland (1992) comments that this explains the continuing, widespread public support for health services and care services for older people in Norway, while there is more division among the Norwegian public about the desirability of egalitarianism and the extent to which taxes and pensions should be redistributive. In contrast, the southern European countries have developed policies that work with a traditional family model: the economic interdependence of the family as a whole, and its role as a source of security for family members. The UK and Ireland lie in between, with the UK more towards the Scandinavian model and Ireland the southern European model.

Overall, the most significant factor in understanding approaches to the care of older people across Europe is welfare culture, and the very different attitudes to the respective roles of the State and the family. The six countries span the range of attitudes. In Denmark, the post-war growth of a large public sector offering professionalized care services to older people has substantially displaced the family from a role in providing care work (Leeson, 1997). Many of the employees in these services are women, and many women who would once have been informal carers are now paid carers employed by the public sector. Rather than seeing the type of concerns evident in the UK and Ireland about whether the current level of family care will continue into the future, both Denmark and Norway face the issue of high turnover and recruitment problems among a care workforce that provides a very high proportion of all the social care older people receive when they cannot care for themselves. There is no evidence, however, that the care systems of Norway and Denmark are unsustainable. Denmark is the most impressive example among the six countries of a care system based on universal coverage of health and social care services, a high level of funding from general taxation, and public ownership and control of services. Norway shares these features to a large extent, but with more emphasis on family care.

The Danish model

If we consider Denmark because of its overall higher spending and strong commitment to social inclusion reflected in the extent of community-based services, to what extent is it an exemplar to which other countries could aspire?

The Danish welfare state is based on an explicit principle of social inclusion for both older people and women of working age, who are relieved of any duty to provide unpaid care work. The UK Royal Commission on Long Term Care (1999b, p. 182) expressed some unease about how this is achieved.

> Danish people are under no obligation to look after or provide care for their older relatives. This has been a deliberate policy stance linked to the equal involvement of women in the Danish workforce.

However, we detected some feeling that the breakdown of extended family structures in Denmark had gone too far, with older people increasingly isolated from the nuclear families of the succeeding generations. However, some felt that this was compensated by increasing autonomy for older people and strong social networks outside the family. In general the support for current social arrangements appears strong, especially from women.

This doubt about the Danish model almost certainly reflect cultural differences in attitudes to the family and personal autonomy, although the Royal Commission strongly endorsed the main features of Denmark's care system but doubted if there would be public support for the level of taxation necessary to pay for this level of provision. Denmark secures a high degree of social inclusion for older people through a developed welfare state that defines inclusion in terms of personal autonomy and citizenship. Other countries with much less-developed welfare states compensate for this, to some extent, with other mechanisms of social inclusion, especially within the family. Previous chapters have identified some of the problems this creates in terms of carer stress, dependency on relatives, variable levels and quality of care, and the stigma attached to using public or charitable services, but have also highlighted some of the advantages when older people can expect family members to have a duty to care for them. In addition, these problems are not unique to informal care, and formal care services can also be associated with carer stress, dependency, variability and stigma. An impressive aspect of Denmark's system is that these problems appear to be minimized by the volume and quality of service provision.

Alber (1995) discusses the factors that have led to Denmark's high level of good-quality public-sector provision. An early secularization of Danish society meant that the principle of subsidiarity was never established, so that voluntary action has not had a major role. Services were expanded through the public sector. Access was based on citizenship rather than employment status, so that common life situations such as ageing and disability came to be fully integrated into public policy. Denmark introduced a means tested state pension for older people in 1891, replacing poor relief and, because pensioners were not allowed to be supported in the workhouses, leading to the establishment of institutional care for poor older people by local authorities. Local authorities were given a duty by central government to provide services, and the integration of community health with social care services has meant that both have expanded together. This expansion and the quality of the services provided have been driven by both central policy and funding, and local democracy. The latter includes a large bloc of older voters and the ability to levy local taxes to supplement central government subsidies. Alber (1995) contrasts this with the more fragmented structures of other countries where co-ordinated expansion is impeded and consumer interests have relatively little weight.

Although Denmark fits the Scandinavian model of a welfare regime, like other Scandinavian countries this regime is essentially a system of local welfare states. Daatland (1997a, p. 24) comments that 'one often talks of the "welfare municipality" rather than the "welfare state" as far as services are concerned'. The notion of a regime essentially describes a framework, and indeed the Scandinavian countries have 'framework' laws which govern their local welfare states. Thus, in Denmark all lower-tier local authorities (municipalities) must provide home help services, home nursing, adapted housing or nursing homes, rehabilitation and preventive home visits. Twenty-four hour services must be available.

Within these national requirements, every municipality decides the coverage, intensity and range of provision, as well as eligibility criteria. Decisions are taken at a very local level: the municipalities can be quite small and over half have populations of less than 10 000 people. This devolution of responsibility leads to differences in local tax rates; the highest local tax rate is about 9 per cent higher than the lowest (Royal Commission on Long Term Care, 1999b). There is variation across local authorities in both the extent and intensity of service provision, as discussed in Chapter 10, but it is variation above a high basic level of provision that applies across the country. In fact, at a more fundamental level, the Danish welfare state is sustained by a wide employment base and relatively egalitarian distribution of income which create the conditions for universal services and common standards, especially as there is widespread public support for high investment in these services and a very direct relationship between local populations and the municipalities they elect and finance.

None of the main features of the Danish care system would be easily exportable to the other countries, except for Norway – where this has indeed happened (Romøren, 1996). This is because these features do not exist independently of the context in which they have evolved and are reproduced in policy and practice. Contextual factors vary greatly across all six countries, depending on history, culture, economic development and political ideology. Policy transfer is much more evident between Norway and Denmark than any of the other countries, reflecting the importance of similar economic and political contexts, and the institutionalization of these similarities in cross-national networks.

In general, despite all six countries facing the common challenge of ageing, there are relatively few signs of convergence on a single type of model or system, although some common developments are apparent. The deinstitutionalization of care in favour of domiciliary services delivered to the older person's own home has gained favour across Europe, and all countries are under pressure to find new ways of caring for older people rather than simply increasing the capacity of existing care services. In Denmark, Norway and the UK distinctions between nursing and residential homes, day and respite care, and various types of supported housing and care provided to 'ordinary' housing have become more blurred. Residential or nursing homes provide day care, and services to supported and ordinary housing are provided in more intensive packages, substituting for institutional care. The discharge of older people with social care needs from hospitals continues to cause problems at times in all three countries, but short-term community and rehabilitation services have been developed specifically in an attempt to address this.

Other common trends, although to varying degrees so that they may be very significant in some countries but still ideas being debated in others, are: recognizing and supporting family carers and volunteers; looking to voluntary and private sector organizations to provide care services more flexibly and cheaply, and to offer more choice; targeting and selectivity, mirrored by some growing concerns about prevention due to the erosion of low level services in favour of provision for a narrower range of more intensive needs; and avoiding negative dependency in care policies and practices.

Some developments have not transferred as much as might be expected. Examples include formal assessment and care management (practised comprehensively only in the UK, Norway and Denmark); the planning and provision of community-based day centres (Norwegian and Danish service centres and Greek KAPIs); and volunteering (Ireland, Greece, Italy and Norway). Day centres are a particularly important example. In Denmark, approximately one in ten people over 60 years old attends a day centre, especially women, those living alone and the very old, and two-thirds of local authorities have an open access day centre. In Norway, one in five people over retirement age attends open access service centres, with many working as volunteers (Daatland, 1997a). These day centres provide opportunities for therapy and club activities, provide cafeterias and restaurants, and are often run by older people themselves. The Greek KAPI centres are particularly impressive examples of preventative day services promoting social interaction, both among older people and with the wider community (see Chapter 8).

There is in general no equivalent provision to senior centres or KAPIs in the UK, with the nearest parallels being either day hospitals, which have a strong medical focus, or day centres, which provide respite care and rehabilitation on a referral basis. The main exception is black and minority ethnic elder centres which have developed in the voluntary sector as important points of access to care services, but their existence largely reflects deficiencies in mainstream social care services for black and minority ethnic groups (Patel, 1999). Ireland has many community-based day centres which provide activities and some services, with active older people working as volunteers and perhaps a paid director who is typically a non-professional or a retired nurse. They are mainly aimed at dependent older people, although not exclusively. The scarcity of community-based day centres in the UK is a gap in provision for older people. In other countries they have been shown to have a key role in providing preventive health care, social activities and support, and educational and recreational opportunities, with strong community ownership among both users and the wider community. Rates of use are high. In America, it is estimated that 15 per cent of older Americans attend senior centres, both as users and volunteers (Lamb, 1999). As Convery (1987, p. 105) comments in a review of the Dublin area's day centre services:

> (D)ay centres are sometimes crucial to maintaining elderly people in the community. At relatively low cost they may offer a lifeline to many old people who live alone (often by choice), and who are not able to look after their own physical needs on a daily basis. Day centres may help to prevent family caring arrangements from breaking down by offering relief from the sometimes constant demands made by frail elderly relations...For some clients, day centres offer some place to go and something to do – escape from an otherwise lonely and tedious existence. Many independent and mobile elderly also derive benefits from the opportunities to socialize and join in activities (and to do volunteer work) that day centres offer. Voluntary day centres, especially, deliver personal care in an informal setting free from the stigma of 'welfare services'.

Decentralization and integration

In Norway, during the middle to late 1980s, all community health and social services for older people were integrated under local authorities (municipalities), including the transfer of nursing homes from the counties. Earmarked state subsidies were also largely replaced with a general government block grant so that a local authority could decide itself on the balance of spending between, say, schools and older people's services. Although central government controlled expenditure more tightly, local authorities were given more power to decide local priorities. The rationale is explained by Daatland (1997a, p. 25) as follows:

> Cost-containment was evidently a major, but not the single, motivating factor behind these reforms. The gathering of services and responsibilities on one administrative level should provide incentives for constructing a better and more integrated chain of services, and as Norwegian municipalities in general are fairly small, they should have intimate knowledge of the needs of the local population, and be in a better position than the county and state administrations to judge what profile of services are the better.

However, this degree of local autonomy caused variations to emerge in the volume and profile of services across local authorities (Lingsom, 1997). Calls for stronger national norms and standards to govern the quality of care have followed, and central government has assumed a more active role in care policies, with commitments to specific service improvements and more direct involvement in monitoring local authority plans and activity (Daatland, 1997a). The most recent national plan for care services for older people makes it clear that government grants to local authorities for expanding care services must be reflected in local planning and new activity, with the sanction of withholding funding if is this is not the case (Ministry of Health and Social Affairs, 1999). The plan is to be reviewed after two years, including an appraisal of the efficacy of the instruments used to implement it.

Denmark's community services are similarly integrated at municipal level. Both countries illustrate the tensions between national standards and local autonomy. Local autonomy is regarded as important because it narrows the implementation gap that can exist between centrally formulated policy and local delivery by bringing decision making nearer to where needs arise and resources are collected. By decentralizing responsibility, policy making is brought closer to implementation, also facilitating opportunities for user and citizen participation in decisions. This does not generate large inequalities in provision in Norway and Denmark, however, because minimum standards are set down nationally and there is a commitment to providing the funding necessary to achieve a relatively high level of basic provision across the country.

In the UK, social care services have been part of the elected local government system, while health services are provided by the National Health Service and managed by boards appointed by central government (except in Northern Ireland, where health and social services are jointly administered by area boards). Integration is beginning. Recent legislation has removed barriers to joint working by allowing social services and health authorities to pool budgets, transfer funds and delegate or integrate some services, and over the next few years it is expected that local authorities will delegate their social care functions to Care Trusts (see Chapter 5). The lack of integration is widely seen as a problem. Joint planning arrangements have sought to address this, and are being strengthened to achieve better co-ordination between primary and community health services, hospitals and social care services. Major changes in the organization, management and governance of health and social services are underway (Department of Health, 1998). These are seeking to achieve better collaboration between health and social services regarding needs assessment, planning and the use of resources, as well as improved scrutiny and accountability, and improved cost-effectiveness. The role of new Care Trusts in moving towards multidisciplinary health and social care teams for populations of about 100 000 people is particularly significant. It is increasingly recognized that policy priorities such as the decentralization of acute services from hospitals to home care requires an integrated program across the continuum of health and social services, as well as addressing forces within the NHS which continue to foster unnecessary post-acute institutionalization (Wistow, 1997).

As in Norway and Denmark, and indeed to a greater extent in the UK, there is a tension between local autonomy and national prescriptions from the centre. For example, local eligibility criteria reflect local priority setting and – ideally – user involvement, but national service frameworks are promising explicit standards and principles for the pattern and level of services, and greater consistency regarding eligibility and charging (Department of Health, 1998). There is much that could be learned from how Denmark and Norway have sought to tackle this issue, although the UK's comparatively low level of public spending is likely to limit some of the options.

Devolution of responsibility is a strategy also evident in Ireland, where powers have shifted from central government to local areas with the aim of improving co-ordination between services. Ireland's social care provision is also integrated with health care under eight health boards but, unlike Scandinavia, social care services are poorly developed and a medical model dominates. Ireland's relatively few home care workers are part of the health care system organized under community nursing. They mostly comprise home helps providing practical domestic assistance; care attendants providing personal care are employed in some areas but are relatively scarce. Traditionally, general hospital care for older people has been well resourced, reflecting the powerful position of hospitals in the Irish health care system, but in recent years community services have received more investment and the use of hospital care has declined.

In Greece, local authorities are increasingly adopting a co-ordinating role among a variety of care providers. They allocate financial support for KAPI centres and have begun facilitating a 'third sector' which uses funds from state, private, and social and private pension sources, administered by the local authorities, to develop not-for-profit services. European Union funding has recently supported an expansion of home care projects linked to the KAPIs and drawing in volunteers. Local authorities are also experimenting with a variety of schemes including sheltered housing, home care and older people's self-help groups.

Central government in Greece has implemented measures to reduce inequality in welfare provision and secure universal access to key services, including new administrative sub-divisions, universal coverage by general medical practitioners, and expansion of health centres and ambulance services. Benefits are also being more directly targeted where needs are greatest. KAPIs have been established in the major urban areas and almost all have started home help services, giving priority to dependent older people who live alone and have no family near to them. But Greece's capacity to develop its welfare provision through taxation and public spending is severely limited by the objective of joining the European Monetary Union, which dictates lower public spending and privatization. This makes it very difficult to establish a national framework governing the types, level and quality of services for older people, and there is a danger that provision will return to a medicalized system in which prevention and rehabilitation have little priority.

Decentralization to Local Health Units (USLs), local government and local centres, combined with integration of services, was an aim of Italy's health reforms in the early 1990s. There was also a focus on prevention. The reforms failed, according to Saraceno and Negri (1994), because the 'clientelist-particularistic' features of the Italian welfare state undermined them: the distribution of social services reflected political bargaining power rather than need, cash benefits were still preferred over services, and inefficiency, waste and corruption were widespread. There was little development of home care or locally based integrated services. A wide implementation gap also undermined the reforms. Policy was developed centrally but implementation was imposed on lower levels of local government, and there was a failure to draw in the voluntary sector, mostly based on the Catholic Church, and social co-operatives.

Later reforms sought to tackle these problems and included attempting to ensure that the granting of social assistance benefits and services was no longer purely a matter of discretion for the individual administrator or social worker. New efforts to improve managerial efficiency and develop linkages between public and private services were initiated in 1992. Local Health Units were given managerial autonomy, but this often decoupled health services from the social care functions of local authorities (communes). There is no legal requirement to provide social care and the extent of provision depends on local policy and spending priorities. Whether health care is organized together with home care varies from region to region. In some, community nursing services are organized by communes and grouped with home care and social work services. In others, community nursing services are organized by Local Health Units together with home care services. Some regions have home care services run separately by the communes. Most communes provide home care at some level, but predominantly for poor older people and with little backing from occupational therapists, physiotherapists or chiropodists, for which older people generally have to pay privately. Home care may be provided directly by the commune or through subsidized co-operatives and voluntary agencies.

Integration between health and social care services is clearly more extensive in Denmark and Norway, and is likely to be so in the UK, than in the other three countries. Developments in health care towards interventions in the community rather than hospital, and the scarcity of family care that is still available in Ireland, Italy and Greece, are the main drivers towards integrated care. In the UK, there is some resistance to integrating social care services into the NHS because of a concern among social care professionals that their distinctive role will be eroded, and concern among local politicians that local authorities would lose control of a major service area. The Royal Commission on Long Term Care (1999a) was not in favour of integrating health and social care services under local authorities because it did not have confidence in their ability to manage health services and especially to avoid the development of major inequalities in provision. The Danish and Norwegian experiences demonstrate how this need not be the case, and their integration of these services at a very local level would almost certainly have advantages for older people in the UK, including the lead role of nurses in community care.

Assessment of need

In Denmark and Norway, older people's needs are assessed by a community nurse, sometimes with a home care organizer. Community nurses are trained in social care as well as health care, and their continuing involvement as care managers with an older service user realizes the integration of services at the individual level. In the UK, assessment and care management are mostly undertaken by a local authority social worker or, generally for users with lower levels of need, by a home care organizer, neither of whom is trained in health care. Health care professionals from the NHS are often only involved in hospital discharge cases (*ECCEP Bulletin*, 1998). Social workers have a comprehensive remit spanning assessment, review and care management, but there is evidence that they under-identify health problems, especially depression and cognitive impairment (Banerjee *et al.*, 1998; *ECCEP Bulletin*, 1998). A recent Audit Commission (2000) report highlights how this problem extends to the organization of services. The Audit Commission found that many older people with mental health problems may receive an assessment in the community but do not access the services they need because most of the resources for specialist mental health services come from health agencies and go on hospital and residential care rather than integrated community services. It concluded that people who would otherwise need residential care could live at home if provided with flexible home-based care by joint health and social services teams. Government plans to integrate services under Care Trusts, with a single assessment process and possibly a nurse lead for the most vulnerable older people, directly address these issues (Secretary of State for Health, 2000).

In both Norway and Denmark, social and nursing care services are both led by nurses, in contrast to the split between social workers and nurses in the UK, but the model of care is a social rather than a medical model. This is particularly the case in Denmark, where nurses receive a strong social care element in basic training, and managers receive further training in social and gerontological aspects of care. Home help workers, who rarely have a care qualification in the UK, are qualified and trained in both social and health aspects of care, and they are integrated under common management with home nursing services. Formal assessment of need takes the older person's whole situation into account and one person, normally a community nurse, coordinates the help provided. The system is similar in Norway, but the medical model remains stronger because both nursing homes and district nursing services are regulated under health care legislation.

The State's responsibility for the social care of older people in Norway, Denmark and the UK is expressed in the universal right to an assessment of need following referral. Despite the different levels of family care in these countries, the existence of assessment means that, in theory at least, there is a safety net for the older person when family care fails. But the effectiveness of this safety net depends on the adequacy of the referral process, especially whether older people in need are always referred; the quality of the assessment, including whether all older people referred are properly assessed; and the entitlements of the older person following assessment by a professional gatekeeper of resources. In all three countries, services are only available to those who 'need' them, that is who are unable to do things for themselves. In the UK, access to free or subsidized services also depends on a financial assessment or means test.

The aim of these processes is to ensure that the provision of social care from public funds is equitable and needs led. In the UK, since the introduction of new assessment and care management procedures in the early 1990s, the equity and efficiency of resource allocation in social care appears to have improved, although there is continuing evidence of general shortfalls in services from the point of view of users (*ECCEP Bulletin*, 1998; Richardson and Pearson, 1995). Highest levels of dissatisfaction and unmet need have been reported as existing among more dependent users (Blackman, 1998; *ECCEP Bulletin*, 1998). There are also major gaps in provision for minority ethnic older people (Patel, 1999). However, despite these resource issues, the system of assessment and care management has much to commend it. In the UK it has been associated with 'new managerialism' and the rationing of resources, but underfunding is a wider issue and, indeed, makes assessment and care management even more important to achieve equity and an efficient use of resources. As Baldock (1999, p. 93) concludes:

> Anyone who knows the history of social services management will know that the 'new managerialism' represents a deliberate effort on the part of the Department of Health to replace the professional social work culture that dominated the provision of social services until the mid-1980s. That approach, built upon the idea that a properly trained and socially committed social worker was the best judge of the appropriate allocation of services, was systematically discredited by research in the 1980s. It was frequently shown that local services were almost randomly allocated, had no clear objectives and produced no measured results that could be used to judge value for money … Within its own terms the 'new managerialism' is logical and had its own integrity. It is difficult to argue with attempts to find those most in need, assess them, arrange services and then measure the outcomes against the original intentions.

In Greece, Italy and Ireland it is the family which provides its members with a safety net rather than the State. This support is not mediated by professional gatekeepers and is unconfined by eligibility criteria and rationing. But the absence of these processes only adds to the fragmented and clientelist features of their welfare systems. The southern model of welfare involves the exercise of a high level of discretion by professionals, managers and politicians in the allocation of welfare resources, heavily influenced by patronage (Ferrera, 1996). For example, in an otherwise positive appraisal of KAPI centres, Stathopoulos and Amera (1992, p. 185) remark that their operation is influenced by political pressures and 'party nepotism towards its clientele by the mayors'. Katrougalos (1996, p. 55) cites evidence that, '50 per cent of patients in the National Health System (in principle free of charge for all citizens) have, illegally, paid some extra money to the medical staff in order to have better care'. One effect of this clientelist use of state power is to reinforce traditional mistrust of the State and suppress popular support for some displacement of family care by state provision.

Many older people need social care, which would benefit their quality of life, but do not have medical or nursing needs. There is no reason, though, why social care should not receive the same attention to achieving universal coverage according to need and a fair allocation of resources as health care. Not only is it a type of provision which in its own right services the aim of countering the social exclusion of older people, but it is an essential complementary provision to health care and, indeed, indistinguishable in many aspects of practice. An absence of medical treatment can cause preventable pressure on social services, just as inadequate social care can lead to preventable pressure on medical care. For example, there is evidence from the UK that older people with depression are not receiving appropriate treatment, and that depression may lead to increased social care use, independent of disability, and higher hospitalization rates (Banerjee and Macdonald, 1996; Walker *et al.*, 1998). Conversely, there is evidence that supported housing in the community may be protective against depression for older people living alone (Walker *et al.*, 1998).

Supporting informal care

Besides the issue of procedural equity – systems and practices that treat people with similar needs in the same way and with different needs in different ways – other aspects of the Danish and Norwegian systems are less transferable for economic and cultural reasons. As Romøren (1996, p. 70) comments, the almost total public funding of care at a high level should be considered 'more as a cultural pattern in the small and homogeneous Scandinavian populations than as a view held by one or other political wing'. In other countries family care will remain of great importance, and the issues are more ones of equity, choice and balance than of a general popular belief that public services should substitute for family care. In the UK, there is widespread acceptance of family care but growing concern that it is inadequately supported. Research has revealed informal caring as often a satisfying and rewarding experience, although it has also demonstrated high levels of stress among many carers (Evandrou, 1996). Studies have focused on the factors that put informal carers at risk, and a particular issue is that households where there is a co-resident carer are less likely to receive social care services than households with an older person living alone (Evandrou, 1996; RIS MRC CFAS, 1998). Recognition of both the costs and benefits of informal care have led the UK to adopt a national strategy for carers, boosting funding for respite care, creating new pension rights and local tax breaks – in other words, working to support informal care rather than displace it (Department of Health, 1998).

The key issue, however, is choice. Ellingsæter and Hedlund (1998, p. 29) write that in Norway, 'Families are allowed some choice: to provide care without public support, to form a care partnership with the public authorities or to relinquish care obligations to the state'. They point out that an important principle underpinning this choice is that all residents are in principle eligible for services. Whether the balance is right can be judged by whether informal carers are denied employment opportunities and lose income, and whether their role is associated with physical and emotional strain that damages their health. Lingsom (1997) reports that the most extensive providers of informal care in Norway are women aged 45 to 66, of whom 30 per cent provide care, on average for just under three hours per week. Most care givers are employed. Lingsom found that the employment and income effects of care giving were generally modest, although negative effects on employment were identified for care givers that lived in the same household as the person receiving care. She also found that most care givers do not experience physical or emotional strain. This contrasts with the UK where there is substantial evidence that care givers experience both loss of earnings and extra expenditure, and that care giving is stressful for many informal care givers, at times leading to a breakdown in informal support (RIS MRC CFAS, 1998). Informal carers in the UK spend an average of 20 hours per week undertaking caring tasks; an estimated 14 per cent provide care for 50 hours per week or more (Evandrou, 1996).

While the UK grapples with finding a balance between family care and public services, the failures of care systems based almost entirely on family care are becoming increasingly evident. The lack of formal care services means that families have to find ways of coping, but this is a difficult challenge when the older person needing care is very dependent. In these circumstances, one coping strategy for families in Greece is to hire an immigrant worker to live with an elderly family member, part of a general increase in demand for immigrant workers to take on household tasks as young educated Greek women turn away from traditional mother and home worker roles (Cousins, 1999a; Fakiolas, 1999). In northern Europe, this option would be unaffordable for all but the most wealthy families. However, it is far from a panacea. Amera (1999) makes the following observations about Greece:

> Lately there has been a lot of criticism directed towards the whole system and even a panel of four previous ministers of health admitted on TV that there are many failures. Elderly people fare worse than all others as there are no geriatric beds and as there is no place for them to go once hospitals have nothing more to offer to them. Social workers in hospitals have a permanent anguish with cases of old, dependent elderly whose families are unable to care for them or

who have no one to go to. Home help and home nursing programs operate only in very few areas but most of them do not have the necessary personnel to care for the type of problems encountered. What is most important is that people in political positions do not have the concept of such services and feel that a visit by a volunteer for companionship alone is enough.

Carer support should clearly be a priority for Italy, Ireland, Greece and the UK. Carer support interventions have been evaluated with positive results in reducing stress in care givers, including complementary home care and respite care provision as well as quite modest resource commitments such as regular telephone contact giving psychosocial support (Bass, Noelker and Rechlin, 1996; Caradocdavies and Harvey, 1995). Care giver training and individual and family counselling have been demonstrated to delay the admission to nursing homes of people with dementia (Brodaty, Gresham and Luscombe, 1997; Mittelman *et al.*, 1996). The effects of dementia on family carers have been shown to be ameliorated simply by providing a diagnosis (Schofield *et al.*, 1998).

Volunteering is an area where there is potential for cross-national learning. As already noted, Norway, Greece and to a lesser extent Ireland offer impressive examples of community-based centres for older people with open access and the participation of older volunteers in providing services and activities for other older people, although mostly at a level of low to moderate needs. O'Shea and Larragy (1999, p. 15) report that many Irish voluntary organizations encourage the active participation of older people: 'they are, for the most part, run by "the not so old" for older people'. Voluntary activity by all older people is common, with over 40 per cent of 66 to 70 year olds estimated to be engaged in some type of voluntary activity, and 20 per cent of 71 to 80 year olds. In the UK, the volunteer contribution to community care is a neglected area in both policy and research (Knapp, Koutsogeorgopoulou and Smith, 1996). However, the new NHS Plan promotes volunteering with a strategy of linking the new network of local Care Direct information points with older volunteer befrienders (Secretary of State for Health, 2000).

A social model

An impressive achievement of Greek KAPIs is their integration of medical and social care, which was an aim from their inception. In Italy, in those localities where integrated social and medical care with case management has been introduced, improvements in cost effectiveness, reductions in admissions to hospitals and nursing homes, and reductions in functional decline among older people living in the community have been demonstrated (Bernabei *et al.*, 1998). In Denmark and Norway, decentralization has been pursued with the explicit aim of integrating and providing better services. The philosophy behind these attempts at integration is the social model of care.

The social model can be applied at both societal and individual levels. At a societal level the social model focuses attention on states of health and well-being as emerging from social and economic conditions. The health and care needs of an individual are seen as largely resulting from the social environment acting on him or her (Brunner and Marmot, 1999). At the individual level, the social model is 'person centred'. It focuses on the person and their capacities and needs, rather than a specific disease or disability which is 'treated' in isolation. It understands a person's capacities and needs in relation to their context, including their family and their wider community and its values (Cheston and Bender, 1999).

The social model is therefore antipathetic to care or treatment, which unnecessarily excludes older people from being able to exercise their capacities, meet their needs and continue living in the context they are used to. In Norway, the social model includes a more recent emphasis on the State taking a supportive role in order to encourage self-care and family care. Like other aspects of the social model, however, there is concern about the extent to which it serves as a legitimization for the State to withdraw from responsibility for meeting certain needs. Daatland (1997a) notes that encouraging self-care and family care has been motivated by the objective of containing costs, especially as improvements in standards and care workers' pay and conditions have increased costs without increasing the volume of services.

Nevertheless, the growing influence of the social model reflects an increasing commitment to social inclusion, despite cost pressures existing alongside its implementation. In Norway and Denmark, nursing homes are frequently providers of domiciliary services and short-term care as well as long-term care for older people; services are planned across the spectrum of levels of need from open access senior centres run with significant community participation to specialist nursing homes; and care services are led by nursing practitioners trained within a social model of care that emphasizes older people's preference to remain in ordinary housing in the community supported by domiciliary services. Hospitals, on the other hand, are run by larger county councils, with the priority on specialist medical treatment delivered within a temporary institutional setting.

Decentralization does not necessarily imply integration within a social model of service provision. Ireland's care services remain relatively medicalized despite the recent decentralization of authority to area health boards. The formal social care services that are provided exist within a health service run by large area boards, and are often fragmented, with poor co-ordination between health and social care planning and delivery. Social work and rehabilitation services for older people remain primarily hospital based.

In all the countries, hospitals have had their role more tightly confined to medical interventions that cannot be efficiently or safely performed in the community. Outside the hospital, the distinction between 'social' and 'medical' care settings in Norway, and especially Denmark, has faded away to a great extent. Social and medical care can be provided in a range of settings and the aim, still tempered by cost considerations, has been to prioritize quality of life. Residential homes have been converted to supported housing and the continuing existence of nursing homes has been justified in terms of quality of care for very dependent older people, backed up by substantial investment in staffing and equipment in these homes.

The negative impact of enclosed institutional life on the autonomy and dignity of older people has been well researched but, as discussed in Chapter 10, the type of care practice is probably of more significance than the care setting. For example, in dementia care, 'person-centred' practices have been found to improve orientation to place, lower social disturbance, lower levels of apathy, and promote 'rementing' (Kitwood, 1997). These practices entail high levels of individual attention, carefully planned activities, close personal support and opportunities for users to participate in general decision making. Social contacts are also important for all older people, and appear to be as valued as functional ability or health status (Farquhar, 1995). If older people have little contact with family or friends, there is a danger that even with relatively well-funded services formal social care cannot secure a decent quality of life, especially when services are increasingly focused on personal care rather than wider quality-of-life criteria. Meretz (1999) comments, on attempts to make the home care services in Denmark more efficient, that:

> There is not enough time for a chat or to go for a walk – maybe to the local shopping centre where the old can choose for themselves

what they want to buy. Several years ago it was normal that the home helper (with or without assistance of the old) cooked dinner. The old chose themselves what they wanted to eat and they could enjoy the preparing and the smell of the food. Today it is meals-on-wheels. It is more effective and cheaper for the municipality. But many old people lose their appetite.

This does not mean that older Danes want to return to dependency on family care, which is widely regarded as undesirable. There is strong support for equal rights to universal social care services but continuing tensions about satisfying demand. Leeson (1997) argues that a 'care gap' has emerged in Denmark, bringing a response from grant-aided initiatives in the voluntary sector, with volunteer visiting for people with dementia, voluntary support for the first few days after hospital discharge and peer counselling. As already discussed in Chapter 10, systems based on familism fare little better in achieving a good quality of life for older people. Karantinos, Ioannou and Cavounidis (1992, pp. 87–88) comment about Greek elders that 'While most of the elderly population have many hours of free time available every day, the only "company" and "activity" available to much of the elderly population today is the television set.'

The integration of health and social care services is an important aspect of the social model, but just as important are opportunities for social contact and activities.

Empowerment

The lack of formal social care provision for older people in Ireland, Italy and Greece does not reflect exclusion from the policy-making process. They are well represented in Italy's trade unions, which are significant political actors (Mirabile, 1999). In Ireland older people are represented at a national policy-making level by the National Council on Ageing and Older People, which advises the minister of health (under whom there is a junior minister for the elderly), and through representatives from older people's organizations on the National Economic and Social Forum. In Greece a government minister is responsible for older people's matters. But in these countries the political issues largely concern pensions, and social care services are a marginal issue.

Older people are regarded as having a strong voice within their families in Italy, Ireland and Greece. O'Shea and Larragy (1995, p. 1) comment about Ireland:

> There is no evidence of any major cleavage between the generations in this country. There have, for instance, been no popular political movements campaigning for either more, or less, opportunities for older people. The general view is that old people are well integrated into the economic and social fabric of Irish society. Whatever pressure exists is concentrated on ensuring that older people's access to health care and pension rights are protected.

Layte *et al.* (1999), however, point out that a significant minority of older people in Ireland, especially older people living alone without occupational pensions or social insurance entitlements, live in deprived circumstances. They also reveal the considerable burden and opportunities foregone experienced by family carers, especially of very dependent older people, and the extent of care provided by older people themselves to their partners.

It is in Denmark and Norway, where social care services are most developed, that older people's representation is strongest. There is a prominent consultative role for councils of older people in local decision-making, as well as influential national organizations. Both countries have experienced direct action by protest groups about care services for older people, supported by the media. About €1.3 million extra (NOK 1 billion) of public spending, for instance, was won in 1990 following a nationwide campaign that grew from local grassroots action in part of Oslo (Daatland, 1997a).

In the UK, while consultation with older people's and carers' organizations is required at local level, and there is a range of initiatives to promote the involvement of older people in local decision making through the Better Government for Older People programme, there is no formal structure or representation at national level (Bennington, 1998). The growing proportion of the electorate who are older, however, is promoting discussion about how older people's interests should be represented in central government.

Conclusion

For the foreseeable future the different social care systems of these six countries seem unlikely to change significantly. The exception could be the UK's current system of social care provision. A major reorganization of the NHS is presently taking place which is likely to lead to social care being integrated with health services under local Care Trusts serving populations of around 100 000 people. Some of the recommendations made by the Royal Commission on Long Term Care (1999a) call for radical changes, in particular the ending of means testing for long-term care in nursing homes and personal care. However, it is unlikely that the UK will shift away from means tested and highly targeted social care services, although a substantial increase in public spending is planned over the next few years, much of it to fund the new commitment fo free nursing care in nursing homes. The key issue remains as to what the costs will be for those older people excluded from publicly funded services. Evidence about the extent of stress and loss of income among informal carers, for example, points to an extensive problem of social exclusion. Better local planning, consultation, assessment and care management practice, and the integration of services will go some way towards addressing this, but the only real solution is a continuing expansion of services.

There is little prospect of family care being displaced to any great extent by an expansion of state provision in Greece, Italy or Ireland. This is not a high political priority and, by and large, families cope with limited support. A feature of the southern European family-based model is a preference for direct monetary benefits rather than services, and in all these countries pension reform is much more significant politically than the provision of social care services (Walker and Naegele, 1999). However, the recent establishment of a National Organization for Social Care in Greece demonstrates that policy inertia is not inevitable. But coping with the care needs of older people who are very dependent remains a major challenge: a key priority is support for family carers and an improvement in provision for when the capacity of family care is exceeded.

In Norway and the UK, ageing pressures on public spending have increased awareness of the benefits of supporting family carers through financial incentives, social support and respite care. Denmark, Norway and the UK can be distinguished from the other three countries because of their procedural rights to social care services, and the national network of service provision which underpins this, despite the more residualist features of the UK system. However, in Greece, Italy and Ireland there is a family duty to care. This duty reflects cultural context, particularly the national religious context and the influence of Catholicism and Eastern Orthodoxy. Only Italy, Ireland and Greece have constitutions which recognize the family and are committed to protecting its role in these societies (Hornsby-Smith, 1999). But both rights and duties are under pressure – from rising financial costs in Denmark, Norway and the UK, and from women's increasing participation in the public spheres of education and work in Greece, Italy and Ireland.

It is bureaucratic processes which enable Denmark, Norway and the UK to achieve some degree of rational matching of services to needs. Family care alone cannot be relied on to produce an equitable distribution of care, nor can quality be assured. Formal social care services exist in Italy, Greece and Ireland, but they have strong client–patron features which distinguish them from the more bureaucratic principles of public administration in northern Europe. As Ferrera (1996, p. 29) comments, 'discretion based on professional or bureaucratic evaluation is not the same as political discretion based on systems of patronage'.

Overall, the six countries represent two worlds of social care: the more family-oriented systems of Ireland, Italy and Greece, and the more individual-oriented systems of Denmark, Norway and – in less universalist form – the UK. These two worlds reflect distinctive welfare cultures, but they are experiencing new pressures from the bottom up as expectations change. In seeking to improve the care of older people in these cultures, resources need to be developed that work with existing sources of care but which also extend the rights of older people, at least to assessment and an equitable matching to needs of the care services available.

Variability in provision, inconsistency of practice and an undervaluing of both paid and unpaid carers are issues that apply to the particular features of the care systems of all the six countries. The different levels of provision of organized social care services are a major aspect of inequality among older people, both within and between the countries. This is a general service development issue for their national government to address, involving political decisions about taxation and public expenditure, and within the EU decisions about the extent to which the equal rights being extended to employees should also extend to the care needs of older people. In Greece, Ireland and Italy the priority is support for the needs of family carers and investment in services for very dependent older people. In Denmark and Norway, the main issue is how to achieve a high quality of life for dependent older people living outside institutional settings, especially people with dementia. The UK shares all these issues to some extent – because private and family care remain significant due to very selective gate keeping of access to formal care services.

While there is little prospect for any wholesale policy transfer across national boundaries, there is potential for selective cross-national learning about the role of social care in tackling social exclusion. Examples include the demonstrable inadequacy of support for family carers in the UK when their stress and loss of income is compared with Norway's family carers; the model provided by KAPIs and senior centres in terms of how to promote healthy ageing, community involvement and volunteering; the extent of variability in resource allocation at geographical and individual levels, and the importance of clear frameworks and monitoring to reduce these variations; the wide range of innovations to promote older people's participation in democratic processes and decision making; and the importance of achieving integration between different types of care at the local level. A clear general lesson, however, is that if older people anywhere are to enjoy rights to care based on equitable needs-led principles, the State must have an active role in taking responsibility for securing these rights within each care system.

References and Further Reading

Abrahamson, P. (1992) 'Welfare pluralism: towards a new consensus for a European social policy?', in Hantrais, L., O'Brien, M. and Mangen, S. (eds), *The Mixed Economy of Welfare*, Cross National Research Papers 6, Leicester: European Research Centre, Loughborough University.

Alber, J. (1995) 'A Framework for the Comparative Study of Social Services', *Journal of European Social Policy*, 5(2), pp. 131–49.

Amera, A. (1990) 'Family Care in Greece', in Jamieson, A. and Illsley, R. (eds), *Contrasting European Policies for the Care of Older People*, Aldershot: Avebury.

Amera, A. (1999) Unpublished notes prepared for this book.

Amera, A. and Maratou-Alibrandi, L. (1988) 'Migration and the Family: the socialization of children in a rural community', in National Centre for Social Research (ed.), *The Rural World in the Mediterranean Region*, Athens: National Centre for Social Research.

Amera, A. and Stournara, A. (eds) (2000) *Home Help Programmes: Implementation Report for the Central Association of Municipalities and Communities*, Athens: Hellenic Society for Social Participation.

Andersen, D. (1995) *Tiden efter tres*, Rapport 95:9, Copenhagen: Danish National Institute of Social Research.

Anderson, R. (1992) 'Health and community care', in Age Concern (ed.), *The Coming of Age in Europe*, London: Age Concern England.

Anttonen, A. and Sipilä, J. (1996) 'European social care services: is it possible to identify models?', *Journal of European Social Policy*, 6(2), pp. 87–100.

Arber, S. and Ginn, J. (1991) *Gender and Later Life*, London: Sage.

Athens Medical Association (1998) *A Social Problem: Medical inflation*, Athens: AMA.

Atkinson, A. B. (1995) *Incomes and the Welfare State*, Cambridge: Cambridge University Press.

Audit Commission (1995) *United They Stand: Co-ordinating Care for Elderly Patients with Hip Fracture*, London: The Audit Commission.

Audit Commission (1996) *Balancing the Care Equation*, London: The Audit Commission.

Audit Commission (1997) *The coming of age: improving care services for older people*, London: The Audit Commission.

Audit Commission (1998) *Home Alone: the role of housing in community care*, London: The Audit Commission.

Audit Commission (2000) *Forget Me Not: Mental Health Services for Older People*, London: Audit Commission.

Baldock, J. (1999) 'Social Services and Contrary Cultures', in Chamberlayne, P., Cooper, A., Freeman, R. and Rustin, M. (eds), *Welfare and Culture in Europe*, London: Jessica Kingsley.

Baldock, J. and Evers, A. (1992) 'Innovations and care of the elderly: the cutting-edge of change for social welfare systems. Examples from Sweden, the Netherlands and the United Kingdom', *Ageing and Society*, 12, pp. 289–312.

Baldock, J. and Ungerson, C. (1994) *Becoming Consumers of Community Care*, York: Joseph Rowntree Foundation.

Baldwin, C. and Lunt, N. (1996) *Charging Ahead: The development of local authority charging policies for community care*, Bristol: The Policy Press.

Baldwin, S. (1997) 'Charging for community care', in May, M., Brunsdon, E. and Craig, G. (eds), *Social Policy Review 9*, London: Social Policy Association.

Banerjee, S. and Macdonald, A. (1996) 'Mental disorder in an elderly home care population: Associations with health and social service use', *British Journal of Psychiatry*, 168(6), pp. 750–6.

Banerjee, S., Shamash, K., MacDonald, A. J. D. and Mann, A. H. (1998) 'The use of the selfCARE(D) as a screening tool for depression in the clients of local authority home care services – A preliminary study', *International Journal of Geriatric Psychiatry*, 13(10), pp. 695–9.

Bartlett, H. (1986) 'Social security policy and private sector care for the elderly', in Brenton, M. and Ungerson, C. (eds), *Year Book of Social Policy 1986–1987*, Harlow: Longman.

Bartlett, H. and Burnip, S. (1998) 'Quality of care in nursing homes for older people: providers' perspectives and priorities', *NT Research*, 3(4), pp. 257–68.

Bartlett, H. and Phillips, D. (1996) 'Policy issues in the private health sector: examples from long-term care in the UK', *Social Science and Medicine*, 43(5), pp. 731–7.

Bass, D. M., Noelker, L. S. and Rechlin, L. R. (1996) 'The moderating influence of service use on negative caregiving consequences', *Journals of Gerontology Series B – Psychological Sciences and Social Sciences*, 51(3), pp. S121–S131.

Bay, A. H. (1998) *Opinionen og eldrepolitikken*, Rapport 24, Oslo: NOVA – Norwegian Social Research.

Benington, J. and the Warwick University Local Authorities Research Consortium Working Group on Local Strategies for an Ageing Population (1998) *Local Strategies and Initiatives for an Ageing Population: Leading to Better Government for Older People*, Coventry: University of Warwick Business School.

Bernabei, R., Landi, F., Gambassi, G., Sgadari, J., Zuccala, G., Mor, V., Rubenstein, L. Z. and Carbonin, P. (1998) 'Randomised trial of impact of model of integrated care and case management for older people living in the community', *British Medical Journal*, 316(7141), pp. 1348–51.

Berry-Lound, D. and Marsh, K. (1996) *Working and Caring for Older People in Europe – A Three Country Comparison*, London: Help the Aged.

Blackman, T. (1998) 'Facing Up to Underfunding: Equity and Retrenchment in Community Care', *Social Policy & Administration* 32, pp. 182–95.

Blackman, T., Durbin, M. and Robb, B. (1998) *Assessment and care planning for older people: A study of the consistency of decision-making*, Oxford: School of Social Sciences and Law, Oxford Brookes University.

Blackman, T. and Palmer, A. (1999) 'Continuity or modernisation? The emergence of New Labour's welfare state', in Dean, H. and Woods, R. (eds), *Social Policy Review 11*, Luton: Social Policy Association.

Blunden, R. (1998) *Terms of Engagement*, London: Kings Fund.

Brodaty, H., Gresham, M. and Luscombe, G. (1997) 'The Prince Henry Hospital dementia caregivers' training programme', *International Journal of Geriatric Psychiatry*, 12(2), pp. 183–92.

Brunner, E. and Marmot, M. (1999) 'Social organization, stress and health', in Marmot, M. and Wilkinson, R. G. (eds), *Social Determinants of Health*, Oxford: Oxford University Press.

Bunnage, D. (1997) *Young Elderly in Denmark in the Mid-1990's*. Report 97:12, Copenhagen: The Danish National Institute of Social Research.

Caradocdavies, T. H. and Harvey, J. M. (1995) 'Do Social Relief Admissions Have Any Effect on Patients or Their Caregivers?', *Disability and Rehabilitation*, 17(5), pp. 247–51.

Carers National Association (1997) *Still Battling? The Carers Act one year on*, London: Carers National Association.

Castles, F. G. (1995) 'Welfare State Developments in Southern Europe', *West European Politics*, 18(2), pp. 291–313.

Challis, D., Darton, R., Johnson, L., Stone, M. and Traske, K. (1995) *Care Management and the Home Care of Older People*, Aldershot: Arena.

Challis, B. and Davies, B. (1986) *Case Management in Community Care*, Aldershort: Gower.

Chamberlayne, P., Cooper, A., Freeman, R. and Rustin, M. (eds) (1999), *Welfare and Culture in Europe*, London: Jessica Kingsley.

Chambers, R. (2000) *Involving Patients and the Public: How to do it Better*, Radcliffe Primary Care Series, Oxford: Radcliffe Medical Press.

Cheston, R. and Bender, M. (1999) *Understanding Dementia*, London: Jessica Kingsley.

Chetwynd, M., Ritchie, J. M., Reith, L. and Howard, M. (1996) *The Cost of Care: The impact of charging policies on the lives of disabled people*, Bristol: The Policy Press.

Chew, C., Glendinning, C. and Wilkin, D. (1994a) 'Annual assessments of patients aged 75 and over: general practitioners' and practice nurses' view and experiences', *British Journal of General Practice*, 44, pp. 263–7.

Chew, C., Glendinning, C. and Wilkin, D. (1994b) 'Annual assessments of patients aged 75 and over: views and experiences of elderly people', *British Journal of General Practice*, 44, pp. 567–70.

Ciocia, A. (1997) 'La redistribuzione previdenziale nelle provincie italiane', in Bartocci, E. (ed.), *Lo stato sociale in Italia*, Rapporto IRIDISS-CNR 1997, Rome: Donzelli.

Cioni, E. (1998) Unpublished notes on social care in Italy.

Cioni, E. (1999) *Solidarietà tra generazioni. Famiglie e anziani in Italia*, Milano: Angeli.

Clark, H., Dyer, S. and Hartman, L. (1996) *Going Home*, Bristol: Policy Press.

Clark, H., Dyer, S. and Horwood, J. (1998) *'That Bit of Help': the high value of low level preventative services for older people*, Bristol: Policy Press.

Classen, J. (ed.) (1999) *Comparative Social Policy: Concepts, Theories and Methods*, Oxford: Blackwell.

CNA (1997) *Still Battling? The Carers Act one year on*, London: Carers National Association.

Coleman, B. (1995) 'European models of long-term care in the home and community', *International Journal of Health Services*, 25(3), pp. 455–74.

Community Care (1999) 'Social services spending goes up', *Community Care*, 27 May–2 June, p. 8.

Convery, J. (1987) *Choices in Community Care: Day Centres for the Elderly in the Eastern Health Board*, Dublin: The Stationery Office.

Convery, J. (1998a) 'Mental Health Social Work with Older People in the Republic of Ireland', in Campbell, J. and Manktelow, R. (eds), *Mental Health Social Work in Ireland*, Aldershot: Ashgate.

Convery, J. (1998b) 'Social Work with Vulnerable Older People in the Republic of Ireland: Factors Influencing Policy and Practice', in Park, J., Campbell, J. and Manktelow, R. (eds), *Mental Health Social Work in Ireland: Conference Proceedings*, Belfast: Department of Health and Social Services.

Corden, A. and Duffy, K. (1998) 'Human dignity and social exclusion', in Sykes, R. and Alcock, P. (eds), *Developments in European Social Policy*, Bristol: Policy Press.

Costanzi, C. (1991) 'Home-care services in Italy (with special reference to Genoa)', in Jamieson, A. (ed.), *Home Care for Older People in Europe: a comparison of policies and practices*, Oxford: Oxford University Press.

Cousins, C. (1999a) 'Women and employment in southern Europe: the implications of recent policy and labour market directions', paper presented at the European Sociology Association 4th European Conference of Sociology, Amsterdam, 18–21 August.

Cousins, C. (1999b) *Society, Work and Welfare in Europe*, London: Macmillan.

Daatland, S. O. (1997) *Social protection for the elderly in Norway* Skriftserie 4, Oslo: NOVA – Norwegian Social Research.

Daatland, S. O. (1992) 'Ideals Lost? Current Trends in Scandinavian Welfare Policies on Ageing', *Journal of European Social Policy*, 2(1), pp. 33–47.

Daatland, S. O. (1996) 'Adopting the "Scandinavian Model" of care for elderly people', in Hennessy, P. (ed.), *Caring for Frail Elderly People*, Paris: OECD.

Daatland, S. O. (1997a) *Social protection for the elderly in Norway*, Skriftserie 4, Oslo: NOVA – Norwegian Social Research.

Daatland, S. O. (ed.) (1997b) *De siste årene. Eldreomsorgen i Skandinavia 1960–95*, Rapport 22, Oslo: NOVA – Norwegian Social Research.

Daatland, S. O. and Svorken, B. (1996) *Eldreråd og eldres innflytelse – et forprosjekt*, Rapport 3, Oslo: Norsk gerontologisk institutt.

Daatland, S. O. and Szebehely, M. (1997) 'Tjenestene og utviklingen i sammenheng', in Daatland, S. O. (ed.), *De siste årene. Eldreomsorgen i Skandinavia 1960–95*, Rapport 22, Oslo: NOVA – Norwegian Social Research.

Dahl, E. and Vogt, P. (1995) *Ensom og ulykkelig? Levekår og livskvalitet blant eldre*, Rapport 185, Oslo: Forskningsstiftelsen Fafo.

Dalley, G. and Dennis, M. (1997) *Patient Satisfaction*, London: CPA.

Daly, M. (1996) *Social Security, Gender and Equality in the European Union*, Brussels: Commission of the European Communities.

Danmarks Statistik (1975–1998) *Statistiske Efterretninger. Social sikring og retsvæsen*, Copenhagen: Danmarks Statistik.

Danmarks Statistik (1990) *Befolkningen i kommunerne 1. Januar 1990*, Copenhagen: Danmarks Statistik.

Danmarks Statistik (1994) *Statistisk tiårsoversigt*, Copenhagen: Danmarks Statistik.

Danmarks Statistik (1997) *Hjemmehjælp. Statistikservice: Socialstatistik 1990–97*, Copenhagen: Danmarks Statistik.

Danmarks Statistik (1998) *Statistiske efterretninger. Befolkning og valg*, Copenhagen: Danmarks Statistik.

Danmarks Statistik (1999) *Statistiske efterretninger. Sociale forhold, sundhed og retsvæsen*, Copenhagen: Danmarks Statistik.

Davis, A. M., Ellis, K. and Rummery, K. (1997) *Access to Assessment: Perspectives of practitioners, disabled people and carers*, Bristol: Policy Press.

Day, P. and Klein, R. (1997) *Steering but not Rowing? The Transformation of the Department of Health*, Bristol: Policy Press.

De Gennaro, E., Palleschi, L. and Zuccaro, S. M. (1997) *1992–96*. 'Progetto obiettivo per la tutela della salute degli anziani: attualità e prospettive', in Federazione Nazionale Pensionati CISL (a cura di), *Anziani '97 tra emarginazione e opportunità*, Rome: Edizioni Lavoro.

De Leonardis, O. (1998) *In un diverso welfare*, Milano: Feltrinelli.

Department of Health (1988) *The Years Ahead: a Policy for the Elderly*, Dublin: Stationery Office.

Department of Health (1989a) *Working for Patients*, Cm 555, London: The Stationery Office.

Department of Health (1989b) *Caring for People*, Cm 849, London: The Stationery Office.

Department of Health (1994) *Shaping a Healthier Future: a Strategy for Effective Health Care in the 1990's*, Dublin: Stationery Office.

Department of Health (1996) *Primary Care: the Future*, London: The Stationery Office.

Department of Health (1997a) *The New NHS: Modern, Dependable*, Cm 3807, London: The Stationery Office.

Department of Health (1997b) *Better Services for Vulnerable People*, EL(97)62/CI(97)24, London: The Stationery Office.

Department of Health (1998a) *Modernising Social Services*, Cm 4169, London: The Stationery Office.

Department of Health (1998b) *Partnership in Action*, London: The Stationery Office.

Department of Health (1999) *The Personal Social Services Performance Assessment Framework*, Internet: http://www.doh.gov.uk/paf/index.htm.

Department of Social Security (1997) *Social Security Statistics 1997*, London: The Stationery Office.

Department of Social Security (1998) *A New Contract for Welfare: Partnership in Pensions*, London: The Stationery Office.

Department of Social Security (1999) *Supporting People: A new policy and funding framework for support services*, London: The Stationery Office.

Department of Social Welfare (1997) *Supporting Voluntary Activity: a green paper on the community and voluntary sector and its relationship with the state*, Dublin: Stationery Office.

Department of Social Welfare (1998) *Review of the Carers Allowance*, Dublin: Stationery Office.

Drew, E. (1994) 'Demographic Change in Europe', paper presented at European Research Workshop in Family, Labour Markets and Gender Roles, European Foundation for the Improvement of Living and Working Conditions, Dublin, 7–9 September.

Drew, E. (1998) 'Re-conceptualising families', in Drew, E., Emerek, R. and Mahon, E. (eds), *Women, Work and the Family in Europe*, London: Routledge.

Duffy, K. (1996) *Final report of first seminar on social exclusion and human dignity in western Europe*, Strasbourg: Council of Europe.

ECCEEP (1998) *ECCEP Bulletin*, No. 2, November, ECCEP team, Personal Social Services Research Unit, University of Kent at Canterbury.

Ellingsæter, A. L. and Hedlund, M.-A. (1998) *Care resources, employment and gender in Norway*, Oslo: Institute for Social Research.

Elstad, J. I. (1997) *Recent Developements in the Norwegian Health Care System: Pointing in What Direction?* Skriftserie 1, Oslo: NOVA – Norwegian Social Research.

Emke-Poulopoulou, H. (1999) *Greek Elderly Citizens*, Athens: Ellin.

Esping-Andersen, G. (1990) *The Three Worlds of Welfare Capitalism*, Cambridge: Polity Press.

Esping-Anderson, G. and Korpi, W. (1987) 'From poor relief to institutional welfare states: the development of Scandinavian social policy', in Erikson, R., Hansen, S., Ringen, S. and Uusitalo, H. (eds), *The Scandinavian Model: Welfare States and Welfare Research*, New York: M.E. Sharpe.

European Commission (1993) *Towards a Europe of Solidarity*, Brussels: European Commission.

European Commission (1998) *Theme 1: Quality of Life and Management of Living Resources (1998–2002) for Research, Technology Development and Demonstration under the 5th Framework Programme*, Draft Workprogramme.

Eurostat (1998) *Labour Force Survey 1997*, Luxembourg: Office for Official Publications of the European Community.

Evandrou, M. (1996) 'Unpaid work, carers and health', in Blane, D., Brunner, E. and Wilkinson, R. (eds), *Health and Social Organization*, London: Routledge.

Evers, A. and Leichsenring, K. (1994) 'Paying for Informal Care: An Issue of Growing Importance', *Ageing International*, March, pp. 29–40.

Eydal, G. B. (1999) 'Child care in a small welfare state: the case of Iceland', paper presented at the European Sociological Association 4th European Conference of Sociology, Amsterdam, 18–21 August.

Fahey, T. (1997) *The Elderly, the Family and the State*, Joint Oireachtas Committee on the Family, Dublin: Government Printing Office.

Fakiolas, R. (1999) 'Socio-Economic Effects of Immigration in Greece', *Journal of European Social Policy*, 9, pp. 211–30.

Falkingham, J. (1998) 'Financial (in)security in later life', in Bernard, M. and Phillips, J. (eds), *The Social Policy of Old Age*, London: Centre for Policy on Ageing.

Fargion, V. (1997) *Geografia della cittadinanza sociale in Italia*, Bologna: il Mulino.

Farquhar, M. (1995) 'Elderly peoples definitions of quality-of-life', *Social Science & Medicine*, 41(10), pp. 1439–46.

Ferrara, M. (1984) *Il Welfare State in Italia. Sviluppo e crisi in prospettiva comparata*, Bologna: Ill Mulino.

Ferrera, M. (1996) 'The "Southern Model" of Welfare in Social Europe', *Journal of European Social Policy*, 6(1), pp. 17–37.

Giarchi, G. G. (1996) *Caring for Older Europeans: Comparative studies in 29 countries*, Aldershot: Arena.

Gibson, D. (1998) *Aged Care: Old Policies, New Problems*, Cambridge: Cambridge University Press.

Ginn, J. and Arber, S. (1999) 'Changing patterns of pension inequality: the shift from state to private sources', *Ageing and Society*, 19(3), pp. 319–42.

Glendinning, C. (1992) *The Costs of Informal Care: Looking Inside the Household*, London: The Stationery Office.

Glendinning, C. (1998) (ed.), *Rights and Realities: Comparing New Developments in Long-term Care for Older People*, Bristol: Policy Press.

Glendinning, C. (1999) 'GPs and Contracts', *Social Policy and Administration*, 33(2), pp. 115–31.

Goodman, A., Johnson, P. and Webb, S. (1997) *Inequality in the UK*, Oxford: Oxford University Press.

Gori, C. (2000) 'Care Allowances for the Elderly in Italy: New Features and Challenges', Paper presented at the Social Policy Association Annual Conference, University of Surrey, 18–20 July 2000.

Green, L. (2000) 'Up to the Mark?', *Community Care*, 1305, 20–26 January, pp. 18–19.

Guimelli, G. (1994) *Anziani e assistenza. Dalla carità verso la sicurezza sociale*, Milano: Angeli.

Gulbrandsen, L. (1997) *Husholdningenes betalingspraksis*, Rapport 12, Oslo: NOVA – Norwegian Social Research.

Gulbrandsen, L. and Langsether, A. (1999) 'Wealth Distribution between Generations: A Source of Conflict or Cohesion?', in Arber, S. and Attias-Donfut, C. (eds), *The Myth of Generational Conflict*, London: Routledge.

Haan, A. de. (1997) 'Poverty and Social Exclusion: A New Research Agenda', Report on Seminar Series: Poverty and Social Exclusion in North and South, Institute of Development Studies. Internet: http://www.ids.ac.uk/ids/research/food/povsem2.html/.

Hansen, E. B. and Platz, M. (1995a) *Kommunernes tilbud til ældre*, Copenhagen: AKF.

Hansen, E. B. and Platz, M. (1995b) *80–100-åriges levekår*, Copenhagen: AKF.

Hansen, E. B. and Platz, M. (1996) *Gamle Danskere*, Copenhagen: AKF.

Hansen, E. B. and Platz, M. (1997) 'Factors Influencing the Well-being of Elderly People in Denmark', paper presented at 9. Nordiske socialpolitiske forskersem-inar in Køge, 6–8 November.

Hansen, E. B., Jordal-Jørgensen, J. and Koch, A. (1991) *Fra plejehjem til hjemme-pleje*, Copenhagen: AKF.

Hantrais, L. (1999) 'Comparing Family Policies in Europe', in Clasen, J. (ed.), *Comparative Social Policy: Concepts, Theories and Methods*, Oxford: Blackwell.

Hardy, B., Young, R. and Wistow, G. (1999) 'Dimensions of choice in the assessment and care management process: the views of older people, carers and care managers', *Health and Social Care in the Community*, 7(6), pp. 483–91.

Haslett, D., Ruddle, H. and Hennessy, G. (1998) *The Future Organisation of the Home Help Service in Ireland*, Report No. 53, Dublin: National Council on Ageing and Older People.

Helseth, A. (1998) *En god hjemmehjelpstjeneste? Brukernes of hjemmehjelpernes syn på kvalitet* NOVA Rapport 19/98, Oslo: NOVA – Norwegian Social Research.

Hirst, J. (1999) 'High and Dry', *Community Care*, 1300, 25 November–1 December, pp. 20–1.

Hornsby-Smith, M. (1999) 'The Catholic Church and Social Policy in Europe', in Chamberlayne, P., Cooper, A., Freeman, R., and Ruston, M., (eds), *Welfare and Culture in Europe: Towards a New Paradigm in Social Policy*, London: Jessica Kingsley.

House of Commons (1999) *Health Committee, First Report 1998/9: The Relationship Between Health and Social Services*, London: The Stationery Office.

Huber, N. (2000) 'Nice plan, but where's the money?', *Community Care*, 1305, 20–26 January, pp. 10–11.

Hugman, R. (1994) *Ageing and the Care of Older People in Europe*, Basingstoke: Macmillan.

Hutten, J. B. F. (1996) 'Home Care in Italy', in Hutton, J. B. F. and Kerkstra, A. (eds), *Home Care in Europe*, Aldershot: Arena.

Hutten, J. B. F. and Kerkstra, A. (eds) (1996) *Home Care in Europe: a country-specific guide to its organization and financing*, Aldershot: Arena.

ISTAT (1990) *Indagine Multiscopo sulle famiglie*, Rome: ISTAT.

ISTAT (1997) *Anziani in Italia*, Bologna: il Mulino.

Jack, R. (1998) *Residential versus Community Care: The role of institutions in welfare provision*, Basingstoke: Macmillan.

Jakobsson, G. (1998) 'The politics of care for elderly people in Scandinavia', *European Journal of Social Work*, 1(1), pp. 87–93.

Jakubowski, E. and Busse, R. (1998) *Health Care Systems in the EU: A Comparative Study*, Luxembourg: European Parliament.

Jamieson, A. and Illsley, R. (eds) (1990) *Contrasting European Policies for the Care of Older People*, Aldershot: Avebury.

Johnson, N. (1987*) The Welfare State in Transition: the Theory and Practice of Welfare Pluralism*, Brighton: Wheatsheaf Books.

Johnson, N. (1999) *Mixed Economies of Welfare: A comparative perspective*, London: Prentice-Hall.

Jura Information (1996) *Nyhedsbrev for œldre og handicappede No. 11*, Copenhagen: Jura Information.

Jura Information (1998) *Ny sociallovgivning 1. juli 1998*, Copenhagen: Jura Information.

Kahn, A. and Kamerman, S. (1976) *Social Services in International Perspective*, Washington: US Department of Health, Welfare and Education.

Karantinos, D., Ioannou, D. and Cavounidis, J. (1992) *EC Observatory on National Policies to Combat Social Exclusion: The Social Services and Social Policies to Combat Social Exclusion – Greece*, Brussels: National Centre for Social Research/Commission of the European Communities.

Katrougalos, G. S. (1996) 'The South European Welfare Model: The Greek Welfare State in Search of an Identity', *Journal of European Social Policy*, 6(1), pp. 39–60.

Keilman, N., Lyngstad, J., Bojer, H. and Thomsen, I. (eds) (1997) *Poverty and Economic Inequality in Industrial Western Societies*, Oslo: Scandinavian University Press.

Keogh, F. and Roche, A. (1996) *Mental Disorders in Older Irish People*, Report No. 45, Dublin: National Council on Ageing and Older People.

Kirk, S. and Glendinning, C. (1998) 'Trends in community care and patient participation: implications for the roles of informal carers and community nurses in the UK', *Journal of Advanced Nursing*, 28, pp. 370–81.

Kitwood, T. (1997) *Dementia Reconsidered*, Buckingham: Open University Press.

Klein, R. and New, B. (1998) *Two Cheers? Reflections on the health of National Health Service democracy*, London: King's Fund.

Knapp, M., Koutsogeorgopoulou, V. and Smith, J. D. (1996) 'Volunteer participation in community care', *Policy and Politics*, 24(2), pp. 171–92.

Koren, C. and Aslaksen, J. (1997) 'A Woman's Perspective on Poverty: Household Work, Income Distribution and Social Welfare', in Keilman, N., Lyngstad, J., Bojer, H. and Thomsen, I. (eds), *Poverty and Economic Inequality in Industrial Western Societies*, Oslo: Scandinavian University Press.

Kosberg, J. I. (ed.) (1992) *Family Care of the Elderly*, Newbury Park: Sage.

Kvist, J. (1999) 'Welfare Reform in the Nordic Countries in the 1999s: Using Fuzzy-Set Theory to Assess Conformity to Ideal Types', *Journal of European Social Policy*, 9, pp. 231–52.

Kyriopoulos, I. (1998) 'More money, worse health', *Kathimerini*, 22 November p. 29.

Lamb, S. (1999) 'The value of Senior Centres in providing opportunities for healthy and satisfying lifestyles for older people in the United States', paper prepared for the NHS Research and Development Strategic Review Ageing Topic Working Group, Oxford: Nuffield Orthopaedic Centre NHS Trust.

Lauvli, M. (1999) *Tilrettelagte boliger – omsorgsboliger*, Skriftserie 1, Oslo: NOVA – Norwegian Social Research.

Layte, R., Fahey, T. and Whelan, C. (1999) *Income, Deprivation and Well-being Among Older Irish People*, Report No. 55, Dublin: National Council on Ageing and Older People.

Leahy, A. L. (1998) 'Moving to a Quality Culture', in Leahy, A. L. and Wiley, M. M. *The Irish Health System in the 21st Century*, Dublin: Oak Tree Press.

Leahy, A. L. and Wiley, M. M. (1998) *The Irish Health System in the 21st Century*, Dublin: Oak Tree Press.

Leeson, G. W. (1997) 'Social Policy and Services for Older People in Denmark – the Experience of DaneAge', paper prepared for the Colloque Européen, Université de Provence, Marseille, 16–17 June, 13pp.

Leibfried, S. (1993) 'Towards a European Welfare State?', in Jones, C. (ed.), *New Perspectives on the Welfare State in Europe*, London: Routledge.

Levitas, R. (1996) 'The concept of social exclusion and the new Durkheimian hegemony', *Critical Social Policy*, 16(1), pp. 5–20.

Lewis, J. (1992) Gender and the development of welfare regimes. *Journal of European Social Policy*, 2(3): 159–73.

Lewis, J. and Glennerster, H. (1996) *Implementing the New Community Care*, Buckingham: Open University Press.

Lingsom, S. (1997) *The Substitution Issue. Care Policies and their Consequences for Family Care* NOVA-rapport, 1997:6, Oslo: NOVA – Norwegian Social Research.

Local Government Management Board (1997) *Community Care Needs 1997 Report*, London: Local Government Management Board.

Local Government Management Board (1997b) *Community Care Trends 1997 Report*, London: Local Government Management Board.

Loux, A., Kerrison, S. and Pollock, A. M. (2000) 'Long term nursing: social care or health care?', *British Medical Journal*, 320, pp. 5–6.

Lundstrom, F. and K. McKeown (1994) *Home Help Services for Elderly People in Ireland*, Report No. 36, Dublin: National Council on Ageing and Older People.

Mabbett, D. and Bolderson, H. (1999) 'Theories and Methods in Comparative Social Policy', in Classen, J. (ed.), *Comparative Social Policy: Concepts, Theories and Methods*, Oxford: Blackwell.

Mapelli, V. (1994) 'Libertà di scelta ed equitaà nel sistema sanitario italiano: un'indagine campionaria', in Costa, G. and Faggiano, F. (eds), *L'equità nella salute in Italia*, Milan: Angeli.

May, M. and Brunsdon, E. (1999) 'Social Services and Community Care', in Horton, S. and Farnham, D. (eds), *Public Management in Britain*, Basingstoke: Macmillan.

McLaughlin, E. (1993) *Social Security and Community Care: The case of the Invalid Care Allowance*, London: The Stationery Office.

McRae, S. (1999) 'Introduction: family and household change in Britain', in McRae, S. (ed.), *Changing Britain: Families and Household in the 1990s*, Oxford: Oxford University Press.

Mestheneos, E. and Triantafillou, J. (1993) 'Dependent Elderly People in Greece and their Family Carers', in Twigg, J. (ed.), *Informal Care in Europe*, York: University of York Social Policy Research Unit.

Ministries of Finance, Housing, Tax, Social Affairs and Economic Affairs (1996) *Ældres indkomster og formuer*, Copenhagen: Ministries of Finance, Housing, Tax, Social Affairs and Economic Affairs.

Ministry of Economic Affairs (1999a) *Familie og indkomster*, Copenhagen: Ministry of Economic Affairs.

Ministry of Economic Affairs (1999b) *Familie og indkomster*, Copenhagen.

Ministry of Finance (1999) *Finansredegørelse 1998/99*, Copenhagen: Ministry of Finance.

Ministry of Health (1993) *Health Care in Denmark*, Copenhagen: Ministry of Finance.

Ministry of Health and Social Affairs (1999) *Security – Respect – Quality: Action plan for care of the elderly 1998–2001*, Oslo: Ministry of Health and Social Affairs, Internet: http://odin.dep.no/shd/proj/eldre/brosjyre/action-plan/.

Ministry of Social Affairs (1998) *Sociale tendenser*, Copenhagen: Ministry of Social Affairs.

Mirabile, M. L. (1999) 'The politics of old age in Italy', in Walker, A. and Naegele, G. (eds), *The Politics of Old Age in Europe*, Buckingham: Open University Press.

Mittelman, M. S., Ferris, S. H., Shulman, E., Steinberg, G. and Levin, B. (1996) 'A family intervention to delay nursing home placement of patients with Alzheimer disease. A randomized controlled trial', *Journal of the American Medical Association*, 276(21), pp. 1725–31.

Morton, M. (1998) *The Senior Help-Line: an evaluation of a new service aimed at isolated and lonely older people*, Kells: Health Promotion Department, North-eastern Health Board.

Moussourou, L. (1985) *Family and Child in Athens*, Athens: Estia.

Mulvihill, R. (1993) *Voluntary–Statutory Partnership in Community Care of the Elderly*, Dublin: National Council for the Elderly.

Munday, B. and Ely, P. (1996) *Social Care in Europe*, Hemel Hempstead: Prentice-Hall.

Musterd, S. and Ostendorf, W. (1998) *Urban segregation and the welfare state: inequality and exclusion in western cities*, London: Routledge.

Næss, S. and Wærness, K. (1996) *Bedre omsorg? Kommunal eldreomsorg 1980–1995*, Bergen: Senter for samfunnsforskning, Universitetet i Bergen.

National Consumer Council (1995) *Charging Consumers for Services*, London: National Consumer Council.

National Council on Ageing and Older People (1998) *The Law and Older People*, Report No. 51 Dublin: National Council on Ageing and Older People.

National Health Service Executive (1999) *Better Services for Vulnerable People*, EL(97)62/CI(97)24, London: Department of Health.

Nijkamp, P., Pacolet, J., Spinnewyn, H., Vollering, A., Wilderom, C. and Winters, S. (1990) *Services for the Elderly in Europe: a cross-national comparative study*, Leuven: Commission of the European Communities.

Nordic Council of Ministers/Nordic Statistical Secretariat (1998) *Yearbook of Nordic Statistics*, Copenhagen: Nordic Council of Ministers/Nordic Statistical Secretariat.

NOSOSO (Nordic Social-Statistical Committee) (1993) *Social Securities in the Nordic Countries*, Oslo: Nordic Social-Statistical Committee.

NOU (Norges Offentlige utredninger) (1992) *Security–Dignity–Care*, abridged version, Oslo: The Ministry of Health and Social Affairs.

NWBMWG (1999) *Managing the Community Care Market – After 5 Years: Regional Commentary and Analysis*, North West Business Management Working Group, Tameside Social Services Department.

OECD (1996) *Caring for Frail Elderly People*, Social Policy Studies 19, Paris: Organisation for Economic Co-operation and Development.

OECD (1998a) *Revenue Statistics, 1965–1997*, Paris: Organisation for Economic Co-operation and Development.

OECD (1998b) *OECD Policy Brief*, 5.

OECD (1998c) *Health Data 98*, Paris: Organisation for Economic Co-operation and Development.

OECD (1999) *Health Data 99*, Paris: Organisation for Economic Co-operation and Development.

Office for National Statistics (1995) *Informal Carers: Results of an independent study carried out on behalf of the Department of Health as part of the 1995 General Household Survey*, London: The Stationery Office.

Office for National Statistics (1998) *Informal Carers*, Social Survey Division, Office for National Statistics, London: The Stationery Office.

Oliver, M. (1998) 'Theories of disability in health practice and research', *British Medical Journal*, 317(7170) http://www.bmj.com/cgi/content/full/317/7170/1446.

Oppenheim, C. (1998) *An Inclusive Society: Strategies for Tackling Poverty*, London: Institute for Public Policy Research.

O'Connor, J. S. (1993) 'Gender, class and citizenship in the comparative analysis of welfare state regimes: theoretical and methodological issues', *The British Journal of Sociology*, 44(3), pp. 501–18.

O'Shea, E. and Hughes, J. (1994) *The Economics and Financing of Long-term Care of the Elderly in Ireland*, Report No. 35, Dublin: National Council of the Elderly.

O'Shea, E. and Larragy, J. (1995) *The Social Integration of Old People in Ireland*, Working Paper No. 3, Galway: Department of Economics, University College Galway.

O'Shea, E. and O'Reilly, S. (1999) *Action Plan for Dementia*, Report No. 54, Dublin: National Council on Ageing and Older People.

Pace, D. and Pisani, S. (1998) *Le condizioni economiche degli anziani*. VII rapporto CERSPI, Bari: Laterza.

Palaiologos, D. (1999) 'The Complementary Role of Private Insurance and the Greek Reality', paper presented at the conference on complementary pensions, Union of Insurance Companies of Greece, Athens, May 25.

Papadopoulos, T. N. (1998) 'Greek family policy', in Drew, E. Emerek, R. and Mahon, E. (eds), *Women, Work and the Family in Europe*, London: Routledge.

Park, J., Campbell, J. and Manktelow, R. (eds) (1998) *Mental Health Social Work in Ireland: Conference Proceedings*, Belfast: Department of Health and Social Services.

Patel, N. (1999) 'Black and Minority Ethnic Elderly: Perspectives on Long-Term Care', in Royal Commission on Long Term Care, *With Respect to Old Age: Long Term Care – Rights and Responsibilities: The Context of Long-Term Care Policy Research Volume 1*, Cm 4192-II/1, London: The Stationery Office.

Pension Provision Group (1998) *We all need pensions – the prospects for pension provision*, London: The Stationery Office.

Platz, M. (1981) *De ældres levevilkår 1977*, Meddelelse 32, Copenhagen: Danish National Institute of Social Research.

Platz, M. (1987) *Længst muligt i eget hjem*, Publikation 157, Copenhagen: Danish National Institute of Social Research.

Platz, M. (1989) *Gamle i eget hjem Bind 1: Levekår* Rappøort 89:12, Copenhagen: Danish National Institute of Social Research.

Platz, M. (1990) *Gamle i eget hjem Bind 2: Hvordan klarer de sig?* Rapport 90: 10, Copenhagen: Danish National Institute of Social Research.

Platz, M. (1992) *Kommunernes ældrepolitik: Fra plejehjem til egne hjem*, Rapport 92:2, Copenhagen: Danish National Institute of Social Research.

Platz, M. (1998) Personal communication, 10 October.

Platz, M. (1999) Unpublished analyses and notes for this book.

Platz, M. and Freiberg Petersen, N. (1992) *Older People in Europe. Social and Economic Policies. National Report for the EC Actions on Older People*, Copenhagen: The Danish National Institute of Social Research.

Plovsing, J. (1992) *Home Care in Denmark*, Copenhagen: The Danish National Institute of Social Research.

Politiken, 15 September 1998.

Politiken, 2 February 1999.

Pratschke, J. (1999) '"Real" Managers or Political Pawns?: Local Management Strategies in the Southern Italian Health Service', paper presented at the European Sociological Association 4th European Conference of Sociology, Amsterdam, 18–21 August.

Prezidenza del Consiglio dei Ministri Departimento per gli Affari Sociali (1998) *Quinta Relazione Biennale al Parlamento sulla condizione dell'anziano 1996–1997*, Rome: PCMDAS.

Prophet, H. (ed.) (1998) *Fit for the Future: The Prevention of Dependency in Later Life*, London: Continuing Care Conference.

Ranci, C. (1999) *Oltre il welfare state*, Bologna: il Mulino.

Rhodes, M. (ed.) (1997) *Southern European Welfare States: Between Crisis and Reform*, London: Frank Cass.

Richardson, S. and Pearson, M. (1995) 'Dignity and Aspirations Denied – Unmet Health and Social Care Needs in an Inner City Area', *Health and Social Care in the Community*, 3(5), pp. 279–87.

Rikstrygdeverket (1998) *Trygdestatistisk årbok 14 årg*, Oslo: National Insurance Administration, Olso: Rikstrygdeverket.

RIS MRC CFAS (Resource Implications Study of Medical Research Council Cognitive Function and Ageing Study) (1998) 'Mental and physical frailty in older people: the costs and benefits of informal care', *Ageing and Society*, 18, pp. 317–54.

Robinson, J. and Turnock, S. (1998) *Investing in rehabilitation*, London: King's Fund and Audit Commission.

Romøren, T. I. (1996) 'International Comparisons of Long-Term Care: Norway and the Scandinavian Solution', *Canadian Journal on Aging*, 15(1), pp. 59–72.

Room, G. (ed.) (1996) *Beyond the threshold: The measurement and analysis of social exclusion*, Bristol: Policy Press.

Rosenmayr, L. and Kockies, E. (1963) 'Propositions for a sociological theory of aging and the family', *International Social Service Journal*, 15, pp. 410–26.

Rostgaard, T. and Fridberg, T. (1998) *Caring for Children and Older People – A Comparison of European Policies and Practices*, Copenhagen: The Danish National Institute of Social Research.

Royal Commission on Long Term Care (1999a) *With Respect to Old Age: Long-Term Care – Rights and Responsibilities*, Report of Royal Commission on Long Term Care: Main Report and 3 research volumes, London: The Stationery Office.

Royal Commission on Long Term Care (1999b) 'Lessons from International Experience', in Royal Commission on Long Term Care, *With Respect to Old Age: Research Volume 1*, Cm 4192-II/1, London: The Stationery Office.

Ruddle, H., Donoghue, F. and Mulvihill, R. (1997) *The Years Ahead Report: A review of the implications of its recommendations*, Report No. 48, Dublin: National Council on Ageing and Older People.

Rummery, K. (1998) 'Changes in primary health care policy: the implications for joint commissioning with social services', *Health and Social Care in the Community*, 6(6), pp. 429–37.

Rummery, K. and Glendinning, C. (1997) *Working Together: Primary care involvement in commissioning social care services*, Manchester: National Primary Care Research and Development Centre.

Rummery, K. and Glendinning, C. (1999) 'Negotiating needs, access and gatekeeping', *Critical Social Policy*, 19(3), pp. 335–52.

Sainsbury, D. (1994) 'Women's and Men's Social Rights', in Sainsbury, D. (ed.), *Gendering Welfare States*, London: Sage.

Saraceno, C. (1998) *Mutamenti della famiglia e politiche sociali*, Bologna: il Mulino.

Saraceno, C. and Negri, N. (1994) 'The changing Italian welfare state', *Journal of European Social Policy*, 4(1), pp. 19–34.

Schofield, H., Murphy, B., Herrman, H. E., Bloch, S. and Singh, B. S. (1998) 'Carers of people aged over 50 with physical impairment, memory loss and dementia: a comparative study', *Ageing and Society*, 18, pp. 355–69.

Schunk, M. (1998) 'Responses to the care dilemma', in International Social Security Association (eds), *Developments and Trends in Social Security 1996 – 1998*. Report to 26th General Assembly, Marrakech, October 1998, Geneva: ISSA.

Schwehr, B. (1999) 'Charging law up-date', Notes prepared for Community Care in the 21st Century: Problems and Resolution, Oxford Brookes University, 8 September.

References and Further Reading   219

Secretary of State for Health (2000) *The NHS Plan*, Cm 4818-I, London: HMSO.

Seligman, M. E. P. (1975) *Helplessness: On Depression, Development and Death*, San Francisco: Freeman.

Sipilä, J. and Anttonen, A. (1999) 'Restoring the welfare mix approach: the ways of producing care', paper presented at the European Sociology Association 4th European Conference of Sociology, Amsterdam, 18–21 August.

Slagsvold, B. (1999) 'Hva med de hjemmeboende?', *Aldring and Eldre* 4, pp. 16–21.

Smed, J. (1997) 'Councils of Elderly and Quality of Age Care', Paper presented at Nordiske socialpolitiske forskerseminar, 6–8 November.

SN (Statistics Norway) (1985) *Norwegian Surveys of Level of Living 1983*, NOS B 511, Oslo: Norwegian Official Statistics.

SN (Statistics Norway) (1989) *Norwegian Surveys of Level of Living 1987*, NOS B 77, Oslo: Norwegian Official Statistics.

SN (Statistics Norway) (1992) *Norwegian Surveys of Level of Living 1991*, NOS C 43, Oslo: Norwegian Official Statistics.

SN (Statistics Norway) (1996) *Norwegian Surveys of Level of Living 1995*, NOS C 301, Oslo: Norwegian Official Statistics.

Socialkommissionen (1993) *De ældre*, Copenhagen: Socialkommissionen.

Sosialdepartementet (1966) *Innstilling om hjemmehjelp for eldre*, Innstilling 1 fra Komitéen, avgitt 28 juni 1966, Oslo: Sosialdepartementet.

Spicker, P. (1984) *Stigma and Social Welfare*, London: Croom Helm.

Spicker, P. (1997) 'Exclusion', *Journal of Common Market Studies*, 35(1), pp. 133–43.

Spinellis, C. and Pitsiou-Darrough, E. (1990) *Violence Against the Elderly: Abuse and Neglect*, Athens: Ministry of Health, Welfare and Social Security.

St. meld nr. 50 (1996–1997) *Handlingsplan for eldreomsorgen*, Government White Paper, Ministry of Health and Social Affairs.

Stathopoulos, P. (1995) *Social Welfare: A General Overview*, Athens: Ellin.

Stathopoulos, P. and Amera, A. (1992) 'Family Care of the Elderly in Greece', in Kosberg, J. I. (ed.), *Family Care of the Elderly: Social and Cultural Changes*, London: Sage.

Sykes, R. and Leather, P. (1997) *Grey Matters*, Kidlington: Anchor Trust.

Tester, S. (1999) 'Comparative approaches to long-term care', in Clasen, J. (ed.), *Comparative Social Policy: Concepts, Theories and Methods*, Oxford: Blackwell.

Thorslund, M. and Parker, M. G. (1995) 'Strategies for an Ageing Population: Expanding the Priorities Discussion', *Ageing and Society*, 15, pp. 199–217.

Tiemann, S. (1993) 'Opinion on social exclusion', OJ 93/C 352/13.

Titmuss, R. (1963) *Essays on the Welfare State*, London: Allen and Unwin.

Titterton, M. (1992) 'Managing Threats to Welfare: The Search for a New Paradigm of Welfare', *Journal of Social Policy*, 21(1), pp. 1–24.

Trifiletti, R. (1999) 'Southern European welfare states and the worsening position of women', *Journal of European Social Policy*, 9(1), pp. 49–64.

Tsakloglou, P. and Panopoulou, G. (1998) 'Who are the poor in Greece?', *Journal of European Social Policy*, 8(3), pp. 213–36.

Turcio, S. (1997) 'La sfida manageriale nell'assistenza sanitaria di base', in Bartocci, E. (ed.), *Lo stato sociale in Italia*. Rapporto IRIDISS-CNR 1997, Rome: Donzelli.

Twigg, J. (1997) 'Deconstructing the "social bath": help with bathing at home for older and disabled people', *Journal of Social Policy*, 26(2), pp. 211–32.

Vabø, M. (1996) 'Quality of Care: Is it Enough to Ask the Client?', paper presented at the international seminar *Developing Quality in Personal Social Services*, STAKES, Helsinki, 12–14 April 1996.

Vabø, M. (1998) *Hva er nok. Om behovsfortolkninger I hjemmetjenesten*, Rapport 8, Oslo: NOVA – Norwegian Social Research.

Vabø, M. (2000). Personal communication, 28 January.

Walker, A and Maltby, T. (1997) *Ageing Europe*, Buckingham: Open University Press.

Walker, A. (1993) *Age and Attitudes – Main Results from a Eurobarometer Survey*, Brussels: CEC.

Walker, A. (1995) 'Integrating the family into a mixed economy of care', in Allen, I. and Perkins, E. (eds), *The future of family care for older people*, London: The Stationery Office.

Walker, A. (1996) *The New Generational Contract*, London: University College London Press.

Walker, A. (1999) 'Political participation and representation of older people in Europe', in Walker, A. and Naegele, G. (eds), *The Politics of Old Age in Europe*, Buckingham: Open University Press.

Walker, A. and Maltby, T. (1997) *Ageing Europe*, Buckingham: Open University Press.

Walker, A. and Naegele, G. (eds) (1999) *The Politics of Old Age in Europe*, Buckingham: Open University Press.

Walker, M., Orrell, M., Manela, M., Livingston, G. and Katona, C. (1998) 'Do health and use of services differ in residents of sheltered accommodation? A pilot study', *International Journal of Geriatric Psychiatry*, 13(9), pp. 617–24.

Warner, L. and Wexler, S. (1998) *Eight hours a day and taken for granted?*, London: Princess Royal Trust for Carers.

Warner, N. (1995) *Better Tomorrows: Report of a national study of carers and the community care changes*, London: Carers National Association.

Wistow, G. (1997) 'Decentralisation from acute to home care settings in England', *Health Policy*, 41, pp. S91–S108.

Wittenberg, R., Pickard, L., Comas-Herrara, A., Davies, B. and Darton, R. (1998) *Demand for long-term care: projections of long-term care finance for elderly people*, London and Canterbury: Personal Social Services Research Unit.

Wright, F. (1998) 'The effect on carers of a frail older person's admission to a care home', *Findings*, York: Joseph Rowntree Foundation.

Yfantopoulos, I. (1999) 'Health and Welfare State', *TO VIMA*, 28 February, pp. 8–10.

Index